Jubilee Jim

Legends of Commerce

The *Legends of Commerce* series breathes new life into classic stories from the world of business and finance. While the topics covered in the series will be broad ranging, all the books will have one common element, they are all great reads that sweep the reader along with factual tales of intrigue and adventure through the decades — all conducted in the name of commerce.

Titles in the series:

Jubilee Jim
From Circus Traveler to Wall Street Rogue:
The Remarkable Life of Colonel James Fisk, Jr.
Robert H. Fuller

1-58799-087-3

The Plungers and the Peacocks
170 Years of Wall Street
Dana L. Thomas

1-58799-109-8

Jubilee Jim

From Circus Traveler to Wall Street Rogue: The Remarkable Life of Colonel James Fisk, Jr.

Robert H. Fuller

TEXERE

New York • London

Original version first published by The MacMillan Company in 1928.

Published by

TEXERE
55 East 52nd Street
New York, NY 10055

Tel: +1 (212) 317 5106
Fax: +1 (212) 317 5178
www.etexere.com

In the UK

TEXERE Publishing Limited
71–77 Leadenhall Street
London EC3A 3DE
www.etexere.co.uk

Tel: +44 (0)20 7204 3644
Fax: +44 (0)20 7208 6701

Designed by Macfarlane Production Services, Markyate, Hertfordshire, England (e-mail: macfarl@aol.com)

Library of Congress Cataloging in Publication Data has been applied for.

ISBN 1-58799-087-3

Printed in the United States of America

This book is printed on acid-free paper.

10 9 8 7 6 5 4 3 2 1

Contents

About the author

A newspaper man by trade, it is no surprise that Robert H. Fuller was drawn to the story of notorious Wall Street plunger, James Fisk, aka Jubilee Jim. Originally published in 1928, Fuller's biographical narrative captures the characters and events that mark 'one of the darkest and strangest periods in American life.' Jubilee Jim's world was unregulated big business, high finance and commercial intrigue in late 19th century America, 'a world where honesty was not even the best policy.'

The story is told through the eyes of Rufus Phelps, a fictional friend and agent of Fisk. The result is an eye witness account that gives readers an entertaining and impartial insight into this flamboyant character.

Based on his own life history, one can only surmise that Robert Fuller would have seen a bit of himself in Rufus Phelps. He was described by his colleagues as loyal, earnest and sensitive to the public interest. Born in Deerfield, Massachusetts on September 18, 1864, Fuller was a graduate of Harvard University. He began his journalism career on the *Worcester Spy* in 1888 and continued to work as an editor and political reporter in upstate New York before joining the *New York Herald* in 1895.

It was his work in Albany that first attracted the interest of New York Governor, Charles E. Hughes. Hughes met Fuller in 1906 and asked him to become Secretary to the Governor the following year. Fuller held this position for over three years, during which time Hughes praised him for his intelligence and sympathetic nature. Fuller went on to become a member of the Merchants' Association of the City of New York and was later appointed a member of the NY State Water Supply Commission.

Robert Fuller published two books prior to *Jubilee Jim*; *The Golden Hope* in 1905 and *Government by the People* in 1907. He died on December 23, 1927 within a week of first revising the typescript for *Jubilee Jim*.

This new TEXERE edition of *Jubilee Jim* for the Legends of Commerce series has been abridged from the original 1928 edition published by The MacMillian Company.

1
Backgrounds

Boyhood

Looking back over many years it seems to me that Ceda Garland was always more of a companion to me than anybody else I ever knew. Sometimes for years I didn't see her or hear from her but when we met again, as we always did, there never was any strangeness. It was just as though we had never been apart. It happens that sometimes in youth we have bosom friends. We tell them our most secret thoughts and hopes but after a few years we are surprised and sorry to find that we are no longer interested in them or their affairs, or they in us or ours. In my own life this has happened to me but I never lost my interest in Ceda Garland and I know she always kept up her interest in me, God knows why!

She was a golden blonde. I don't mean that her hair was golden in color, for it wasn't. It was a shade or two darker than gold and it grew still darker as she grew older. Like the rest of us, she changed from year to year, but always the most noticeable thing about her hair was its thickness and the way it lay on her head and across her forehead, waving a little. There was a flame in it when the light fell on it. The straying threads, at any rate, were golden enough in the sun.

Her eyes were not especially large, nor were they deep-set, but they were the shade of blue that the sky is on a cloudless Spring day. Anyway, she had those eyes. It was almost impossible to look at anything else when she was there. It wasn't just their beautiful color; they were candid, with something appealing and trusting about them. And they almost always looked happy.

She belonged to my boyhood just like Bald Mountain, with its naked granite ledge along the top of the ridge against the sky. It was a great thing for us to climb up there and it was wonderful to look down from the height of that ledge. The bright thread of the Walloomsac River ran along the broad valley south until it made an elbow westward in order to join the Hoosic and in that way reach the Hudson. We used to think how the waters of Roaring Branch, which ran past our houses, were carried down through miles and miles of country until they came to the great City of New York, a wonderland in our minds. It seemed as far away as China.

South we could see Mount Anthony and further on, over the line in Massachusetts, the heights of the Berkshires. On the West were hills and ridges in New York State. North, the Valley lay between the hills. It is a beautiful valley. It used to look peaceful enough with its meadows and its rounded elm trees, but even the smallest of us knew that it had once been a battleground where the English Red Coats and German Hessians were slaughtered and driven off by the brave Green Mountain Boys under General Warner and other heroes in cocked hats and laced coats and satin knee breeches. This famous victory somehow tinged Bennington. It set the town apart. The people who lived there never forgot it and they took credit for themselves and the town in a dauntless and military way.

———♦———

Ceda was the girl I knew best and Jim Fisk was the boy. Probably all the other boys of our age in Bennington would say the same thing about him, though not about her. He had a personality. It impressed everybody and he liked to make an impression. In fact he never lost a chance of doing it. That was his mainspring. Jim had plenty of energy. Say what you like, he got what he wanted. Most of us want things that we haven't got the stamina to work for. When we don't get them, we try to salve our self-love by explanations founded on 'ifs.' He never did that.

There were two sides to Jim, though in his case the world saw only one and that wasn't his best. I knew him. There wasn't a mean hair in his head. Everybody liked him. He was the leader among the boys in the village in spite of the fact that his father, who was an unprosperous tin peddler, owed everybody who would trust him. Jim was well built and strong. He was the best wrestler among us and the best jumper. I could run faster than he could and Walter Perkins – 'Frog' we called him – could throw a stone farther. But Jim would not compete with us in these things. He stuck to wrestling and jumping. He liked to win. But if he got beaten, he didn't sulk over it. He laughed and went on to something else.

He had a fair skin, with red in his cheeks and wavy chestnut hair that turned brown when he was older. He had plenty of self-confidence – 'cheek' we used to call it. He was smart in school, especially in arithmetic. I admired him for this because I could never get my examples to come out right. He used to help me do them. He was always willing and he never made you feel that you were under obligation to him for it. He just did it and then forgot it. It did him good, gave him the feeling of superiority that he liked.

He was never at a loss for something interesting to do; he had energy to carry out his ideas and daring where courage or impudence were needed. We were willing followers, all the more because he wasn't an exacting master. He didn't abuse his authority. He didn't maintain his position by force but by popular favor, so to speak. We all liked Jim; nobody was afraid of him.

Bennington was a center for the country round about. The stages stopped there going north and south, and later the railroad ran through there to Rutland. We had a grist mill where the farmers brought in their wheat and corn to be ground, and a sawmill where the lumber came to be cut up. They hauled it down from the mountains mostly in the winter. The big logs of pine and spruce were chained on bob-sleds drawn by yokes of steers. In the summer the same steers drew loads of hay from the fields. Folks weren't in so much of a hurry then about their work, but they managed to get it all done. The houses were solid; they stood up against the wind in winter and they were warm enough, though we had only open fires. The post office was in the town and there was a blacksmith, where the horses and oxen were shod, and stores. When we were boys every man was a carpenter. A good many could mend a harness or a pair of boots, or solder a leaky pail. Painting a house was not a thing to hire someone to do, nor was laying a stone wall, or building a chimney, or digging a well.

We could have got along all right even if all the roads into Bennington had been blocked. There were vegetables in the cellars, corn and wheat in the bins, salt pork and corned beef in barrels, and smoked hams in the chimneys. There were sheep to supply us with wool and mutton, calves for veal and spinning and weaving had not yet been forgotten.

The Garlands didn't live exactly in the village but half a mile or so away up the Branch. Ceda was one of a brood of tow-heads, and the only attractive one. They were as poor as Job's cat. That didn't make any difference. Poverty wasn't regarded as a fault – scarcely a misfortune. The family lived in a weather-beaten house on a strip of land beside the stream, and an upland pasture above, among the ledges. It was a meager farm and the women had to hoe the potatoes and corn and vegetables while Garland worked out his yoke of steers to earn money to buy what he lacked land to raise.

♦

My father was a Unitarian minister and I think he must have been a rather uncommon man. His marriage was a love match, of which I was the only offspring. He died of typhus fever before I was a year old.

He gave me one thing of great value and that was the ability to enjoy books, and especially poetry. The reading of books has always been my most valuable resource. Perhaps it has helped to make me a spectator, rather than a man of action; but when all is said and done it has enabled me to enjoy my life and at least to relish what I have seen and heard.

We lived, my mother and I, just at the edge of the village, where the Roaring Branch road comes in from the east, and the Fisks lived a little farther along, between us and the Garlands. My mother had a small income, paid to her by her brother Joel, from the rent of some farm land her father had owned, and she increased it by giving music lessons and sometimes by dressmaking. She and I lived alone in the small weather-beaten pleasant house which stood under a large horse-chestnut tree close to the road. At the back of it was the kitchen. Next to that was the woodshed, overgrown with woodbine and facing the South, looking out upon the vegetable garden. There was the well and the well-sweep that we continued to use for drawing water long after a good many other people were using pumps. There were apple trees further along and a barn in which we kept our cow, 'Daisy,' and the pigs. My boyhood existence was centered here.

My name among the boys was 'Rabbits.' Jim gave it to me on account of two rabbits I caught one winter in a boxtrap that I set in the pine grove just over the stone wall behind our house, in the pasture. They were common gray rabbits and I kept them in a cage I made out of an old wooden box by putting wires across the front of it. I began by keeping them in the kitchen, but they smelt so that my mother had me carry the cage out into the woodshed. These rabbits were objects of much interest. Jim thought up a plan to take advantage of it by forming what he called the Bennington Fur and Skin Company. His idea was that my pair of rabbits would breed and he figured out the average growth of the family and the length of time it would take for them to get large enough to be killed and skinned. Members of the company were enrolled upon payment of twenty-five cents each to Jim and all were required to sign an agreement that these contributions should be invested in the business, and that the contributors should not expect to get them back. Each member of the company was to provide himself with a pair of rabbits and encourage them to produce their kind for the benefit of the company.

It was a great scheme. We elected Jim president and treasurer. He knew more about it than anybody else because he had invented it, and he was constantly adding new details which kept us interested and aroused debate. At one time we had twelve members, though not all of them kept rabbits. We used to hold meetings in an underground resort that we constructed at the top of Squaw Hill, which was a mound of sand and clay on our farm not far from the pine grove. We dug a square pit there about seven feet long, five feet wide, and five feet deep. Then we laid poles across the top, put brush over them, and replaced the turf so that no sign of the hole was left. To reach the retreat it was necessary to crawl through a tunnel which began on the side of the hill. We had a piece of rusty stove pipe which we pushed up through the roof when we wanted to make a fire inside, and there we assembled to discuss the plans and progress of the company.

The hill got its name from a story that an Indian Squaw had buried the body of her child there before she migrated to Canada with her tribe after the Englishmen won in the French and Indian War, and that she came back for the bones years later when she was nearly a hundred years old, and carried them away with her to Canada in a bag. This story gave the little hill a romantic, slightly ghostly reputation which, with the concealment of our underground chamber, inspired us with the idea of organizing ourselves into a secret society, with signs, passwords, and initiation ceremonies. We called ourselves the United Redskins and our regalia consisted of headdresses of chicken feathers.

The heyday of the United Redskins was short – but more delightful than we knew at the time. Our ages ranged from thirteen to fifteen and our company began to break up almost immediately. Vivid are the recollections of that fall, the last when we were all together. I can shut my eyes and see the Valley – a carpet of yellow and brown and green in a thousand shades of earth and withering vegetation, with the ring of dark blue hills around it, lying against the pale, misty sky.

One October night, when the Hunters' Moon was full, I remember we made an expedition to the lowlands along the Walloomsac in search of skunks. The affairs of the Fur Company had been stagnant all summer and Jim had an idea that we might revive them by capturing skunks on the moonlit plains where they were in the habit of ranging for the purpose of digging white grubs out of the dry turf. Jim admitted that it was a hazardous business to hunt skunks with only the short clubs that we carried, but he had the plan of campaign all reasoned out. 'They can't throw any stink unless they're facin' your way,' he assured us. 'They put it on their tails and then they jerk their tails forwards and sprinkle it on you over their own heads. The thing to do when we see one will be for some of us to stand in front and keep him facin' our way, while Rabbits, here, or Frog, creeps up behind and whacks him with the club across his back. Once you hit him on his back, he can't do nuthin' more.' This seemed plausible, but nevertheless I was secretly very much afraid we might find a skunk and I was relieved when we came home without having seen any.

Jim made one more attempt, a little later, after winter had set in, to get the Fur Company going. He projected the capture of a Canada lynx that had been seen by a teamster beside the road along Roaring Branch some distance above the Garland place. The Garlands had an old shot-gun that had once been a flint-lock and had been made over for percussion caps. We got a little powder, which we poured into a powder horn, and a box of caps. We loaded the gun with nails and screws as being more deadly than shot, and set off to find the 'link.' We allowed Ceda to go with us in view of the fact that she had supplied the gun. We found the tracks of the animal in the snow and followed them through the woods but we didn't catch up with the 'link.' Darkness ended the hunt. As we turned back, Jim showed us what would have happened if we had overtaken the lynx. He aimed the old gun at the trunk of an oak tree and fired. The missiles that it contained tore the rugged bark and buzzed off through the air in every direction. The next day a snow storm covered the lynx's tracks.

That spring the Fisk family moved to Brattleboro. The United Redskins and the Fur and Skin Company went out of existence. With them went our boyhood.

I have given only a faint idea of the many activities and events that filled our long days. The river was a source of endless pleasures. It is not a large river. It comes down from Camel's Hump and the North in a succession of rapids and shallows from pool to pool. I knew not only every foot of it, but all the trout brooks for miles around. We swam in the pools and we built rafts to sail on. We made fires and roasted our fish on forked sticks and ate them. We got as sunburned as it was possible to be. Sometimes Ceda was with us. She did everything that we did, including swimming, but this wasn't often and we never 'told on her' because we knew her mother wouldn't approve of it.

Perhaps it is just as well that I haven't detailed the tricks and pranks that we played in the village. These were constant and various and Jim, who always loved practical jokes, invented most of them. Anybody who has lived in the country knows how filled with events are the uneventful lives of country-folks! All that part of our lives ended for me too soon.

Change

That summer of 1850 after Jim, with his father and stepmother and his half-sister Minna, moved away, I saw a good deal more of Ceda Garland. I was sixteen years old in February that year and she was sixteen in April. My voice finished changing, and I began to look anxiously for signs of a moustache. I was made conscious of the fact that Ceda's being a girl made a great difference between us.

In other ways, too, that year for me was a year of change. I stopped going to school and went to work, hiring out to anybody that would pay me. I wasn't specially strong but I was willing and I wanted to help my mother all I could. So I worked for what I could get, and that was more often under than over a dollar a day. It was hard work but it did me more good than harm because it taught me how to do a lot of things that I picked up from the different men I worked for. Most of my work was for farmers, but some of it was in the village. I clerked in a store one month and helped in the post office for a while.

I didn't feel much like going out evenings when I got through; I was mostly glad enough to get into bed. But I don't think I would have gone even if I hadn't been so tired. My mother began to feel the long strain of taking care of herself and me for so many years, ever since my father's death. Sometimes I could get her to laugh again, but as time went on, it was harder and harder. Maybe she had feelings that she never told me about and knew that she wouldn't live much longer. But I had no idea of anything of the kind. She was a young woman yet – only thirty-nine. I hadn't been eighteen more than a month – it was in March, 1852 – when she caught cold from getting her feet wet in the slush. The cold turned into pneumonia and she died. It came all of a sudden, before I could get my mind ready for it. It was a grief to me such as I never knew anyone could feel. The sharpness of it wore off in time, but I have never gone back to what I was before it happened. My thoughts grew older after she left me alone.

———♦———

When the doctor saw that my mother couldn't get well, he told Mrs. Evander Thomas, a neighbor, who had been my mother's best friend, and Mrs. Thomas sent to Rutland for my Uncle Joel Winslow, who lived there. He took charge of everything. His business was to buy cattle and sometimes horses in the northern parts of Vermont and York State. Sometimes he sold them in Albany and sometimes he drove them to New York and sold them there. This was before the West was enough settled to supply the eastern part of the country with beef and pork and grain.

———♦———

My Uncle Joel's house in Rutland was comfortable and almost new. He had taken in a couple to look after him and to take care of the house when he was away. The man's name was Henry Rodman. He was a thin man, with quick brown eyes and a wide mouth. He was fond of joking and he was a great checker player. His wife was cheerful and plump and a very good cook.

He wasn't a man of impulse, Uncle Joel, I mean. After my mother's funeral, he considered what was to be done next and when he had made up his mind, he told me what decision he had reached. We were to sell what I had in Bennington and I was to come to live with him in Rutland and learn to be a drover. I agreed. I was too miserable to think of the future or to care much what became of me.

I couldn't bear to attend the auction of my mother's house when the day came. Instead, I went up the Branch to the Garlands' and asked Ceda to come out with me. I brought her up a sealskin coat that had belonged to my mother. Such garments were much more common then than they are now, but my mother had always taken great care of this coat and it was the most highly prized of her treasures. I didn't want anybody else to wear it, but it was too useful to be thrown away and I wouldn't sell it. I decided that I'd rather give it to Ceda than to anyone else. She was overjoyed to get it.

We walked up on the hill and sat down there under a pine, tree. 'What do you expect to do?' Ceda asked, when I told her I was going to live with my uncle.

'I don't know,' I said, 'I haven't thought about it yet. He wants me to go into his business with him.'

'Does it pay him?'

'Yes, he's done pretty well, I guess.'

'I should like to travel all over, the way he does. Will you go to New York?'

'I shouldn't wonder. He has to take his cattle there, sometimes.'

'Ain't you wild to see it?'

'No.'

'Why not? I should think you would be.'

'I don't know why, but I ain't.'

She was silent for a moment. 'When shall you be coming this way again?' she asked at last.

'Maybe never,' I replied.

'Don't you want to?' she insisted.

Her inquiry brought the future before my mind and a wave of lonesomeness and self-pity swept over me. My nerves had been worn by wakefulness and grief. I tried to speak and could not. 'Poor boy!' said Ceda. She put her hand on my shoulder and pulled my head down into her lap. Her sympathy made me all the worse. I sobbed while she stroked my hair, saying nothing, but waiting quietly until I had regained control of myself.

The City

Behind a drove of sixty-three head of cattle we set out down the river through Pownall in the fall of 1852. The driving was done by a young man named Thomas Jefferson Hayden and his shepherd dog Randy, assisted by myself. Uncle Joel rode along behind in his chaise. Jeff and I rode two bony horses of middle age but still capable of outfooting a straying cow or an obstreperous steer when Randy failed to keep them in order, which was seldom.

Jeff was an experienced drover. He had already made the trip to New York three times and he liked to astonish me with accounts of what was to be seen, heard, desired, and feared in the great city. He was an accomplished liar. I soon discovered that weakness in him but I carefully concealed my discovery. It took us a long time to make that drive. We were something like three weeks on the road. I enjoyed it all. The far prospects that we got when we came out into the Hudson Valley were a new thing to me. The distant blue shapes of the Helderbergs and later of the Catskills were quite different from the views of our own mountains, which never could get so far away from us. The great river beside which we travelled was always a source of interest. The towns along its banks looked prosperous. I envied the people who lived in them. The sails of vessels carrying merchandise to and from these towns aroused my wonder; still more the steamboats that swept past, with the smoke pouring out of their funnels.

But even more wonderful were the trains that ran upon the tracks along the edge of the river. The railroad had just then been opened from New York to Albany. Jeff told me some remarkable lies about Commodore Vanderbilt who owned the steamboats. He said they called him 'Commodore' because he had been a pirate in his youth, plundering ships not only of other countries but also of the New England coast, especially those in the oriental trade; and that it was with the money gained in this bloody business that he had grown so rich.

♦

One afternoon we drove the cattle into their pens behind the Bull's Head Tavern, which was then on the edge of the city among the farms of the Boston Road, where Twenty-sixth Street now crosses Third Avenue. As we straightened those creatures out in the pens, I little dreamed of the important role one of the owners of the Bull's Head was to play in the story I am now telling. That man was Daniel Drew.

Uncle Joel didn't have much trouble getting rid of his cattle. He happened to arrive when the market was pretty bare and prices were high. Before night of the day after we got there, the last of our steers had been weighed and turned over to buyers. The next morning at sunrise we undertook to drive into the City about a dozen head that we had agreed to deliver.

This ended our job and my uncle proposed, by way of celebration, to buy me a ticket to Barnum's American Museum, which then stood at the corner of Ann Street and Broadway. Nobody paid the shilling required to get into that Museum without getting his money's worth. I lost myself in contemplating the wonders. I stared at them with open-mouthed absorption. I was standing before a case in which strange birds of brilliant plumage were seeking in stuffed alarm to drive a wicked-looking snake and several ugly lizards away from their nest filled with eggs amid the branches, when I felt a sudden slap on my back and a gruff voice exclaimed: 'Here, young feller! You can't stand here all day unless you pay another shillin'!' I turned and there stood Jim Fisk! He was taller and bigger, but his face had changed very little and it was grinning all over. 'Where in the name of Jenny Maria Jones did you drop from?' he inquired.

I was astounded. He was the last person I expected to meet there. As soon as I could recover I explained, and in a few minutes I told him all that had happened since I saw him last. He was very sorry to hear of my mother's death. Everybody liked her. 'How did you happen to get here yourself?' I demanded in my turn. 'Business!' he replied, expanding his chest and squaring his shoulders. 'Business, my boy! I'm working for Van Amberg. You know who he is. He couldn't do without me, says I'm necessary to his happiness. We're in Brooklyn this week.'

'Van Amberg!' I exclaimed. The reputation of that showman's collection of wild animals was known all over the country. 'What do you do?'

'What don't I do, you'd better ask!' he said. 'It would be a lot easier to tell you that. If I really tried to tell you all I do for that show we'd be standing here until people took us for wax works.'

'Do you like it?'

'You bet! I've got so attached to the animals that they won't eat unless I'm there. That's a fact! The keepers just can't make 'em, 'specially the lions.'

'How did you get the job?'

'Well, it's a long story. After we moved to Brattleboro, the old man started out to run a hotel there. You know what a genius he is. He ran it so darn fast that mighty few were quick enough to get into it. At last he ran it into the ground. Van Amberg had his show up there and he put some of his help into dad's emporium. One of his men, he was a young fellow, got homesick or somethin' and he slid out for Maine. I told Van I might be induced to take the place and of course I got it. I've travelled all over with 'em.'

I looked at him with admiration. It didn't seem possible that I had been his chum in Bennington. He seemed to know all about everything. He was as much at home amongst the marvels of the Museum as he had been in the Bennington school house. I asked him if he ever saw anything of Ceda Garland. Seeing him reminded me of her.

'Ceda' he replied, 'Yes, I've seen her since we moved. She came to Brattleboro and took a job as waitress there in the hotel for a while. Maybe she's there yet; I haven't been there for quite a spell and I never hear anything. Ceda's a smart girl.' I felt pleased somehow to hear him praise her. While we talked, we were walking slowly through the rooms of the Museum. We came to a room at last in which a crowd of people was gathered round a stout man in a long black coat who was explaining to them about something in a glass case. 'That's him; that's Phineas T. Barnum!' Jim informed me. 'Come up closer and let's hear what he's sayin'.' Barnum was telling them a story about a withered-looking thing with the tail of a fish that he had in the glass case. He called it a mermaid – the only one that ever had been caught.

'He's a cheerful liar!' Jim said in my ear, after we had listened for a while. 'Come on! I've got to get along back to work.' In the next room he declared that the mermaid they were making such a fuss over was only a monkey-body with the tail of a fish sewed onto it. I didn't believe it. I didn't want to. I preferred to believe I had seen what once had been a real, live mermaid.

'All right, Rabbits, believe it if you'd rather,' Jim said. 'You don't hurt anybody believing it. But if you want to see something that's worth seeing, come on over to Brooklyn tomorrow afternoon and I'll show 'em to you. Shan't cost you a cent. Bring your uncle, too. Just ask for me and I'll get you in for nuthin'.'

Travels

In this narrative I shall cover a good deal of time, since the background must be reckoned in to a certain extent. My memory is fairly good for some things and not so good for others.

Anyone can gain a good knowledge of these important years from the history books. There was the Civil War, for instance, and the time that is usually called the Period of Reconstruction. Those were the big events. The steamboat was just beginning to crowd the clipper off the seas; railroads were replacing canals; the first ocean cable was laid; oil was struck in western Pennsylvania; the common school system was becoming a gospel and corporations were beginning to range with very little restraint over the richest field for plunder in the whole world. In short, the American life that we are living to-day had begun.

♦

At that time in my life the controversy over slavery had been fanned by the struggle between the North and the South for possession of the new territory west of the Missouri River. The situation in Kansas was growing daily more acute. New England was sending out companies of Free Soil settlers to occupy the land. The South sent its men out to uphold the institution of slavery. My uncle made up his mind that it was his duty to join this frontier guard of freedom and I decide to go with him. We set out in the spring that followed our cattle drive to New York, reaching the Ohio River through Pittsburgh.

Cincinnati gave me my first experience of the spirit of the West, confident, animated, and boastful. We put up at the Burnett House. After supper I strolled out alone to get some idea of the city. My attention was attracted almost immediately by large posters announcing the presence that day of Van Amberg's circus and wild animal show. This was the show that Jim Fisk had told me he was with. I wandered on through the town, stopping at the store windows, until I reached a large vacant field on the outskirts where a number of brightly painted wagons were drawn up. I realized that this was the place where the circus had been and that the show was being packed up. While I stood watching the bustle and confusion, someone laid a hand on my shoulder and a voice said: 'If it isn't Rabbits, by all that's sacred!' It was Jim Fisk. He held out his hand. 'Where did you come from?' he asked.

'From Pittsburgh,' I replied, 'with my uncle.'

'Where you going?'

'To Kansas.'

'Kansas? Why don't you go to Timbuctoo?'

'Because they've got slavery there already, I suppose.'

'Oh, slavery, is it? You had better let it alone, Rabbits; it's a bad business.'

'What are you doing here yourself?'

He waved his hand toward the bright wagons and the moving shapes of the men loading the carts with the paraphernalia of the circus.

'I'm runnin' the show,' he said.

'You mean to say that you're still associating with those animals that I've been looking at on the posters?'

'That's what I'm doing. They all eat out of my hat.'

'Is it a good business?'

'Best in the world. Besides, they couldn't get along without me for a week. Looking after the animals isn't all of it, by a long shot.'

'What else do you have to do?'

'Why, I furnish them with ideas. If it wasn't for me the whole blessed show would go up the flue. Van Amberg's all right, but let me say to you I don't know how he ever got along as well as he has.' He proceeded to tell me instance after instance of how he had come to the rescue of the show when matters looked serious. By careful questioning I discovered that his real occupation was taking tickets at the entrance of the big tent.

Jim stayed with the show for several years after that before he started a business of his own that made him known all over the western part of New England, and even across the border in York

State. At that time his upper lip had begun to be shaded by a blond mustache and his outlines were showing a little of the roundness that became more characteristic as he grew older. He was as self-confident and full of energy as ever. We stood talking together until he had to climb on one of the wagons which was going to lumber along through country roads all night toward Columbus, their next town. He waved farewell to me from the rear of the circus wagon as it jolted away down the street into the darkness.

Next day, my uncle having concluded his business in Cincinnati, we boarded another riverboat, which carried us down the Ohio to Louisville, where we awoke the following morning. We went on past Paducah and Evansville, and finally reached Cairo on the flat at the meeting of the Ohio and the Mississippi.

———— ♦ ————

This is intended to be the story of Jim Fisk and it isn't the place to tell in detail what happened to my uncle and me in Kansas. We settled in Lawrence, where we built a log cabin for ourselves. In that cabin, Uncle Joel was shot and killed by a band of drunken ruffians from Missouri when Lawrence was sacked during the following year by a mob under the leadership of the sheriff. I wasn't born to be either a pioneer or a reformer. I like the conveniences and comforts of civilization. I never felt the indignation over slavery that most of the New Englanders in Kansas felt. I didn't like Kansas. It wasn't safe there. I wanted to go back to Rutland; I knew I wasn't a hero and I didn't want to try to be one. Hatred filled the air and it made me uncomfortable. I didn't want to hate anybody, not even the men who killed my uncle. They didn't know any better, and my hating them wouldn't bring him back. Uncle Joel willed me everything that he had, and his death left me without relatives in this country, so far as I knew.

———— ♦ ————

I came back East as far as Cincinnati by the same route as we had taken when we went out but from Cincinnati I went up across the

State of Ohio and reached Schenectady by way of Lake Erie and the Erie Canal. At Troy I took the Rutland stage and surprised the Rodmans, Henry and his wife Becky, whom my Uncle Joel had left in charge of his house when we set out for the West. They gave me an enthusiastic welcome home; Henry insisted on starting a checker tournament that very night.

I probated my uncle's will and then began to consider what I should do next. I had just about income enough to keep me but I didn't like the idea of doing nothing for the rest of my life.

♦

I was walking home one evening thinking about my future and admiring the carpet of bright October leaves which covered the path, when I heard a great commotion down the street. It was caused by four white horses drawing a wagon resplendent with paint and varnish and polished brass. I stared like everybody else and as soon as I saw the face of the driver, I recognized him as Jim Fisk. He didn't see me, but I knew he must be going to the hotel and I followed him there. The wagon, from which the horses had been unhitched, was standing in front of the stable when I arrived. On the side of it, in gold lettering, I read:

JAMES FISK, JR.
jobber in Silks, Shawls, Dress Goods, jewelry
Silver Ware and Yankee Notions

I read this inscription with a mixture of envy and admiration. While I had been hesitating over what to do, he had gone ahead and done something. I was looking at the wagon when Jim came up behind me. 'Pretty, ain't it!' he said. We shook hands. Jim was as glad to see me again as I was to see him. He unlocked the different compartments of the wagon to show me how he had got it arranged and what he had in it. He talked a blue streak all the time. While he was telling me about it, a tin peddler's wagon, of the old-fashioned kind, such as his father used to drive, turned into the yard

'That's mine, too,' said Jim. 'Hello, Dan. What luck?'

'Purty fair,' the driver replied, as he climbed down from his perch and spat on the ground. 'I've got two more of 'em on the road,' Jim told me. 'The others'll be here to-morrow. Where are you staying?' I told him and invited him to come with me to supper, and he came. As we walked along, I told Jim in a few words what had happened to us in Kansas, and why I had come back. I asked him then to give an account of himself.

'Well,' he said, 'the last time I saw you was in Cincinnati. That's a great town. I wish we had it in Vermont. I liked the show business. There was always sunthin' new in it – either the elephant would get a belly ache, or we'd get stuck in the mud, or the hands would try to get their pay raised, or the bareback lady would elope – always sunthin' going on. I got a lot of practice fixing things up, first one thing and then another. They all liked me there. I'd have stayed with Van Amberg and maybe I'd have bought the show off him some day, if it hadn't been for Pop takin' that hotel in Brattleboro. You know Pop isn't exactly what you'd call a financial wizard. He's got good ideas, but somehow they never seem to work out the way he thinks they're going to. He had a notion that he could run the hotel and tin peddlin' business too, and make money out of both of 'em. Well, he wasn't makin' any out of either when I dropped in to see him on leave of absence.

'Pop was way down in the dumps. He'd been figgerin' things up and the only thing he could see ahead was bankruptcy and darned little for his creditors in that, even, to say nothing of himself. I'd saved up some money, and I'd just made some more bettin' on a horse race in Syracuse, that one of the circus men told me about. It was enough to stave off the sheriff for the time bein' and I looked things over. To come to the point, it ended by my buying Pop out of the peddlin' end of his business and our rentin' the hotel for a year to Hank Sayles.

'That gave us a chance to turn around and then I told Pop my notion of how the peddlin' business ought to be run, that cart you saw up at the hotel and the four white horses, you know. He didn't believe I could make a go of it. Well, I planned the cart all out and got a man to make it, and I took a trip to Boston and ordered a lot of stuff on three months' time from Jordan and Marsh. They're a big firm in Boston. The Lord only knows how I got 'em to give me credit, but they did. Of course Van Amberg said a good word for me and Pop got some folks in Brattleboro to say I was all right.

'My idea was to do a jobbin' business as I went along. I go to all the storekeepers in a place and if there's anything in my wagon that they like, as there most usually is, I get it for 'em from Jordan and Marsh, and collect a commission on the sale. Of course I sell to them at wholesale prices, lower than the retail prices that I sell for out of the cart, and I make a good many sales that way, too.

'I didn't intend to lose the retail trade. I had Pop's old cart shined up, got him a good stock, and sent him out with it. I agreed to pay him twenty dollars a week and expenses. That worked so well that I put on two more retail carts, with the best men I could get to drive 'em.'

'That sounds good,' I said. 'You say it works well?'

'Like a charm,' Jim replied. 'Why, we made so much money the first year that Pop's gone back to the hotel business. He's got Hank for manager though; I had to insist on that.'

♦

By this time we had reached the Rodman's gate. They took to Jim right off, and he to them. While we were eating supper he told some stories about his adventures when he was with Van Amberg and I told about some of the things that had happened in Kansas. Jim asked what I was going to do and I told him what I'd been thinking about. 'Why don't you come in with me?' he asked. 'I don't know anything about selling,' I replied. I hadn't thought of joining him. 'Sell nuthin'!' said Jim. 'I want you to keep things straight for us. We get mixed up all the time because there's nobody to keep track of what's going on. We ought to have some books. I can't remember everything, especially when somebody else remembers it different. What do you say? I can make it worth your while.'

'Where would you want me to be?'

'In Brattleboro, where we've got our main head-quarters. You'd live with Pop in the Revere House. Ceda Garland's there.'

'Is she? What's she doing?'

'She's got charge of the grub – the kitchen and dining room.' It occurred to me that she and Jim were going to get married and I felt a strong dislike for Brattleboro.

'Ceda's a great friend of my wife,' he remarked.

'You married?' I exclaimed.

'Since last fall.'

'Congratulations!' I cried, slapping him on the back with a little extra heartiness, because I was relieved about Ceda. 'Who's the lucky girl?'

'She was Lucy Moore – Lucy D. Moore, in fact,' said Jim. 'She lived in Ashland, and she came up to Brattleboro to go to boarding school there. She and I got acquainted and when you see her, you won't be surprised at what happened.'

'Who are her folks?' I inquired.

'Her father and mother are both dead,' he told me. 'She's got a guardian, a man named Sanderson, who lives in Springfield. You'll like her, Rabbits.'

The more I thought about Jim's offer, the more attractive it seemed. I talked it over with the Rodmans after he'd gone, and they liked it, too. Jim had impressed them by his personality, as he usually did impress people. They had confidence in his ability to make good in anything he undertook.

2
War and Profits

The Yankee Peddler

It was agreed that I should go to the Revere House in Brattleboro as soon as I could arrange matters in Rutland. Jim promised to join me there and show me what he wanted me to do. I left Rutland a few days later and stopped overnight in Bennington at the Catamount Tavern. I was quite a hero. Everybody wanted to hear what was going on in Kansas, and what I thought would probably happen out there. The ancient warlike spirit of the Benningtonians was stimulated by the developments on the border.

I saw some of my old companions in Bennington next morning. A good many of them I found had left the place for new homes in York State and further west. I understood that the Garlands had located somewhere out on Lake Ontario. Ceda hadn't gone with them.

The stage took me to Brattleboro over the hills of Glastenbury. Old Pop Fisk welcomed me. He had improved. He'd been a broken-down, worried-looking man when he was trying to make a living out of the countryside with his tin peddler's cart. He was now fat and self-confident, with plenty of easy talk and cordiality. While he talked about Jim, he showed me the Revere House. I wanted to ask him about Ceda, but I didn't have the courage. He gave me a comfortable room at the back of the hotel. Jim wouldn't get there until the following day. I was dying to find Ceda again, but I didn't want to seem too eager. I thought maybe she might have changed. I expected to see her at supper time. While I was waiting for my beefsteak I glanced up and there she was, superintending operations near the entrance to the kitchen.

Her figure had filled out and she seemed to have grown taller. She looked more mature and self-possessed. I made observations by snatches, pretending to eat my supper. Apparently her duties made it necessary for her to keep an eye on the kitchen as well as upon the dining-room, and while she was out of the room I sneaked away and took refuge on the veranda. The dining-room gradually emptied and some of the guests of the hotel came out and sat down near me. Among them was a brisk-looking drummer with short side whiskers who used a gold toothpick.

'Nice lookin' gal!' he said to a companion. 'Which one?' the other man, a fat, pasty-faced person, inquired. 'The head waitress,' the first man said. 'There she goes now! Goodbye!' He got up from his chair and walked quickly down the street. Looking in the direction he was taking, I saw Ceda lingering under the trees which shaded the sidewalk. The drummer joined her and took off his hat with a show of ceremony that made me sick. Without waiting to see more I got up and went into the hotel. I was very much depressed. The talk and laughter in the barroom annoyed me. I went out for a stroll in the darkening town. At the first corner I came face to face with Ceda. She was alone.

'How are you, Rab?' she asked, holding out her hand and smiling.

'Hello, Ceda!' I said gloomily.

'What's the matter with you?' she asked.

'Nothing,' I replied.

'Come along. I want to talk with you,' she said putting her hand through my arm. 'Where's the drummer gone?' I blurted out. She laughed.

'I don't know,' she said, 'he hasn't been with me.'

'He went out to meet you,' I couldn't refrain from saying.

'Maybe he did,' she admitted, 'but I'm too busy to waste time on folks like him.' My spirits began to rise. 'I saw you in the dining-room,' I said, after a pause. We were walking along together. 'Of course you did, and I saw you,' she replied, 'only I didn't think that was much of a place to talk and I want to have a good talk with you.' She pressed my arm in a friendly manner. The world began to seem more cheerful.

———♦———

It turned out that we had a great deal to say to each other. Ceda told me how matters had gone from bad to worse with her family, until at last they'd left the house on Roaring Brook for a westward migration. She had a thousand things to tell me about mutual acquaintances and old schoolmates and on my side I had a thousand things to tell her of my experiences. I was surprised and pleased to find how easy it was to talk to her about myself. That I should be interested in what she had to tell me seemed entirely natural. I found myself telling Ceda all of my plans and hopes. I held her hand and I wanted to kiss her, but I didn't dare to try it without encouragement. She didn't give me any.

'What kind of a girl is it that Jim has married?' I asked.

'I like her very much,' Ceda replied. 'She comes from down near Framingham. Jim loves her to death. I don't think she knows much about housekeeping and that sort of thing. She's never had any chance to learn. Jim got going with her while she was in school here in the Female Seminary. She was only a young girl when they were married. Her father and mother are both dead. She thinks the world of Jim.'

'What sort of a looking girl is she?' I asked.

'She's a little bit taller than Jim is,' Ceda told me, 'and she has beautiful brown hair; I never saw anything to beat it.'

'It can't be as pretty as yours, Ceda!' I said.

'Don't talk nonsense,' said Ceda. 'Come along, it's time that we got back to the hotel.'

Thus ended my encounter with Ceda. Of course I saw a great deal of her during the months when I was keeping track of Jim's business affairs in Brattleboro. She was the same Ceda she'd always been, only she had grown more self-reliant and more acquainted with the world.

In a day or two Jim came back and explained the part that I was to play in his affairs. He showed in the management of his peddling business the same qualities that afterwards made him so successful in much larger enterprises. He liked to do things with a flourish and on a liberal scale. He liked the change and variety of driving round the country in his glittering coach. Very often he took Lucy, with him perched high up on the seat beside him. Her presence always had a softening influence on Jim. While he was never a profane man, he carefully avoided any swearing while she was there. His fondness for her had in it much of the protective element. They seemed made for each other.

I don't think Jim was ever happier than he was during the summer of 1857 when I became a member of his organization. Everybody liked him. Nobody ever made a complaint that the things he sold were not what he represented them to be or that anything he said about them was not true. He paid his bills promptly and he was scrupulous in all his dealings. His cart, his pretty wife, and his horses became famous all through western New England and eastern York State. His enterprise and his methods attracted attention all over that region and there were descriptions of him even in the New York and Boston newspapers. Jim liked all this. He believed that advertising was necessary to success. Barnum believed the same thing. In this Jim was like Barnum, as he was like him in some other ways.

———♦———

Jim spent a good many days in Brattleboro with his father and stepmother and Lucy. His half-sister, Minna, was going to the Brattleboro Female Academy. She had the greatest admiration for Jim and she never would allow anybody to say a word against him without bristling up like a setting hen.

Jim and I had a good many talks together in the Revere House. Once I asked him how he happened to leave home and join Van Amberg's show. 'It was the first dollar I earned that did it,' he said. 'Pop never liked to clean out the stables, and as soon as I got big enough to lift a dungfork, he took me out to the barn and let me watch him do it. Next day he asked me whether I thought I could do what he'd done. "I don't know whether I can or not," says I; and then he pulled a silver dollar out of his pocket. "That's yours if you do it the way I did," he says. I took the fork and I managed somehow to get the job done. Pop was tickled to death. He gave me the dollar and patted me on the back. "You did well, boy," he says. "I couldn't have done it better myself. You've done it so well," Pop says, "that I'm a-goin' to let you keep on doin' it all winter."

'That settled things for me. I made up my mind it was time for me to strike right out into the cold, wide world the first chance I got, and Van Amberg was the chance.'

Jim Goes to Boston

Ceda Garland was almost like one of the family, just as I was. We were together most of the time when we were not at work. Gradually we got to feeling that we belonged to each other. I was always ready to take her anywhere or do anything she wanted, and she never thought of going with anyone but me. She looked after my clothes and mended them when they needed it. It wasn't strange under the circumstances that I should fall in love with her, and I did.

There wasn't any moon the night when I asked her to marry me, but the sky was full of a million bright stars. Well as I knew her, I didn't somehow find it easy to propose. I'd thought out the words I was going to say, but it was a tough job to say them. I suppose she knew what was the matter with me and tried to stave me off. When I finally managed to ask her I hardly recognized the sound of my own voice; but anyhow, I did it.

'O Rab!' she said, 'Why not let things be the way they are? Aren't we having a good time?'

'Yes,' I admitted, 'but I want it to keep on like this always.'

'That's much more likely if we don't get married.'

'Do you think that, Ceda?'

'I know it. I've watched a good many marriages.'

'But I want you!'

'Haven't you got me now?'

'I don't mean that way. I want you for my own.'

'I don't want to be anybody's own, Rab; how would you like it, yourself?'

'But you're a woman.'

'Suppose I am; what difference does that make?'

'I want to take care of you.'

She laughed and put her hand on my arm, so it wouldn't hurt my feelings. 'I don't need anybody to take care of me; I can take care of myself,' she said; and I knew it was true.

'But, Ceda, don't you see – '

'Now, Rab, let's talk about something else; that's a good boy.'

'Does that mean "no," Ceda?'

'No, it doesn't. Do you want me to say "no"?'

'Of course I don't; I want you to say "yes".'

'Well, I shan't say either – not now, anyway.'

No matter how hard I begged, or how much I told her I loved her, she wouldn't budge from this. She made me understand that I'd have to leave the situation the way it was or go without. Of course that didn't prevent me from talking about it. She didn't seem to mind that; I think she rather liked it.

♦

It was natural that Jim's operations as a new-style peddler should attract attention to him and they did. Jordan and Marsh, the ambitious young Boston house from which he bought his supplies, began to take notice of him. He was one of their best customers and they asked him to move down to Boston and go to work for them.

Jim considered the offer. It appealed strongly to his imagination. He didn't like to stay long in one place. We'd been doing a good business peddling, but when we came to foot up the profits, there wasn't much to brag about. Jim couldn't save. He didn't want to. He never cared about money for its own sake. He had made a big investment in his showy carts and horses and he spent a lot on Lucy. He wanted her to have the best of everything.

'I'll tell you how I feel about it, Rabbits,' he said when we were talking it over. 'It strikes me that we've got about all the glory there is to get and it don't appear that we're any of us goin' to get very rich out of it. How much is it we're payin' for interest?' I told him. It was a good deal.

'What I'm thinking about is whether we'll ever have a better chance than we've got right now to sell out,' he continued. 'It don't seem to me that the business is goin' to be any more thought of than it is. What do you think?' I hadn't looked on the business as something that Jim was building up to sell. I had been regarding it as a permanent thing, when I thought about it at all but now that Jim asked me, I had to say that, if he was going to sell, the time to do it was then, before the novelty had worn off.

'There's another thing about it, too,' said Jim. 'First we know some cuss'll come along and do the same as we're doing. I s'pose most everybody thinks we're makin' a lot of money. If they put on a competition against us, we'd have to let down our prices, and where would our profits be then?' That was something I hadn't thought about, either.

Jim began to inquire around and before he got through he found where he could sell his main route – the wholesale route, we called it – for enough to let him pay up his loans with something over. He'd still have his three retail routes left. 'You and Pop can manage the retail trade,' he explained, 'and I can try my luck in Boston. If I shouldn't make a go of it there, I'd have some place to come back to, and Lucy can stay here with the rest of you until we see how things turn out.' So he did it, and early in 1860 he was in the wholesale department of Jordan and Marsh's store trying to sell goods by the carload. We stayed behind in Brattleboro.

♦

Jim wasn't a success as a salesman, taking instructions from a sales manager and competing with a lot of other salesmen. He wasn't cut out for any such job. When he set out to do a thing, he had to do it in his own way and usually that was different from anybody else's way. Jim needed a free hand.

There was too much politics that year for business, anyway. The new party was nominating and electing Abraham Lincoln president; the jealousy between the North and the South over slavery was about to end in the open break that precipitated the Civil War. Maybe this had something to do with Jim's failure as a salesman and Eben Jordan took him aside and told him he'd better go back to Brattleboro and take up peddling again. He liked Jim, but he didn't think Jim could succeed on the larger stage.

That's where he made a mistake. The thought of coming back to Brattleboro as a beaten man made Jim feel sick at the stomach. He couldn't bear to contemplate such a thing, much less do it. 'I know I'm a failure,' he told Jordan, 'but you can't make a silk purse out of a sow's ear. I can't stand a man up against a pile of goods and make him buy 'em. As soon as he starts to haggle over the price and tell me that he can get the same thing from so-and-so for less, I want to give him my blessing and tell him to run right along and buy 'em off so-and-so if he feels that way about it.'

'I see how it is,' Jordan commented.

'All right,' Jim went on. 'That doesn't mean I can't sell anything. I know darned well I can. But I've got to sell in my own way and not under orders.'

'I don't see how that can be managed,' Jordan put in.

'Look here,' said Jim. 'You just let me alone for another six months and I'll show you how to do it. I don't care a darn whether you pay me a salary or a commission. Turn me loose and I'll demonstrate for you.'

'He didn't know what to say at first,' Jim said when he told me about it, 'but they talked things over amongst themselves and yesterday they told me to go ahead on a commission.'

'Do you expect to make anything?'

'Say! They'll look sick before I'm through with 'em! You just watch me! I'll be a partner in that firm before I'm through!'

'How are you going about it?'

'Look here, Rabbits, there's going to be war before very long. The South will never stand Abe Lincoln.'

'Suppose there is?'

'Why, as soon as war's declared you can sell anything to the Government at almost any price you've got the guts to ask for it. Commissions! Holy cats!'

Jim knew what he was talking about. We had all grown so accustomed to hearing the brags and insults that were exchanged between the Abolitionists of the North and the slavery champions of the South that we had come to believe that vocal hostilities could go on indefinitely; but Jim saw what was coming and his shrewdness in this shows how to get ahead. He saw things before other folks did, that's all.

War Contracts

War was declared in the spring of 1861, about a month after Lincoln moved into the White House. He called for volunteers to put down the Rebellion, and they came to the defense of the Union faster than equipment could be provided for them. As Jim had foretold, you could sell the Government almost anything. He was all ready to act. He applied without losing a moment to Boutwell for a chance to offer supplies to the Government. He learned that Mrs. Wilkins, a Boston woman, had secured through political favor the disposal of a large contract for shirts and underwear for the troops. He hastened to get an introduction to this agent. He told her that his firm was able to deliver the merchandise at the lowest price and on the shortest notice. In a flood of enthusiastic language he appealed to her patriotism, her vanity, her humanity, and her self-interest. Before she knew it, she had assigned to Jim all her contract but a small part which she had already promised to somebody else. Jim found out that nothing had been signed and next day he came back and got her to take this fraction away from his rival and give it to him.

'There!' he said as he laid the contract, duly signed, before Eben Jordan. 'What do you think of your sow's ear now?' Jordan looked at the agreement and shook Jim's hand.

'Good boy!' said he.

'I told you I could,' said Jim, swelling with self-satisfaction.

'I wish we could sell 'em those blankets we've got in the warehouse,' Jordan remarked. Jim knew that he was referring to several hundred cases of blankets that the firm had bought a year or two before because it could get them at a low figure. All efforts to dispose of these blankets had failed. The house was stuck with them.

'I'll sell 'em for you,' said Jim. 'I shall have to go to Washington and the operation will cost you something. I don't want anybody checking up my expense account.'

'Why can't you sell 'em here?' Jordan asked.

'I don't know why, but I can't,' Jim replied. 'Maybe one of your regular salesmen can do it. If you want to try it that way, all right, go ahead; only if you're ever going to sell 'em, now is your chance. I wouldn't handle 'em myself after someone else had tried to work 'em off.'

Jordan laughed. He was beginning to understand Jim. 'All right,' he said. 'Can you get started to-morrow?'

'I'll take the midnight train to-night,' Jim said. 'Send a case of blankets by express in charge of a messenger to me at the best hotel there. I don't know which one it is.'

'It's the Willard,' Jordan told him.

'All right; send 'em to the Willard, then,' Jim said. 'Just make sure there's no moths in the case.'

It was around noon when they had this talk. Jim spent the afternoon getting letters of introduction to the right men in the War Department and in completing other preparations. He overlooked nothing. He'd telegraphed ahead in the name of his firm and he managed to get a suite of rooms in the Willard. Before he unpacked his bag, he ordered supper to be served in the suite that night. 'I hadn't any idea who'd be there, if anybody,' he said afterward, 'but it's always just as well to be ready.'

As a matter of fact, with the aid of some Massachusetts members of Congress and the member from the Brattleboro district, who was a friend of his, Jim got together the men he wanted and he gave them such good things to eat and drink and smoke that they forgot their cares and enjoyed themselves. Not a word about blankets! It was just an informal little get-acquainted party. He wanted them to drop in whenever they felt like it; to get in the habit of dropping in. They could be sure always of finding a quiet place where they could talk things over and relax.

Of course, they did drop in. Jim was first in the field in providing a snug refuge where government officials on small salaries could always find a welcome, a good cigar, and a drink of the kind of poison they preferred. He let the right people in and kept the wrong ones out. He conducted everything in person, with unfailing suavity and tact. Not a word about blankets; but the soldiers had to have them and inevitably the problem of where they were to be found came up. Blankets? Of course they were necessary. Too bad there was a shortage. Maybe Jim could help his friends to get hold of some. He knew where there had been some blankets, quite a good lot, in fact. He didn't know whether they had been disposed of. He promised to inquire and let them know as soon as he could get word from Boston. They told him to hurry and they'd wait for him.

So the blankets were sold, down to the last case, and at a price about three times what Jordan and Marsh had dreamed of getting. The firm shipped the cases out of its lofts, approved Jim's expense account without stopping to verify his addition, and wired him to keep his headquarters in the Willard House open until further notice.

Jim did that, but he didn't stay in Washington all the time. He had a bright young man sent down as assistant to relieve him when he wanted to go away. Army officers seem to have been much less scrupulous then than they are now about making a little money for themselves on the side. Jim knew how to distribute little presents, as he called them, and always attended to such matters himself.

But if Jim bribed an officer to award him a contract, say for shoes, that didn't mean that he filled it by supplying an inferior grade of shoes. His goods were always up to specifications. He might get good prices, and he did, but his shoes were good shoes, fit to march in. His vocabulary failed when he set out to express his contempt for the contractors who cheated the soldiers in the quality of their supplies. He expressed himself freely on this subject, no matter who heard him. Furthermore, he always insisted that his deliveries must be made before they were due under his contracts.

———♦———

It wasn't long after Jim sold the blankets that he began to buy cotton in the South and send it to the starving cotton mills of New England. There was a good deal of cotton to be had in the territory along the Mississippi on both sides of the river that was held by the Union troops. There was a whole lot more behind the Rebel lines and around New Orleans after Ben Butler got down there. A great deal of this could be bought in spite of the immense amounts that were burned by the Rebel officers to prevent our getting hold of it. Cotton was worth twelve cents a pound down South and as much as two dollars a pound up North. Jim made a preliminary investigation and then hurried on to Boston to report to his firm. Eben Jordan saw the point, but he didn't have capital enough alone to swing what Jim proposed. He offered William Dwight and the firm of Francis Skinner and Company, of Boston, a chance to come in with them and they came.

They told Jim to organize his field force. He proposed to scour all parts of the South that could be searched. He knew there'd be a swarm of speculators down there before you could say Jack Robinson as soon as this golden opportunity became known. He wanted to get there first and buy the cotton before anyone else could. He sent for his father and for Ceda and me and explained his ideas to us. He told us we were going to Nashville. He also hired a dozen shrewd Yankee buyers for the region around New Orleans. I was astonished at the magnitude of his plans and his self-confidence in carrying them through. He was beginning to blossom out.

We went to Nashville – or at least, I didn't, but Pop Fisk and Ceda did. I started out with them, but everywhere the bugles were blowing and the drums and fifes were working overtime. I wanted to enlist as soon as war was declared. I put it off then because we all thought the thing was going to be a matter of only a few months. The Rebels, we felt sure, would have to surrender. Jim laughed at that notion and the more I learned about it, the more I was convinced that he was right. The drum and fife music did the business for me. I enlisted in Cincinnati and left Ceda and Pop to go on alone. I might not have done it if Ceda had tried to persuade me not to but she didn't. In fact, she approved.

♦

The first boatload of cotton went up the Ohio River from Tennessee to Pittsburgh on April 22, 1862. It came in charge of army officers and it was consigned to the Quartermaster General in Washington. Before long other boats loaded with bags and bales of cotton followed it. But it wasn't consigned this time to the Quartermaster, but to Jordan, Marsh and Company in Boston. Jim's plans were working. The stream of cotton that began to flow through the battle lines, past the sentinels on both sides, into the New England warehouses of Jim's associates soon made Jordan and Marsh Company the chief cotton house in the North. Thousands of bales went up to the Boston firm. The risk of loss during transportation was so great that the insurance companies charged five per cent premium and they lost a lot of money at that.

Admiral Farragut captured New Orleans on April 25, and General Butler took command of the city on May 1. Jim's agents were close at his heels and they combed the Louisiana plantations for cotton. The retiring Rebs had burned all they could find so that we shouldn't get it, but Jim managed to clean up a fair harvest there. Most of this New Orleans cotton was shipped direct to England.

Jim went down to New Orleans himself when his friend General Nathaniel P. Banks began operations for the Red River expedition into rich cotton territory. His cotton purchases at this time ran from one hundred to five hundred thousand dollars a day on the average. Some days he bought as much as eight hundred thousand dollars' worth. 'It was a trifle more than I'd been used to handling when I was drivin' the wholesale cart up home,' he said when he told me about it afterwards.

———♦———

He expected to get a raft of cotton out of the Red River country and he bought a steamboat in New Orleans, named the *Joseph Pierce*, to bring it down the river. He paid about three hundred and fifty thousand dollars for her. She brought out several loads of cotton and everything looked rosy; but one day some jackass of a Union officer came aboard and demanded transportation for himself and his men and a lot of ammunition. Jim wasn't there and the officer paid no attention to the protests of the captain. He got his men and ammunition on the boat and ordered her on her way. Inside of half an hour, the ammunition blew up and the obstinate officer and his men just managed to save their lives. For some reason Congress would never allow Jim a cent of damages for this boat.

———♦———

Jim's energies were not all devoted to cotton buying in the early years of the war. On a Saturday in the middle of September, 1862, the armies of McClellan and Lee met on the banks of Antietam Creek and fought a drawn battle. Next day, Sunday, the telegraph spread the news through all the North that thousands of men lay wounded, many of them dying, on the battlefield over which they had struggled. Jim happened to be in Boston. His active imagination pictured the scene; he saw the wan faces of men whose life blood was draining away; he heard the moans of soldiers who lay half conscious in the trampled mud. He read that there was a shortage of hospital supplies and medicines needed to relieve the agony of the wounded, and that even food was short. He hastened at once to Eben Jordan's house.

'See here! We've got to do something to help those poor devils down there!' he exclaimed.

'What can we do, Jim?' Jordan asked. The air was full of the sound of church bells summoning congregations to worship. Jim heard them.

'Let's ask the dominies to call on their flocks for volunteers,' he proposed. 'Have 'em adjourn to Tremont Temple. We can put 'em to work there.'

'What will they do?'

'Do? Well, first of all they can make bandages and pick lint to keep men from bleeding to death. They can beg and give clothing and food and collect it, and they can pack the stuff in boxes; medicines, too. There's plenty they can do. I'll keep 'em busy!'

'Where are the supplies coming from?'

'I can't tell you that, but there'll be all we can handle. God knows we can afford to contribute the supplies ourselves out of the store if there ain't enough – we're making plenty out of it, Eben.'

'I guess you're right, Jim; let's get to work.' Inside half an hour messengers had carried the appeal to all the ministers who could be reached. The invitation was read in every church and the response was immediate. Boston loves that sort of thing and Jim knew it. He knew very well that the famous house of Jordan and Marsh and also the Company, which was himself, wouldn't lose anything by leading in such a work of mercy and humanity. There he was, with his coat off and the sweat running down his red face, bossing the job. Tremont Temple was filled with crates, boxes, barrels and bundles of food and supplies. Jim was the center of everything.

———♦———

He didn't entirely give up getting war contracts, either. He found time to bring in a good one now and then. When he was in New York one day, he learned that the Government was going to need a large quantity of a certain kind of cotton cloth. He happened to know where this cloth was made – at Gaysville, in Vermont. He had often seen the mill while he was peddling. He also knew that it was the only mill in the country that could make that particular kind of goods. Without losing a minute, Jim sent off a long telegram to his firm telling them to rush a man to Gaysville to buy the mill. The contract for the sale had hardly been signed before a telegram came from New York offering five thousand dollars more for it than the agent had bought it for. It was a narrow squeak. Jordan and Marsh ran the mill for two years and made upwards of a hundred thousand dollars a year out of it. Then they sold it back to its old owner for a little more than they had paid him for it. A neat stroke of business!

Besides this sort of thing, Jim did quite a bit of exporting while the war was going on. He shipped a good deal of butter and cheese from the New England region he knew so well, and one time he sent over a thousand bales of hops from York State. But all this was done, or at any rate, most of it, without me. I was in the Army, fighting for the Union under General Grant.

Vicksburg

Vicksburg was a hard nut to crack, but of course we had to have it because its capture would cut off all the Rebel States west of the Mississippi from which the Confederacy was drawing supplies, men, and even munitions shipped in through Mexico. We tried half a dozen different schemes all through the fall and winter of 1862, but when we found ourselves in camp early in April, 1863, at Milliken's Bend, the great fortress seemed as far from capture as ever. The parlor strategists at home were howling for Grant's removal from command, and the politicians were pulling their wires to get him out. President Lincoln was about the only friend he had left, and the best even he could do was to give him one more chance. So that was the situation when we spread out on the plains at Milliken's Bend.

The order came to get ready to march and we knew that we were going to try from the west and south. We marched down on the west side of the river to New Carthage, floundering along swampy roads, pulling artillery out of mudholes, and scrambling on as best we could. The amount of cursing we did in that week or ten days was enough to keep the sky blue. But when it came to swearing we had to take our hats off to Colonel Rawlins, Grant's Assistant Adjutant General.

Rawlins was a lawyer and he had been a townsman and friend of Grant's in Galena before the war began.

We had almost got to New Carthage late in one afternoon and half a dozen of us had fallen out to see whether we couldn't pick up a few chickens or a small pig, perhaps, for supper. We were hoofing it along Indian file when we heard voices and stopped where we were, knowing that nobody could see us in the undergrowth. We made out two voices. One was harsh and angry and we could hear what it said. The other was only a mumbling.

'Now, God damn your soul, you stop and listen to what I got to say,' the angry voice came to us from the invisible speaker. 'You know God damn well what you promised me by all that was holy that you wouldn't take another God damn drink while the war lasted. Did ye, or didn't ye?' There was an apologetic sound of mumbling and the angry, anxious voice went on.

'Yes, you know you did! You can't deny it! An' here ye be, drunker'n a fiddler's bitch! That's a hell of a way for a soldier to act. For Christ's sake, how long do you think it's goin' to be before they git ye if ye act like such a God damn fool? The hull damn army dependin' on ye, too! Give me that bottle o' whiskey!'

There was a feeble remonstrance from the mumbler and the sound of something like a brief struggle, and then we heard the passage of an object thrown through the leaves and a splash in the mud pretty close to me. Jud Hudson got down on his hands and knees and began feeling around for it. The rest of us stood in our tracks to listen. We knew that the angry voice was Rawlins – 'Grant's nurse' we called him – and that the mumble was Grant, our Commander-in-Chief. Rawlins was Grant's backbone.

'There! That's gone!' the angry voice went on. 'So help me God, if I catch you drinkin' anything stronger than coffee before we get into Vicksburg, I'll beat you until you can't stand up! I've got a hell of a good mind to do it right here and now! Are you goin' to let it be?' A mumble.

'Raise your right hand, God damn ye! Do you solemnly swear that you won't touch liquor again until the end of this God damn war, so help you God?' Another mumble.

'All right; I'll let it pass this time, but if you do it again, by the Jumpin' Jehovah, may I be eternally damned if I don't beat you within an inch of your life! You hear me! I mean what I say! Now come along!'

There was a creaking of saddle leather and a sound of horses' hoofs, which was lost in a multitude of hoofbeats in the wood from which they had ridden into the brush along our path for the dialogue we had overheard. Hudson found the bottle and we each had a swallow of Grant's whiskey while we waited until the coast was clear. It was good liquor.

♦

We always had a good many camp-followers, civilians, who came along to see what they could pick up. Speculators came down, loaded with money, to search for a stray bale here and there. When this cotton famine closed down the big English mills in Manchester, thousands of workers were brought to the edge of starvation. We had to send relief ships over while we were fighting, to help feed them. In 1863 cotton had got so scarce that it was selling for somewhere around a dollar a pound and it could be bought for anywhere up to fifteen or twenty cents a pound – usually for much less. At first the trade in cotton was open, but so many were attracted by it and they made so many secret agreements with officers in the army to share profits with them when they helped get it, that the President issued an order forbidding all trading excepting under regulations to be issued by the Secretary of the Treasury. Chase issued the regulations on March 31, 1863, but not much attention was paid to them.

♦

We were camped on the bank of the Big Black River one night in early May on our way north from Grand Gulf. There were no fighting men left in the country we had come through – only old men, women, and children. We were living on what we could forage. Grant had cut loose from his base of supplies so that he could move more quickly. He wanted to prevent the Rebs in Jackson from joining the Rebs in Vicksburg and he did it. We didn't have any tents or any other such luxuries with us and we were sleeping under blankets – or trying to, for there was a cold drizzle that night which kept us cursing. Just as I was dozing off, I was roused by the rumble and rattle of a lumber wagon in the road which ran through the patch of woods in which we were bivouacked. In a minute the wagon apparently fell into a mudhole, for the rattling stopped, and presently a thin, high nasal voice disturbed the air. 'Git up, ye gol durn shoat! Git-up!' This exhortation was followed by a sound of blows and a floundering and creaking, but the wagon didn't move.

I knew at once that the voice belonged to Pop Fisk. His manner of addressing his team left no doubt in my mind. I never heard anybody else call his horse a shoat, but he often did when he was driving his peddler's cart. He wouldn't swear outright, but he knew a lot of synonyms. I crawled out of my blanket and went out to the road. It was the Old Man sure enough. He had a one-horse lumber wagon loaded with four bales of cotton and drawn by a rickety mule. The wagon was stuck in the mud and he was pulling the mule by the bridle and yelling at him. The mule knew it couldn't be done and he lay back in the mudhole, refusing to make another try without reinforcements. A lanky youth in a torn cotton shirt held a feeble lantern to light the scene. Neither saw me until I was close to them.

'Hello, Pop Fisk!' I said. He dropped the bridle and stared. 'Who be you?' he asked suspiciously'

'Don't you recognize me?'

'Never seen ye before to the best o' my knowledge an' belief.' Even after I told him who I was he continued suspicious for some time, until my talk finally convinced him. He had a pass for his cotton and he was anxious to get it through before morning. Nobody knew what the Rebs were doing or exactly where they were.

'If ye can get ten or a dozen of the boys to help me out of this, I'll make it worth their while,' he said.

'How much?' I demanded, knowing him of old.

'Five dollars a-piece,' he replied with some hesitation.

I got the boys and we pushed and pulled until the wagon finally crawled out of the hole. Pop paid off, and I walked along with him in front of the mule while the lanky youth drove. 'What in thunder are you doing down here?' I asked. 'Where's Jim?'

'I'm down here scoutin' for cotton,' he replied, 'an' Jim's here an' there – mostly there. He's in Boston right now, or he'd oughter be.' He went on to tell me that Jim had made arrangements with Eben Jordan and some others in Boston – rich men – to buy cotton and sell it to the mills or send it to England, whichever would pay best. 'We've been doin' fust rate, but cotton's gittin' almighty scarce an' this new order don't help us none,' he told me. 'I dunno's it hurts much, neither; Ceda's looking after that end of it – permits an' passes.'

'Ceda!' I asked. 'Where is she?'

'She's stayin' mostly at headquarters in the Gayoso House, in Memphis,' he explained. 'You'll hardly know her when you see her next time. She's a wonder. She's got a head on her shoulders; an' she ain't bad-lookin', neither.'

I saw him and his mule across the bridge over the Big Black and then went back to my company. I didn't mind the rain so much, thinking of Ceda and all the news the Old Man had given me about people I had known in Vermont and what had happened to them. I mused on the fact that he had not recognized me at first and I wondered whether Ceda would find me so changed. I saw her in imagination just as she had been, with her warm skin and her blue eyes looking at you steadily from under her yellow thick hair. Anyway, she wasn't married!

I was shot in the left leg just above the knee early in the day on May 16, when we attacked Pemberton's army and drove it from the strong position it had occupied on the wooded ridge. My wound became inflamed, and when they sent me up to the hospital in Memphis, with several thousands of other wounded men, I didn't expect to live and didn't care whether I did or not.

Pop Fisk had told Ceda about me and she made inquiries which led to her finding me in the hospital. When I came to, I discovered that she had saved my leg. The doctors would have cut it off if she hadn't insisted that amputation wasn't necessary, and sat beside me for hours keeping the bandages moist and cool by pouring cold water over them out of a cup. This treatment finally drove out the inflammation and I still have the leg.

Ceda and I had a great deal to tell each other. She gave me all the time she could spare from her business of looking after the cotton. I was astonished at her development. She had always been level-headed and cool. She could see things as they were and not as she wanted them to be, as so many women do, or as somebody else wanted her to see them. She was handsomer than ever. In my convalescent weakness of course I fell more in love with her than I had ever been.

'How's Jim getting on?' I asked her. 'When do you expect him?'

'He ought to be here in a week or two, but you never can tell,' she said. 'You'll be surprised to see how he's grown. I don't mean in size, though he's getting fat too, but in his ability. I think he's going to be a rich man if he can learn not to take too many chances. He loves the excitement and he really doesn't care about money; he spends it as fast as he makes it.'

'In what ways has he developed?'

'He takes a larger view of things than most men. You'll find he'll know all about the war out here in the Mississippi Valley and all about what's going on everywhere else. Besides that, he'll have a good idea of how people are feeling about it in the North and even, probably, in England.

'You mean he reads the papers.'

'No, I don't mean that. I don't think he reads the papers more than most men. I don't know where he picks things up. And it isn't so much the things he knows, after all, but his judgment about what's going to happen next. Jim understands men – all kinds – and somehow he understands human nature in general. He's smart. He just seems to feel which way the cat's going to jump, and he isn't afraid to act accordingly. He gets there first and he's usually right.'

'He was always a great worker, but I never thought he was as smart as you say.'

'I didn't either, and I don't think he had any idea of it, or that he has now, for that matter. He takes things as they come, that's all; just the same as I've been doing. If anybody had told me two years ago that I'd be doing what I'm doing here, I'd have laughed at them. But here I am, and I like it.'

'How did it happen? Tell me about it.'

'Well, Jim got in with these rich folks in Boston, and at first he did the buying himself. Pretty soon, he had to have folks to help him and it wasn't so easy to get hold of them. Some didn't have the brains and energy and some were thieves. Finally, Jim put Pop in charge. He said if there was going to be any stealing, he wanted it kept in the family. And he told me to watch Pop, to help him, and keep track of the money.'

'But you're really the manager now.'

'Well, I've had to take in more than I expected to, or ever thought I could. Pop looked to me, and when I knew what was to be done I did it, that's all; and mostly it has come out all right, so far.' She let me hold her hand while she talked and that was agreeable. She knew I still loved her. I didn't talk to her about it. I didn't have to.

♦

Before long, Jim turned up, making a tour of the border, inspecting his sources of supply. He was glad to see me. He asked a hundred questions about how I got hurt and all that had happened to me. Then he wanted to know all about the situation around Vicksburg and what the outlook was there. I told him about how Rawlins had pitched into Grant for drinking. Jim laughed. 'Drunk or sober, he's the best general we've got!' he said. 'There are too darn many theorists and amateurs on our side, and a darn sight too much politics. We couldn't lose the war if we tried; but politics would lose it for us if such a thing was possible.'

Jim was going to stay in our part of the country for a week, at least. His scouts had located a batch of cotton and had negotiated for its purchase. A lot of money was involved – too much, Jim thought, to trust to anybody else. He got a leather wallet that hung around his chest by a strap and in that he proposed to carry the cash for the cotton. He showed that wallet around the hotel and explained its advantages. He carried a bunch of money in it when he left to buy that cotton – three hundred thousand dollars, he said. I didn't count it. When he came back a week later, the wallet was gone and he didn't have any cotton. He told us he'd lost all the money.

'The plantation where the cotton was is between the lines,' he explained. 'I'd got almost to it and I was dodgin' towards it through a piece of woods when I got sight of a Rebel patrol comin' from the place and headin' toward where I was. Those Rebs were a hard lookin lot – as though they wouldn't mind takin' a shot at their grandmothers if they didn't have anything else handy to shoot at. I didn't think it was either the time or the place for formalities and when I put the question to myself whether it wouldn't be wise to effect an immediate retreat, I found the vote was unanimous. The Rebs weren't more than forty rods away. If they should see me, I knew I was a goner. So I slipped into the foliage as fast as I could and at the same time unslung the bag of money and threw it into a clump of bushes. When it comes to parting with your money or your life, there's no trouble about makin' the choice.

'I thought I'd have no trouble in findin' that wallet again, but when I went back to look for it next day, it was gone. Neither hide nor hair of it could I find and I looked for it high and low. Oh well, there's more where that came from!' There were envious people around Memphis who said that Jim's story was made up out of whole cloth and that he'd salted the money down somewhere for a rainy day.

As soon as I could be moved from the hospital, Jim had me taken to the Gayoso House, where he managed to get a comfortable room for me, though the place was crowded to the roof with speculators of all kinds. There I could be near Ceda and it was a happy time for me. The surgeons found that my hurt would put an end to my military service. In a few weeks, I got an honorable discharge from the army, a month or two before my term of enlistment expired, and Jim sent me up to Brattleboro to look after things for him there.

———♦———

When it became evident, to Jim's way of thinking, that the war couldn't last much longer, he planned a stroke that would have made him a rich man if it had been carried out as he wanted. Millions of dollars worth of Confederate bonds were owned by Englishmen and they were being bought and sold every day on the London Stock Exchange. Jim got together a few of the rich acquaintances he had made in his cotton operations and took them into his confidence after dinner.

'The war's on its last legs,' he said to them. 'One more good slam from this man Grant and there won't be enough left of it to sweep up. They're trading in Rebel bonds in London. They ain't worth a hundred cents on the dollar in the market there, but they're worth a darn sight more than they will be when the Britishers hear that the Rebs have thrown up the sponge. My idea is to get a fast boat and send her to Halifax to wait orders. Put a man on her who ain't afraid of the cars. I'd like to go myself, if I could. When we know for certain that the Rebs have come into camp, we send this man a telegram that he'll understand, and nobody else. As soon as he gets it, he'll put out for Liverpool as fast as he can; and as soon as he gets there, he'll sell all the Confederate bonds they'll take, at any price they'll pay. When the mail gets there, and they find out that Lee's surrendered, those bonds will go down until our man can buy 'em almost for nothing, and then he'll make delivery and we'll pocket the difference between what he paid for 'em and what he sold 'em for.'

'Great head, you've got, Jim; there's only one drawback that I know of to that scheme,' one of the capitalists remarked.

'What's that?'

'Why, the last I heard there wasn't any telegraph wire through to Halifax. There's a gap of about fifty miles where the wire doesn't go.'

'How much are you worth?' Jim demanded. 'You and all the rest of us here?'

'Oh, I'd say fifteen or twenty millions,' the capitalist replied, smiling. 'What's that got to do with it?'

'Well,' Jim said, 'of course you're all my friends, but I wouldn't hardly have let you in on this if I hadn't expected you'd want to do something to earn your money. I had a kind of notion that after you'd bought or hired the fastest boat you could find and sent her down there to wait, you wouldn't let a little thing like fifty miles of telegraph wire prevent you from making your everlasting fortunes.'

The capitalists laughed. 'I guess you're right about that, Jim,' said the fellow who raised the objection. 'Be sure you're right, then go ahead, as Old Hickory, my favorite President, used to say, has always been my motto,' Jim returned. 'I furnish the idea and the information; you furnish the cash and the boat, and we share alike. Is it a go?'

'It's a go.'

Then Jim told them the reason why he knew the war couldn't go on much longer and he explained just what was going to be needed. 'Our man has got to have plenty of nerve and he's got to know the game,' he insisted. 'He's got to begin selling as soon as he gets there and never quit while he can find a man fool enough to buy. He may be able to sell as much as we're all worth.'

There was some demur at so extensive an operation. Suppose something should go wrong after the ship sailed? Suppose some plan for redeeming the bonds should be adopted? They'd all be ruined!

'You've got to take some chance, you know,' Jim said. 'I don't want any million if it's goin' to be handed to me so I don't have to hold my breath before I get it.'

'But you can't lose anything if you don't put any money in,' one of the guests reminded him.

'O yes, I can,' Jim said quickly. 'I can lose my reputation and that's worth more to me than any of you or all of you together will contribute.'

♦

The capitalists were convinced that Jim's plan offered a practically sure way to make money and they went ahead with it. They chartered a fast boat with a good skipper and put a smart young man, named Hargreaves, on board of her after explaining to him what he was expected to do. They told the skipper to proceed to Halifax and wait there with steam up, night and day, so he could sail at a minute's notice. His instructions were to wait in Halifax and to take his orders from Hargreaves.

Hargreaves was accustomed to stock deals. He was, in fact, broker for the cautious member of the group of backers, and this partner of Jim's, who had complete confidence in Hargreaves, had undertaken to explain to him what he was to do for the syndicate when he got to the other side.

Gangs of linemen were sent out to string a temporary wire over the fifty-mile gap. It took about ten days before a message came through from Hargreaves saying that he was all ready. Jim was as nervous as a flea on a scratching dog. He had his men with Grant's army with instructions to wire him as soon as Lee was beaten. When word came over the wires that Lee was through, Jim sent the message that started Hargreaves on his race across the Atlantic. It consisted of one word – 'Go.' Hargreaves had waited only thirteen days. He reached Liverpool in six and a half days, which was five days before the next boat, the one that brought official news of the Rebel defeat. In these five days he might have sold Confederate bonds enough to satisfy even Jim but the cautious capitalist who had given him his instructions, unbeknown to the others, had told him not to sell more than five million dollars' worth and so he stopped there. Rage and disappointment for once in his life made it impossible for Jim to express himself when he learned the truth.

By the time I saw him he had recovered his self-possession. I went back to Brattleboro when I got my discharge from the Army and there I continued to run the peddling business and to look after Jim's orders at the mills that were located in that part of the country. 'This thing has taught me one lesson,' Jim declared, 'and that is not to depend on anybody. If you want to do something, do it alone.'

♦

Jim's step-mother, Love, was in Brattleboro and Lucy was with her most of the time; Jim never stayed in one place long enough for her to join him. We were shocked one day in August, 1864, to get a message from Ceda telling us that Pop Fisk had had a sunstroke while he was out down there hunting cotton. That night his wife and I started for Memphis. Ceda got to Jim somewhere south of Washington and he arrived there almost as soon as we did. We found Pop very ill in the hospital, where Ceda had had him sent. He had been unconscious ever since they brought him in, but ice-packs on his head finally saved him.

I didn't know that Jim was as fond of his father as he showed himself to be when he found Pop there in the hospital. Money was no object. He got everything that it would buy to make the old man comfortable and as soon as he was well enough to be moved, he sent him in a private car all the way to Boston, where he could have the best treatment. Pop regained consciousness and some of his strength came back; but his mind had been impaired and he didn't know anybody but his wife and Jim. He had to be taken care of all the time. Jim had nurses for him day and night and a doctor went up with us to Boston.

When they had examined him in the Boston hospital, they decided that his recovery could be brought about best in an asylum and so Jim had him committed but he provided everything on the same regardless scale. No son could possibly have done more than Jim did. He had to put up with a lot of abuse in later years, but nothing that was said of him really hurt him except the taunt that his father was crazy. Astonishing as it may seem, this slur was used against him only by the 'better element' of Boston and other New England centers of culture and high thinking. They sneered at Jim because he'd been a peddler. He didn't mind that. He was proud of it. But when they sneered at him because his father's mind had broken down, that enraged him and he made them pay for it.

♦

In spite of the distressing circumstances of our meeting, it was a pleasure to me to see Ceda again. She had been writing to me, of course, but that wasn't like seeing her. She was just the same. My being wounded, I found, hadn't made me love her any less – more, in fact. I told her so and she seemed pleased; but I couldn't go any further. She was still not ready to say either 'yes' or 'no.'

'Do you know, Rab,' she said to me one day, 'you're the only one of us that gave something in the war instead of getting something out of it. All the rest of us have been making money.' I was glad to hear her say that. I hadn't thought of it that way myself. Really Ceda did a lot in the war while she was buying cotton in Tennessee. Many a poor wounded devil remembered her and many a distracted wife or mother got comfort and help from Ceda.

Dry Goods and Wall Street

Jim didn't stay in the Jordan and Marsh Company long after the war ended. He didn't fit when there was no longer need for a human steam engine. He could get them government contracts, buy up mills for them, and supply them with cotton smuggled out through battle fronts; but he couldn't run on the track like the business steam engines of peace.

They all liked Jim and they appreciated what he had done toward boosting them into the foremost position; but they felt safer with him outside the firm. Jim wasn't much surprised when they told him so. 'It's all right, Rabbits,' he told me. 'I know just how they feel about it. I dare say I'd feel the same way if I was in their shoes. But just between us, they're makin' a mistake. I could double their business in a couple of years.'

The more Jim thought about the things that Jordan and Marsh ought to do but didn't, the more convinced he was that anybody who did do them would be bound to succeed. The upshot of it was that he made up his mind to try them himself. He had made a lot of money in cotton that he hadn't been able to spend, and the firm was liberal when he got out of Jordan and Marsh. He had money enough for his experiment.

He opened his store at the corner of Summer Street and Chauncey in Boston as a dry-goods jobber. He did it on his usual scale. It was a big place and over the door was a big sign with the name 'James Fisk, Jr.' on it in big gold letters. He laid in a stock of goods that he'd found in his peddling experience to be popular. He put a lot of money into his stock and his fittings. That was one of the things that he had wanted Jordan and Marsh to do – have their store fitted up in a more showy and elaborate way.

Maybe he was right. Nobody ever will know because he didn't have a fair chance to test his theory. He hit on a bad time. The period of deflation that follows every war had set in. The price of his stock fell so fast that he couldn't have sold it to the trade even if there'd been any demand for it, which there wasn't. Everybody was taking in sail and selling what they could. Nobody was buying anything. All values were shrinking and Jim was left with a large stock on his hands that wasn't saleable for what he had paid for it. As soon as he realized the situation he made up his mind what to do. 'No use crying over spilt milk,' he observed. 'This is a false start, Rabbits, and we've got to crawl out of it the best we can. There's other ways of making a living besides selling dry goods to retailers.'

He sold everything for what he could get, and that was less than half what he'd put into the enterprise. He paid every cent he owed – but he always did that. So far as Boston was concerned, his record was above reproach. Yet Boston hated him – later I mean – as it hated few other men.

———♦———

Jim wanted me to come with him when he left Jordan and Marsh. He could talk like a streak, but he couldn't write so well. The bent of my mind and my reading had given me a familiarity with composition that he wanted me to use for his purposes. One of the things he believed in and had intended to test in his store was advertising. He wanted me to look after that end of it for him. When he had to abandon his role as a jobber, he still insisted that I stay with him. 'You see, Rabbits,' he said, 'people take you pretty much on what they hear about you. Very few of the great and glorious public ever have a chance to see or hear you personally. Their idea of you is taken from what they read in the papers. That's why I like to be talked about in the papers and why I want them to tell the truth about me. They can't tell the truth unless they know it, and that's the reason I want you with me – to tell 'em what the facts really are.'

'But suppose they print something else, things that aren't true?' I suggested.

'We can't help that, of course,' Jim said. 'But in the long run, if they print anything about you, the public is going to get a pretty good idea of what the truth is. I've noticed it lots of times. Even when the editors try to give the wrong color to the facts by putting in a word here and there, their readers see through it and draw their own conclusions. That's why it's better to have 'em print what isn't true than nothing at all.'

So I stayed with Jim and I did my best to have the truth made known. That's really the reason I am telling his story – telling the truth about Jim as I see it. The trouble was that he was always making enemies and they were forever lying about him so that the picture projected by the papers on the public imagination was always more or less a caricature.

We went to New York with what was left of Jim's superfluity. I can't call it savings, because he never saved anything. The experiment with the Confederate bonds in London and some haphazard speculating he had done in the stock market turned Jim's mind to Wall Street as a suitable theatre. He had so little capital that I offered to add mine to it; but he wouldn't consent.

'It isn't enough to save us,' he said, 'if our luck's bad; so what's the use risking it? You hang on to it, Rabbits, and when we get things goin' we'll roll it up into a small fortune.'

With a slender knowledge of how the Wall Street game is played, only a few acquaintances in New York, and no financial backing, Jim hired an office in Broad Street on the ground floor, furnished it in elaborate and expensive style, nailed his sign up over the door, laid in a stock of cigars and whiskey, and sat down to wait for customers. It didn't take them long to nose out the fact that a greenhorn had set up shop amongst them. Jim never concealed anything about himself, not even his ignorance. Speculators came to him and opened accounts on collateral that nobody else would accept. 'Insiders' gave him marvelous sure-thing tips that turned out wrong. It was Jim's nature to take the bull side of the market, that is, to buy stocks for a rise in price rather than sell them for a decline. The times were against him. The tendency of all values was downward.

The men who seemed most friendly, who sat around his office, smoked his good cigars, and drank his good whiskey, were really betraying him, as we learned too late to do us any good. If they found out that he had bought a stock, they laid their heads together and put the price down until he was forced to throw his holdings overboard. They bought his stock then at a profit to themselves for less than they had sold it for, and delivered it to the buyer. This was a favorite among the dirty tricks they played on him.

Under the circumstances, it wasn't long before they had stripped Jim reasonably bare. The office was closed as suddenly as it had opened, the sign with 'James Fisk, Jr.' on it disappeared, and another name was displayed in its place. For the second time, we had failed.

But this time, Jim wouldn't admit defeat. When he shut up shop, he had money enough to pay up all that he owed, with a few thousand dollars over. 'Well, Rabbits, they've taken us into camp; but I ain't through with 'em yet – not by a long shot,' he said as we boarded the train that was to take us back to Boston. 'We went in on a shoestring and they cleaned us up. But the money we lost is really invested, and it's a darn good investment, you'll see. We know the ropes now and if Wall Street has ruined me, Wall Street's goin' to pay for it, you mark my words!'

♦

It was true that Jim had learned the ropes. He was an apt pupil. He never burned his fingers twice at the same fire. I had a lot of confidence in him, but not so much as he had in himself. That would have been impossible. Nobody who saw and heard him on that journey to Boston would have believed that he'd just been cleaned out. I was more discouraged than Jim and after a while grew tired of the talk and laughter and the stories with more smut than wit in them. I retired to the end of the smoking car and sat down.

After I had reflected for a while upon our unsatisfactory financial prospects, I heard a sigh and became aware of a weak-looking, sandy, thin-faced young man with anxious blue eyes who was sitting in the seat on the other side of the card table and looking at me with evident sympathy. At last he observed: 'It's a nice day.' I knew from the way he said it that he came from down East. You might as well have tried to resent the advances of a shy and awkward pup. I confessed that there was nothing in the weather to complain about, and then I answered his friendly questions about what my business was, where I lived, where I was going, how long I'd been in New York, whether my parents were living, where I had been born, and the other usual inquiries employed in New England as a preliminary to acquaintance. 'I've bin to New York myself,' he admitted finally. 'It's a pretty big place, I guess, but I don't like it. I'd ruther a good sight live in Portland, Maine, where I was born. 'Tain't likely I'll go there again very soon.'

'What's your name?' I asked.

'John Goulding.'

'What have you been doing in New York?'

'Been tryin' to sell a patent.' He smiled ruefully.

'Did you?'

He shook his head. 'It's still mine,' he replied. 'I couldn't seem to get those folks interested in it.'

'Is it good for anything?'

His blue eyes kindled and he proceeded to tell me all about it. It appeared that the patent was for an invention that his father, John Goulding, had made. It was a simple device to be used in textile weaving. He unbuckled his carpet bag and showed me the drawings of it. He showed me also numbers of the *Congressional Globe* in which was set forth an act of the 37th Congress, second session, for the relief of John Goulding the elder. This act renewed for seven years the Goulding patent 'on the manufacture of wool and other fibrous substances' with the proviso that the act 'shall not restrain persons using it from continuing to do so, nor subject them to any claim for damages for having so used it.'

The son also showed me the report made in the *Globe* for 1861 of the explanation of Representative Rice when he put the bill before the House with a recommendation for favorable action on it. Goulding had been an inventor all his life, Rice told the House, and he had never made a cent out of this patent because there had been so much litigation over it. A little while before the expiration of the life of the patent, he wrote to the Commissioner of Patents in Washington asking when he should apply for an extension. The Commissioner told him any time before the expiration of the patent. On the strength of this information, he wrote again a few days before the expiration date and the Commissioner then calmly told him it was too late. His bill for relief had been ten years before Congress, and Goulding was then seventy years old, Rice said.

'You see, father's idea was useful,' the son explained. 'He wasn't exactly what you'd call practical. He invented dozens of things that weren't worth much. But this one was, and all the mills in New England began to use it as soon as they found out about it. When he tried to make 'em pay something, they jest laughed at him and told him to go ahead and get what he could. He didn't have a chance in court, an' even in Congress they wouldn't let him have his relief bill until they'd put in there that he couldn't stop the mills from keepin' on usin' it without payin' him anything if they was usin' it when the bill passed. Congress says to the thieves that had been robbing him all those years that they could keep right on. Father, he was tickled when he come home with the relief bill after such a long fight as he'd had to get it; but he didn't last long after that; so it didn't make much difference to him.'

He'd got so far when Jim came down the aisle of the car to where we were. 'Hullo!' he said, 'What's all this conspiracy about, Rabbits?' I told him and he sat down right away beside Goulding and began to quiz him. He made him tell the whole thing over again and he looked at the drawings and the *Congressional Globes*. 'Well,' he said finally, 'what are you askin' for the contraption?'

'Twenty-five thousand dollars,' Goulding said. 'But I guess that's a good deal for it.'

'I'll give you twenty,' Jim said. 'What do you say?'

Goulding looked at him half scared to death, but when he saw Jim really meant it, his eyes filled up with tears. 'It's more'n I hoped to get,' he said.

'Then it's a go,' Jim said. 'Shake on it!'

They shook hands. I never saw such a transformation as took place in Goulding. He was like a different man.

'Can you draw up a bill of sale for the thing, Rabbits?' Jim asked. 'Put in it that we pay a thousand down and the balance inside of three months.' Goulding signed the bill of sale and handed it to Jim, who handed it back to him.

'Don't be a darn fool,' he said. 'You don't know me from Adam and you haven't got a cent from me yet. You jest hang on to that paper until you count the first thousand. Where do you stop?'

'I generally go to the Revere House.'

'All right; go there again and I'll come there to see you with the money at one o'clock tomorrow.'

'That suits me to a T,' young Goulding answered; and so it was settled. As soon as I could get Jim away from Goulding I asked him how in the name of Sam Hill he expected to get twenty thousand dollars in three months. 'Don't worry, son!' he said. 'I'll make more'n that out of this thing in one month. You wait and see.'

He was right. He got the first thousand out of Eben Jordan, who undertook to finance the purchase in return for a quarter interest in the patent. Then he disposed of another quarter interest in return for more capital, hired the best lawyers he could get hold of, and turned them loose on the mills that had been robbing poor old Goulding. He gave them a bellyful of litigation and he got a lot of money out of it, first and last. He got something else and that was the hatred of almost all of the rich and dignified mill owners in New England. It filled them with permanent rage to be called to account for what they had done and were doing, and they lost all control of their emotions when they thought that the man who was doing it was a miserable tin peddler from Vermont! That was the way they spoke of Jim. Old Goulding would have smiled in his grave if he could have known what Jim was doing to the men who had downed him.

Enter Uncle Dan'l

Jim made a good beginning before he got back to Boston when he bought the Goulding patent, but it wasn't this that put him on his feet again. It was the purchase of the Bristol line of steamboats. Jim knew a good many men in Boston from his dealings in cotton – capitalists, I mean. We hadn't been back there two days before we found out that a New England combination had got control of railroads that gave them a through line to Bristol. They wanted the boat line from there to enable them to send their passengers and freight on to New York.

It happened that Jim had been told when he was in New York that Uncle Dan'l Drew, who owned the Bristol line, wanted to sell it if he got a fair offer for it. This was just the sort of chance that Jim liked. He didn't lose a minute in getting the Boston crowd to make him their agent in buying the boats. With their contract in his pocket, he went to New York and allowed it to become known that he and his Boston friends were engaged in starting a rival line of boats to Bristol to connect with their railroad. Uncle Dan'l was the kind of man who always believes the worst. That's why he was such a bear on stocks – the Great Bear, they called him in Wall Street. He believed the story about the new line. It was just the sort of thing he thought would be most likely to happen to him. He forgot all about the trick he played on the Hudson River syndicate when he was one of its directors and sold it a boat he'd secretly put on the river to compete with it. That was a sharper trick than Jim was playing on him.

Jim put up at the Fifth Avenue Hotel. He had brought over a pocketful of money and he took a suite there. He wanted to give an impression of affluence in view of his retreat with empty pockets from the brokerage business such a short time before. He didn't wait for Uncle Dan'l to make a move. He sent for shipping men to come and see him and he visited them in their downtown offices. He talked big wherever he went; but not too big, either. He had some ideas about the new line that were new and he explained them. His ideas aroused comment and got into the newspapers.

Uncle Dan'l was suspicious. He hadn't lived sixty-nine years without finding out that things are sometimes not what they seem to be. He waited and watched but no approach was made to him. He and his steamboats didn't appear to exist in Boston. On the other hand, he heard something every day that showed him how the plans for the new line were getting ahead. He began to lie awake and reckon up how much money he was losing. Jim, on his side, was beginning to wonder why he didn't hear from Drew.

'I thought maybe I'd made a mistake somewhere,' he said when he told me about it, 'but I couldn't make out what it could be. I was just goin' to say my prayers and go to bed one night when a boy came upstairs to tell me that a man wanted to see me. Said his name was Drew. I sent down word for him to come up in ten minutes and I used them to fix things so he'd think I'd had some men in there to see me – tobacco smoke, empty glasses, papers, chairs, and all that sort of thing.

'He came in with his high hat in his hand lookin' as solemn as if he was attendin' his own funeral. He's an ignorant old cuss. He talks like a farm hand and he couldn't write more'n his own name to save his neck. Well, he comes in kinder slow and cautious as though he expected somebody to ask him for a loan. I shook him by the hand and told him how sorry I was to have to keep him waiting, and I asked him what I could do for him. He sat down and blew his nose – wouldn't have a cigar. "I hear you're fixin' to put on a new line of boats to Bristol," he says. I told him we were – almost ready to sign contracts, in fact. "What d'ye want to put another line on there for?" says he. "I got a line there already. Why don't ye buy it?" I rubbed my chin a little an' told him we'd thought about makin' him an offer and had decided not to do it because, in the first place, we wanted everything up to date, with all the modern improvements, and in the second place we'd heard he'd been losin' money on the line and my partners were superstitious about takin' his boats on that account.

'We talked until after midnight and the end of it was that I agreed to hold up for a few days while I went over to Boston to consult my folks there about it. He told me to come and see him next day before I went and I did. He wanted to make me some kind of an offer if I could at his price for the boats he wanted to sell, but he didn't quite like to come to the point about it and I didn't help him much. When he began to hint around it, I told him I thought his price was reasonable and that I'd do my best to get it for him. As a matter of fact, the Boston folks had told me I might pay a couple of hundred thousand dollars more than he asked. I'd got him down to a million three hundred thousand for his two best boats.

'My principals thought I'd done a good piece of work when I told 'em what I'd done, and when I went back to New York I carried a certified check for the purchase money. Uncle Dan'l almost smiled when he saw it. He felt so good over it that he wanted to boost his price for the seven other boats that he had on that line, but I held him down to a million and that's the price we paid for 'em after I'd been to Boston again. He was satisfied and more. He seems to have taken quite a shine to yours truly, and I shouldn't wonder if it was goin' to lead to somethin' worth while.'

———♦———

Jim told me all this in Brattleboro where I'd gone the day after he got the Goulding patent in Boston. He wanted me to see how everything was getting on up there, and I wanted to see Ceda again. If I didn't see her once in so often, I missed her. The trouble was that whenever I saw her, I couldn't help urging her to make up her mind to marry me and when she refused to tell me whether she would or not, I always felt sad. And that was as far as I could get with her. I had to make the best of it, as usual.

♦

Pop Fisk was gradually getting better, the doctors said, and that pleased Jim more than anything else. The Revere House was doing fairly well. I'd been puzzled to find another hotel in Boston bearing the name of the celebrated silversmith, but I discovered later that for some reason the name seems to exert a sort of fascination over hotel proprietors everywhere.

I felt more at home in Brattleboro than anywhere else and I'd have been glad to stay for a while, at any rate; but Jim sent for me to come to New York, where he had gone. 'Great doings here, Rabbits,' he wrote. 'They need a historian, or I'm mistaken.' I smiled to think of Jim as an historical figure, like Caesar and George Washington. Of course I don't mean to compare him with such great men as they were, but he had a place and an influence more than most other men in his own time. It was a pleasing thing to see Jim and Lucy together. She, at any rate, had no doubt that he was a great man and that he would some day become an historical character. She was always of an even temperament, but when he was there, she became animated and her happiness shone in her smiles and sounded in her laughter. As for Jim, he beamed upon her and bragged a little – he couldn't help it – to impress her. He was very proud of her.

♦

When I got to New York, I found that Jim had arranged to try his luck again in Wall Street. I was astonished at the quick change in his fortunes. What had happened was that Uncle Daniel Drew had taken a fancy to him. That cautious, timid, treacherous nature had been impressed by Jim's frank boldness and by his energy. Uncle Dan'l needed a broker to do business for him in Wall Street and so he decided to set Jim up in business. But he insisted on giving him a partner of experience in the ways of the market and the man he picked out was William Belden. He had affiliations and sources of information that were certain to be of value, and his acquaintances in the financial district enabled him to select the right men as accomplices in carrying out the devious schemes that Uncle Dan'l was constantly hatching out like a spider lying in wait for flies.

Drew was at that time sixty-nine years old. He was a notable man in the world then, far more dreaded than his great rival, Commodore Vanderbilt. These two had been trying for years to get the better of one another. The essential difference between them was that Vanderbilt was a builder and organizer while Drew was a gambler. Vanderbilt relied upon pay for services rendered while Drew sought fortune in speculations in which he attempted by trickery to gain the advantage.

No doubt there's room for a lot of moralizing in the careers of these two men, but I don't care to indulge in it. It is my intention to set down what happened so far as my abilities will allow me and let others draw such morals as they like. But Uncle Dan'l's correct family life and his devotion to church affairs hadn't earned him public respect at three score and almost ten. The plain truth is that Uncle Dan'l had no friends in Wall Street because he'd cheat a friend as soon as he would a stranger – a little sooner, perhaps, because it was easier. And he was the way from which Jim launched his second venture into the financial whirlpools of Wall Street.

Uncle Dan'l himself had been a broker. He was the senior member of the firm of Drew, Robinson and Company, which he founded in 1850. Nelson Robinson, who once was a circus rider in Carmel, was a partner, and the 'Company' was Robert Weeks Kelly, who had married one of Drew's daughters after she was left a widow by the death of Chamberlain, Drew's barkeeper in the Bull's Head Tavern, where Jeff and I had left our horses on my first visit to New York with the cattle. Drew got an interest in the Erie Railroad as early as 1854, in a characteristic manner. He bought the steamboat line that the Erie used to send its freight on from its Lake Erie terminal at Dunkirk, and he told the Erie people that unless they took him in and treated him right, he'd give the rival New York Central better rates than he gave them. They couldn't help themselves. He had them where the hair was short. So they took him in and made him a member of the board of directors and treasurer of the road, an office which he resigned three years later, although he had continued to be the ruling power in Erie. He got out of the brokerage business, too, after a few years, but not out of Wall Street.

The Erie was Uncle Dan'l's gold mine. Like most of the great railroads, its early days were filled with trouble. It always wanted money to lay rails, buy cars, and equip itself to do business. It had just managed to open its line through from the Hudson to Lake Erie when Drew became its treasurer. After that, whenever it needed money, he was always ready to supply it with loans, taking stock, or bonds that were convertible into stock, as his security. His close connection with the road and his relation to it as creditor gave him inside knowledge of coming events that would be favorable or unfavorable to it and thus make its stock go up or down in Wall Street. He took advantage of this advance knowledge to buy or sell blocks of the stock, upon which he made large profits.

But he wasn't satisfied with this. He was continually manipulating Erie stock in such ways as would put money in his pocket. He did this by circulating false stories about it and by using other methods of getting other speculators to buy stock from him when he knew it was going down before long, or to sell it to him when he knew it was due for a rise. For the purpose of influencing its price one way or the other, he didn't hesitate to use the collateral security of stock and bonds that he held for his loans to the road. These tricks earned him the Wall Street nickname of The Speculative Director.

———— ♦ ————

Uncle Dan'l didn't confine his speculations entirely to Erie, by any means. He gambled in any stock when he thought he saw a chance of profit, but he mostly took the bear side – that is, he sold stocks short in the expectation that they would decline so that he could buy them back at a lower price. It was this pessimistic bent of his mind that made people say of him: 'His touch is death.' This wasn't always true. A very conspicuous instance of when it wasn't befell Uncle Daniel when he tried to put down the price of Harlem railroad stock about 1864, a few years before we came on the scene.

Vanderbilt and Drew began to buy Harlem stock at eight dollars a share and it wasn't long before they had control of the road. The Harlem ran to Brewster and horses drew its cars down from Forty-third Street, where nobody much lived then, to Twenty-sixth Street. There was a clause in its charter permitting it to extend its tracks down Broadway when the city gave consent. Uncle Dan'l saw a chance to turn an honest penny; so he went to William M. Tweed, who got the consent through the Common Council. Of course the stock went way up. Drew and Tweed sold what they owned and put their profit aside. Then they sold the stock short and had the Common Council rescind the consent, expecting the stock to go down. But Vanderbilt, who had bought the stock that cunning Uncle Dan'l sold, had begun to lay tracks down town and he refused to stop. So Drew went to the Court of Common Pleas and got out an injunction against him to make him quit. Still the price of the stock didn't go down. The Commodore knew what Drew and the Tammany crowd were up to and he didn't propose to let them make money out of him. He kept up the price of the stock by taking all that was offered at a figure high enough to keep the short-sellers from covering – that is, from buying the stock back for less than they had sold it for. Then he got Uncle Dan'l's injunction dissolved and went ahead. The Commodore was a hard man to stop after he got going.

But Uncle Dan'l and the politicians had a trick or two left. A report came down from Albany that the Legislature was going to give the Harlem a franchise to get down town, which would make it independent of the City Council. Upon this, the stock jumped up to one hundred and fifty dollars a share. At that figure, Uncle Dan'l and his friends sold large quantities more of the stock short. Then they had the franchise defeated in the Legislature. The stock went down fifty dollars a share. The conspirators reckoned up and found they had sold twenty-seven thousand shares. They had a profit of a million three hundred and fifty thousand dollars – on paper. In order to convert it into cash all they had to do was to buy back at a hundred dollars a share the stock they had sold for one hundred and fifty dollars a share.

Uncle Dan'l's name carried such terror in Wall Street that when Vanderbilt's brokers found out that the short selling came from him, they asked the Commodore whether they shouldn't stop buying. 'Not by a damn sight!' the Commodore replied. 'Buy every share that anybody offers to sell, I don't care a damn who he is.' Not satisfied with having issued these orders, or perhaps distrusting his brokers, he sent a bosom friend of his, John Tobin, to bid for Harlem stock after the stock market closed. Tobin had made a million dollars following the Commodore's lead in speculation. Bred to the knock-down and drag-out practices of salt water, he took his stand on the Broad Street doorsteps of his office and stood there in his shirtsleeves, with rumpled gray hair, tobacco juice running down from the corners of his mouth, bellowing for Harlem stock at one hundred and fifty, and buying all that was offered at that price or any other, for cash. To tell the truth, there wasn't much offered. The speculators saw that the Commodore was aroused and they prudently left Drew and the politicians to fight it out with him.

When the conspirators went to buy the stock, they couldn't get any for a hundred dollars a share. Nobody seemed to have any to sell. They tried to buy it for a hundred and ten, twenty, even a hundred and forty dollars a share; no use; they couldn't get it. Then they realized that the Commodore had all the stock there was. In the Wall Street slang, it was a corner. As soon as they understood this, it was devil take the hindmost. The price of Harlem shot up to two hundred and eighty-five dollars a share.

Uncle Dan'l had to surrender. He was caught in a vise. He went to the Commodore and owned up that he was beaten. 'I thought the stock was a-sellin' too high, C'neel,' said he, 'but I guess it ain't.'

'Not by a jugful it ain't!' said the Commodore. 'It ain't half high enough. When you goin' to deliver the stock you sold me, Dan'l?'

'That's what I came to talk to ye about. C'neel, I ain't got that stock.'

'Then go out an' buy it for me, Dan'l; I need it.'

'I can't find none to buy, C'neel – nary a sheer.'

'That's too bad, ain't it? Ye shouldn't sell what ye ain't got, Dan'l.'

'Ye've beat me fair an' square; how much be ye a-goin' to let me off for?'

'How much be you worth, Dan'l? I guess that'll be about it.'

Uncle Dan'l cringed at the thought of losing his fortune and he begged and pleaded for terms. He pointed to the good works he was doing in propagating religion; but the Commodore, who wasn't much of a hand to go to church, only snorted at that. He gave Uncle Dan'l a sleepless night and in the end, let him go for a ransom of nearly a million dollars. He lived to regret it. So did everybody else who had shown mercy to that merciless old man. That was the Commodore's first corner in stocks and it paid him well.

♦

With a share of Uncle Dan'l's speculative Wall Street business to help it, and the experience of William Belden to keep it from making mistakes, the firm of Fisk and Belden did well from the start. Nothing could prevent Jim from following the methods that were natural to him. He still kept open house, with whiskey and cigars on the table in the back room of the firm's office, where the regular customers congregated daily to watch prices. There he swapped stories with them and picked up information. The money that he had lost a few months before soon began to come in again. 'I told you I'd make 'em pay!' he said to me triumphantly.

We began the year 1866 with good prospects. That was an eventful year. It marked the beginning of Jim's real career, the career that made his name known all over the world. The impression that he made on his contemporaries was described in a paragraph written by a biographer a few weeks after his funeral.

'His life was like the sweep of a fiery meteor, or a great comet, appearing suddenly in the sphere of the terrestrial atmosphere, plunging with terrific velocity and dazzling brilliancy across the horizon, whirling into its blazing train broken fortunes, raving financiers, reckless speculators, corporations, magnates and public officers, municipal, state and national, civil and military, judges, priests and Presidents.'

This was florid and robust language, but it wasn't so far from the truth after all is said and done. Another contemporary writer who had known him and who happened to be a euchre player said 'Colonel Fisk's right bower was shrewdness; his left bower was pluck; and his ace of trumps was good nature. And with the right and left bowers and the ace in his hand, or even in his boot, or up his sleeve, a man cannot easily be euchered.'

Of course, I thought the world of Jim. I couldn't help it after what he had done for me when I was wounded. But I didn't realize then what a remarkable character he was. He was only thirty-one years old when he began the fiery meteor stage of his life and he had quite a record behind him then.

♦

My job was to see that the fountains of public opinion, the newspapers, were not poisoned against him. I made it my business to get acquainted with the reporters and all the editors I could reach. They always knew where to find me and I was always ready to do them favors when I could. I spent my evenings in Pfaff's, in Broadway, where they congregated to drink beer and smoke.

New York in those days was wide open in fact. The stores along Broadway below Fourteenth Street were interspersed with saloons and gambling houses; the side streets harbored houses of prostitution. There was no police interference. The proprietors simply paid and were allowed to run. Many of the reporters whom I met at this time became my friends for life. The Scotchman, James Gordon Bennett, who started the *New York Herald* in 1835, first made a specialty of financial news in his newspaper. I knew Joe Howard, Jr., of the *New York Times* when he was a star writer on that paper and later managing editor of the *Brooklyn Eagle*. Charles Nordhoff, of the *Evening Port* often drank beer with us. So did Manton Marble, editor-in-chief of the *World*, and William H. Hurlburt of the same paper. Of course, everybody knew the benevolent-looking owner and editor of the *Tribune*, Horace Greeley.

I paid particular attention, of course, to the financial writers – the Wall Street men. Caleb C. Norvell, of the *Times*, was one of the foremost among them. I knew Allan Nevins of the *Post*. Albert

Brisbane, an advocate of the doctrines of Fourier, who was much in the *Tribune* office and who influenced Greeley to take stock in Fourierism, was an interesting figure in the Pfaff group of talkers.

Gould and the Erie

The new firm of Fisk and Belden was a success from the start. It became known as 'Drew's brokers,' which gave it a standing and brought it plenty of business. Of course, we got to know everybody in the financial district, and, among the rest, an undersized, rather effeminate looking man of thirty – a year younger than Jim – with very black eyes that searched you through, whose name was Jay Gould. He had been in Wall Street since 1859, starting alone. He was a member of the firm of Smith, Gould, and Martin when Fisk and Belden appeared.

The contrast between Jim and Gould was complete. Jim was florid and fond of the table, a weakness that was beginning to show in his figure. Gould was abstemious. Jim was loud and self-confident; Gould was silent and seemed diffident. Jim was bold; Gould was cautious. Jim said what he thought; Gould kept his mouth shut. Jim liked to spend his money; Gould kept his. Jim was generous and open-handed; Gould wasn't. But both men had an inexhaustible capacity for work and both were unusually intelligent. They made a formidable combination when they joined forces.

Gould had been as poor as Jim when he was a boy. He was born in a little house in the town of Roxbury, in the Catskills, and his father tried to make a living on a small, stony hillside farm. A settled conviction that money was the only thing in life worth having must have become established in little Jay's mind as soon as he was able to understand that the lack of it was the cause of the deprivations he had to endure. That conviction was the guiding principle of his life. He made every sacrifice to gain riches and to keep them. He succeeded, although if he hadn't had Jim's help at one crisis, he would certainly have gone under, and whether he could have recovered is a question. He had an extraordinary mind and he always played a lone hand, no matter what associates he had at one time or another. The closest of them, not even Jim, who was closest of all, knew what went on in the dark recesses of his brain. I have always thought that he made use of

Jim's personal peculiarities – his love of show, his contempt for hostile public opinion – to make him the scapegoat in transactions where both of them were equally concerned and where Gould usually carried off the lion's share of the profits. Jim felt this sometimes, I believe, but he never complained.

It was Gould who saw the possibilities of an alliance with Jim and he made the advances. It didn't take him long to ingratiate himself. Jim soon grew to respect his remarkable powers of mind and he became very fond of him. Gould had the faculty of carrying in his memory every detail of the most complicated transactions. He didn't have the organizing and executive genius that Jim had, but his judgment of popular feeling was unerring and he knew how to appeal to it, even when he had a bad case. Through Jim, of course, he got into the confidence of Uncle Dan'l. Nobody knew better than he did how to turn this acquaintance into money.

♦

The year 1866 was notable for other things besides the formation of the firm of Fisk and Belden. Central Park was laid out that year; Cyrus Field at last succeeded in laying an Atlantic cable after ten years of failures; Commodore Vanderbilt bought the New York Central Railroad. Finally Uncle Dan'l loaned the Erie three million four hundred and eighty thousand dollars upon the security of three million dollars in Erie bonds, convertible into Erie stock at sixty cents on the dollar, and twenty-eight thousand shares of Treasury stock. This last transaction was destined to have far more interest for us than any of the other events I have mentioned.

♦

There was a short railroad, the Buffalo, Bradford and Pittsburg, running down into Pennsylvania. Uncle Dan'l bought the stock – it was Gould's idea – for two hundred and fifty thousand dollars and then issued two millions of bonds. Then he had the Erie lease the road for four hundred and ninety-nine years and assume the bonds.

A law had been passed in 1861 reorganizing the Erie. This law limited the Erie stock to the amount then outstanding and the unsecured debt at that time. That seemed to set a limit on the total supply of Erie stock, a matter of great importance to speculators in it. But the General Railroad Law, while forbidding railroads to increase their capital by a direct issue of stock, allowed them to borrow money by bond issues to complete, equip, or operate their roads. It also allowed the railroads to provide for the conversion of their bonds into stock. This privilege was intended to make the bonds more desirable by permitting bond holders to convert them into stock in case the stock went up above par. It was supposed that the conversion could be exercised only when money had been actually borrowed by the sale of bonds, but Uncle Dan'l and Gould took the ground that the bonds didn't have to be sold to be converted – only issued; and they acted accordingly.

In order that he might have enough ammunition for what he contemplated, Drew had the stock of the leased Buffalo, Bradford and Pittsburg road converted into Erie stock, as the law allowed, and this provided him with ten thousand more shares of Erie. The two million dollars' worth of bonds of the leased line also were legally exchanged for two millions of convertible Erie bonds. All this was done early in the year 1866. Erie stock was then selling at ninety-five. Uncle Dan'l, little by little, sold thousands of shares around that price, and the Commodore bought a good part of it. Jim and Gould, to whom Uncle Dan'l explained what he was about, sold all the Erie stock they dared to sell short.

To outsiders it looked as though Uncle Dan'l had lost his wits. Old friends shook their heads over his recklessness, and bought a few of the Erie shares he was offering so lavishly. They were sorry for him, but they didn't see why they should refuse his money.

The Commodore ought to have seen the trap. He knew about the Drew loan and the security that had been given for it. Perhaps he didn't suspect that Uncle Dan'l would dare to sell this security, which really didn't belong to him and which he was bound to return if his loan was repaid. But if he thought that Uncle Dan'l was going to stick at trifles with so much money in sight, he was mistaken. The old man hadn't forgotten how the Commodore had made him pay in the Harlem corner. He had made up his mind to get even, and he did.

Just when everybody was watching to see him try to buy fifty thousand shares of Erie stock in order to deliver it to the men to whom he had sold it, he distributed among them the crisp new certificates of stock into which his bonds had been converted. He didn't have to buy a share. He had them already.

A cold chill ran through Wall Street when this unsuspected stock appeared. The price yielded and broke before the flood and the quotation went to fifty dollars a share. In the process five million dollars were transferred from Vanderbilt's pocket to Drew's.

When the Commodore realized that the wily Uncle Dan'l, on whom he had taken pity in Harlem, had made him repay five for one the million he had exacted, he frothed at the mouth. His rage was a sight to behold. It was whispered through the Street that he had taken a vow, confirmed with strange and vigorous oaths, to get that money back again and to teach Uncle Dan'l a lesson he wouldn't forget. I don't know whether he did take such an oath, but anyhow he got after Uncle Dan'l without a moment's delay.

♦

There was a sickly railroad in New England, the Boston, Hartford and Erie, which had been surveyed to run from Boston to Fishkill, three hundred miles, or four hundred if you counted the curves. The year before Uncle Dan'l sheared the Commodore, Richard Schell, one of the Vanderbilt family circle, proposed an alliance between this corporation and the Erie.

John S. Eldridge, a Boston financier, was president of the Boston, Hartford and Erie. The company had spent twenty millions in building two hundred and forty-five miles of track as far as Hartford. It had a debt of ten millions and it had exhausted the generosity of the Massachusetts Legislature in the way of subsidies. Its reputation could hardly have been worse. We bought some stock in this road – Gould and Jim did, I mean. Jim knew some of the men who were interested in it, and Gould knew something about all railroads. It had been planned to connect it with the Erie and to carry Erie coal over it to Boston. Why shouldn't the Erie help it to complete its line? This seemed logical to Eldridge. To Gould it seemed a thing that perhaps might be worth considering.

The Commodore's state of mind at this time was interesting. He had decided upon the details of his plan of railroad development and it didn't include the Erie. He would push through to Chicago over the Lake Shore and Michigan Southern. His only interest in the Erie was to prevent it from becoming a competitor. The Commodore didn't believe in competition. So he thought it would be a good idea to buy the Erie and confine it to the New York and Pennsylvania field, leaving the western business for his own system. Besides, that ungrateful scorpion, Uncle Dan'l, had just stung him for five million dollars. It would gratify him to get even with Uncle Dan'l by putting him out of Erie and thus depriving him of his source of income.

It was Gould who first called the Commodore's attention to the advantages that he might gain from an alliance with the Boston crowd. He and the Boston adventurers had bought a lot of Erie stock. At Gould's suggestion, Eldridge went to the Commodore and offered him proxies on this and other stock within their control, for the Erie election on October 8, 1867. The Massachusetts Legislature had promised to give the Boston, Hartford and Erie three million dollars to keep it alive if it could raise four million dollars outside. The Eldridge offer of proxies was conditional upon his agreement to make the Erie guarantee the interest on four million dollars of Boston, Hartford and Erie bonds at seven per cent. They talked the matter over and made the Commodore see that together they could swing the election if Uncle Dan'l could be prevented from voting the stock he held – his fifty-eight thousand shares of collateral security. The Commodore promised to do what they asked and he undertook to get an injunction to keep Drew's collateral out of the election. He had the papers drawn up without delay. Uncle Dan'l somehow smelled a rat and he went straight to Vanderbilt.

'What's all this about you an' the Airy, C'neel?' he asked.

'All what?' asks the Commodore.

'Why, I heered tell you was out arter the Airy. Mebbe twarn't true?'

'I ain't after it – I've got it,' says the Commodore, slapping his breeches pocket.

'Be ye sure of that, C'neel?' Drew asked in his melancholy voice, looking at him from under his eyebrows. 'Be ye sartin? Ye know I've got a few shares myself.'

'I know ye have, Dan'l; and I know just how many ye've got. And I know that ye won't vote them shares. Look here.' He showed Uncle Daniel the papers he had drawn up, giving the reasons why Drew should not be allowed to vote his collateral stock. Drew, after looking at the petition, asked Vanderbilt to read it to him.

'I left my glasses to hum,' he remarked. The fact was, he couldn't read well enough to be sure of what it meant.

The Commodore spread the petition out on his desk and read it over slowly, pointing out the words to himself with his gnarled and bent forefinger. Uncle Daniel shut his eyes and listened, no sign of emotion on his wrinkled old face.

'Ye wouldn't do that to an old man like me, would ye, C'neel?' he asked when Vanderbilt had finished.

'Old man!' Vanderbilt snorted. 'Why, damn your eyes, ye're no older'n I be!' The fringe of whiskers that grew up out of Uncle Daniel's stock around his withered neck trembled as he swallowed. 'Ye c'n say what ye please, C'neel, but it don't make me no younger,' he said sadly. 'I ain't got long now an' I don't know's I'm sorry. I feel as though the Lord might call fer me enny time, a'most.'

'Gammon!' said the Commodore. 'Come to the pint an' stop yer damn nonsense. You seem to ferget, Dan'l, that I've known ye now a-many years.' Uncle Daniel had not forgotten this fact; but then, he knew the Commodore, too. He wasted no more words, but told the Commodore that he didn't want to be put out of the Erie as things stood – couldn't afford it, in fact. He had always been a good friend to the Erie and he hated to see it get into the hands of its rival; but if he must, he must. Eldridge and the Boston crowd were no good; they'd skin the Commodore alive if he didn't look out. Better throw 'em overboard and work together as they used to do when they were running steamboats on the Hudson and on the Sound. That would save any trouble over the collateral stock. If he wasn't taken in, he'd fight, and maybe the courts would let him vote the stock after all.

The Commodore took a chew of tobacco and spat into a box of sawdust on the floor. 'All right, Dan'l,' he said. 'I'll leave ye where ye be for a while; only I hate to break my word – allus did – an' we'll have to find out some way.'

What he meant was that all Wall Street knew that Uncle Daniel was going to be dropped off the Erie Board. If he wasn't dropped, then everybody would think Vanderbilt had been beaten and he didn't want that. So it was agreed that Drew should actually be dropped, but that after the election a member of the Board should resign and that the Board should then elect Drew to fill the vacancy, putting him back where he was before. Drew was pleased with this. 'You can pass the word to Eldridge, Dan'l,' said the Commodore. 'I will, C'neel,' said the old man, and he told Jim, who, of course, told Gould.

Eldridge and Gould were struck all of a heap and they went to see the Commodore about it at his Washington home. They were inclined to be indignant at first and they protested against being left out in the cold after the Commodore had agreed to take care of them. They found him in great good humor. He laughed at their complaints. 'Hell fire!' he said. 'Did you think I'd forgotten you? Not by a damn sight, I didn't! Come on over to Dan'l's and we'll see what we can scare out of the old cuss.'

They went over to Union Square and talked it out there in Drew's parlor. When they got through it had been agreed among them that the Erie should not compete with the New York Central; that Drew should hold his office as a Director and Treasurer of the Erie; that Eldridge and Gould should have a guarantee from the Erie for interest on four millions in bonds of the Boston, Hartford and Erie road, and that they, together with Frank Work, the Commodore's representative, and James Fisk, Jr., as Drew's friend, should be elected to the Board of Directors. Everybody was happy.

Not a word was said about all this in the Street. After everything had been settled, written down, and signed, Uncle Daniel suggested that they might as well make a little money; so they made up a bull pool to buy nine million dollars of Erie stock, and appointed Uncle

Daniel pool manager. The Commodore was in it and so were Richard Schell, John Steward, and James H. Banker.

The election was held according to schedule and the changes that had been agreed upon were made in the Board. It was a proud day for Jim and Gould when they saw their names in the papers as directors of the Erie. They gave Gould's name as 'J. Gould' and some of them gave Jim a final 'e' on his name while two of them called him 'James Fish, Jr.' This carelessness didn't last long. The names were soon known familiarly in every newspaper office in the country.

Eldridge was elected president. Berdell didn't like being dropped, but the Commodore wouldn't listen. Out he went. Jim got Eben D. Jordan, his old friend, made a member of the board of directors, on which Boston was strongly represented. Frank Work was put on as the Commodore's personal representative. Uncle Dan'l, as everybody had anticipated, was not re-elected. It was plain to the most inexperienced that Vanderbilt was in control of Erie and that Uncle Dan'l was out. But before the numerous victims of Drew's devious ways had finished congratulating each other on the downfall of the Speculative Director, a newly elected member of the Board – his name was Levi Underwood, an ex-Lieutenant Governor of Vermont – resigned and the other members joined in electing Drew to fill the vacancy. This made a new sensation in Erie. Meanwhile the pool was at work. The stock went up; but it didn't go as far as most people expected it would. Richard Schell began to get impatient. He went to Drew and asked him why Erie didn't go up faster.

'Plenty o' time,' said the manager. 'There ain't nothin' in crowdin' the mourners.'

'But it's going up, isn't it?' Schell insisted.

'That's one o' them things ye can never tell,' Daniel told him, 'but it looks cheap to me.'

This was enough for Schell. He confided to Uncle Dan'l that he'd been buying Erie and declared that he'd buy more if he had the money. 'I've got some pool money I c'd lend ye,' Uncle Daniel suggested. This struck Schell as a good idea. He borrowed from the pool funds on the security of the Erie stock he had already bought, and proceeded to buy more. The stock kept fluctuating, and still it hesitated to make the upward jump that was expected of it. Schell came back for another loan and bought more stock. Still no marked advance took place and at last Schell grew tired of waiting. He made some inquiries and before long he was startled by the discovery that the stock he had bought had been sold to his brokers by the firm of Fisk and Belden. This seemed so suspicious that he complained to other members of the pool, and they decided to appeal to Drew for assistance. He listened sadly while they unfolded their story. They suggested that an upward movement in the price of Erie not only would help him in selling the pool stock at a profit, but would also be of advantage to Mr. Schell, who, as Mr. Drew knew, had bought several thousand shares of Erie in anticipation of the rise.

'The pool ain't got no Airy stock,' Uncle Daniel informed them in the voice of a man who has just attended the funeral of his last, best, and only friend. 'It ain't got none, and it don't want none.' They couldn't believe their ears. They exploded in questions. It was true. In a melancholy way Uncle Daniel told them that the pool had sold out all its 'Airy' at a handsome profit and that he was about to divide the proceeds. 'Then you've been unloading the pool stock on me, you old hellion!' Schell exlaimed. 'There! There! Don't ye get excited now!' said Uncle Daniel, raising a deprecatory hand. 'I never told 'em to sell any Airy stock to you – I just told 'em to sell it. Mebbe you bought it; there's no law agin that. Nobody ain't done ye no harm. Didn't the pool lend ye the money?'

You couldn't get the better of Uncle Daniel. You couldn't even find out where he was, most of the time.

The Commodore Goes to Law

While this lesson in speculation was being given to the sanguine Schell, the Commodore was preparing to collect his part of the bargain. He wanted his profits. He called a meeting of representatives of the Erie, the New York Central, and the Pennsylvania Central roads and proposed that they should form a combination, put up rates on a non-competitive basis, and each road take one-third of the proceeds. But the Erie objected to this on the ground that it was earning more than half of the total earned by all three roads and that therefore it ought to get more than one-third. When the Commodore insisted, he found Jim, Gould, and Eldridge with the Boston crowd, lined up with Drew against him. He swore and stormed and threatened, declaring that he was only asking for what they had all agreed upon in Drew's parlor; but it was in vain. He choked with anger to find that the nimble Erie had again escaped him.

Commodore Vanderbilt didn't like to be beaten, not a bit. So he started in again to buy the Erie in the open market. He didn't intend to have any mistake about it this time. He would own a majority of the stock himself. His first move was to try to tie up Drew, hand and foot, in court orders. His relations with Tammany were of the best.

He sent Frank Work to Justice George G. Barnard, a subservient whom Tammany had put on the Supreme Court bench, to ask for an order requiring Drew to return to the Erie treasury the fifty-eight thousand shares of Erie stock and the three millions of convertible bonds that had been given to him as security in 1866. Justice Barnard issued the order on February 17, 1868, at the same time restraining the Erie from repaying the money it had borrowed from Drew and directing all hands not to do a thing excepting what he had ordered. This wasn't enough. Justice Barnard two days later, on February 19, 1868, issued a second order in which he suspended Drew as a director of the Erie. So far, so good.

There was one more Vanderbilt suit, this time brought in the name of the people of the State by Attorney General Marshall B. Champlain. It further restrained the Erie from issuing any more of the four millions of seven per cent guaranteed bonds of the Boston, Hartford and Erie Railroad. Some of these bonds still remained in the possession of Drew and of J. C. Bancroft Davis, an Erie director. This injunction was granted on March 4, 1868.

Uncle Dan'l never said a word. In the face of all the sapping and mining against him, and despite the boom in Erie stock caused by the Commodore's buying, he kept on selling Erie short and he didn't care who knew it. But on the very day when the Attorney General entered the fray on the Vanderbilt side, Mr. Drew's two sanguine young fellow-directors, James Fisk, Jr., and Jay Gould, applied to Justice

Ransom Balcom, in Binghamton, for an order restraining Work and all others concerned, including Justice Barnard and the people of the State of New York as represented by Mr. Champlain, from prosecuting the Erie or even interfering in any way with Uncle Daniel Drew. Work was summoned to show cause in Cortlandville on April 7, why he should not be removed from the Erie board as a Vanderbilt spy. Gould made oath, in support of this application, that Vanderbilt was trying to get his hands on the Erie's throat for monopoly purposes, and that Work, when he was elected a director, knew all about Drew's fifty-eight thousand shares of Erie and the rest of the things he was complaining about before Justice Barnard. This affidavit showed how complete was the division between the Commodore and his late ally.

All these suits and counter-suits were known to everybody. What was not generally known was that between the two Barnard injunctions of February 17 and February 19, the wily treasurer had got the board to authorize the executive committee to issue ten millions of Erie bonds for construction purposes. They were convertible, as usual, and before Drew was suspended by Justice Barnard's order of February 19, they were converted into a hundred thousand shares of Erie stock. Drew kept half of these shares and gave Jim the other fifty thousand.

Both of them nursed this secret supply of new stock until the last day of February – the twenty-ninth. Erie was then selling at sixty-eight dollars a share. Drew had sold a lot of it short. He threw his fifty thousand shares on the market expecting to force down the price, but the Commodore had given an order to buy all that was offered, and his brokers took Uncle Dan'l's stock without winking. Instead of going down, the price actually went up that day to seventy, seventy-two and then seventy-three, where it closed. Uncle Daniel was flabbergasted.

♦

Richard Schell, Vanderbilt director of Erie, came to the front on March 9, with a request for an order forbidding the board of directors to hold any meeting unless Work was present and restraining them from increasing the capital stock of the road by converting bonds or issuing new stock. He got the order, of course. But on the same day, William Belden, who had been Jim's partner, appeared before Justice Gilbert with Thomas G. Shearman as attorney, and charged that the Vanderbilt crowd had been speculating in Erie stock and that the suits they had brought were intended to influence the price of the stock and to prevent the Erie from interfering with Vanderbilt's railroad monopoly by depriving it of the money that it needed to extend its line to Chicago. Belden and Henry N. Smith swore that Justice Barnard was a stock speculator, and Belden asked for an injunction against the whole Vanderbilt faction. He got it, of course.

But the Belden complaint, in which it was easy to find Jay Gould's line of reasoning, touched a responsive chord. The Commodore was too autocratic to be popular. One of the newspapers had an editorial about the suits. 'Now if this contest affected only the gamblers in stocks,' it said, 'it would not much concern the public; but, as it appears to us, every citizen has the deepest interest in its being terminated as soon as possible by the discomfiture of Mr. Vanderbilt. Let him once get the Erie into his power and the tariff of freights along its whole length will be raised and not only that, but the freights in all the western roads connecting the two.'

———♦———

Justice Barnard was one of the boldest men that ever abused judicial power for personal ends or to oblige his friends. He stuck at nothing. 'He's a bad man to have against us,' said Jim. 'We've got to get him if we expect to keep on doing business in this town and stay out of jail!' Gould agreed with him. Meanwhile, they had no time for anything except the business before them, which was to keep the Erie out of Vanderbilt's strong box.

On March 9, the day Thomas G. Shearman got an injunction against the Commodore and his lieutenants forbidding them to proceed against Uncle Dan'l, the Commodore had John Bloodgood get an injunction from Judge Cardozo against Drew.

All these court orders and injunctions may sound academic, but they were real enough at the time. They were moves in a desperate fight for control of the Erie and the establishment of a railroad monopoly. This was the situation in Erie stock – Vanderbilt was trying to buy it in order to get control of the railroad; Drew had sold thousands of shares short and had disposed of the fifty thousand shares that had been issued to him; Vanderbilt was putting the stock up and Drew was hoping it would go down; Jim had fifty thousand shares which he could either sell and thereby depress the price, to Uncle Dan'l's advantage, or keep.

Of course, Jim wanted to get as good a price as he could for his stock. He didn't intend to keep any; it was too dangerous. Gould and he laid a plan to make the two elder rivals pay. Gould began to play on Uncle Dan'l's fears. He dropped dark hints to the effect that Jim wasn't going to sell his fifty thousand shares – that he feared some pretext would be found in the manner of their issue to put him in jail; that Vanderbilt was going to put the stock up to two hundred dollars a share, as he did in the Harlem corner. Drew lost sleep. Perhaps he'd better cover his short stock while he could. The price was seventy-nine and the demand was strong on March 10. Uncle Dan'l, with a sore heart at the heavy loss he was about to take, gave instructions to his brokers – though not to Fisk and Belden – to buy.

Gould found out what Uncle Dan'l was doing and he told Fisk. Of course, when Uncle Dan'l had covered his short contracts, the demand for Erie stock would be decreased and the price would go down. Jim and Gould knew that the price at which it was then selling would probably turn out to be near the top and they prepared for action. Jim had Belden parcel out his fifty thousand shares in lots of five thousand shares or less, secretly, among brokers whom they could trust to keep quiet. They were ordered to hold the stock until they got word to sell it, and then to throw it on the market for whatever it would bring.

Having set this trap, they awaited developments. All was quiet on the Exchange that morning when the calling of the list began. Then came the call of 'Erie' and in a second a young riot broke loose. The Vanderbilt brokers, under orders from the Commodore, bought all the stock that was offered and yelled for more. Uncle Dan'l's orders helped to advance the quotation. In ten minutes Erie had jumped a full point, to eighty dollars a share.

Then the gavel fell and the vice-president called the next stock on the list. But nobody paid any attention to him or to it. All together the brokers rushed out of the Exchange, down the stairs into the street, where they could continue trading in Erie without breaking the Exchange rules. They poured out across the sidewalk in a human torrent, still yelling like madmen, leaving an empty room behind them. On the street, the Vanderbilt and Drew brokers became centers around which eddied the tide of other brokers, who formed a great whirlpool of buyers and sellers, in which each man sought frantically to find a fraction in his favor.

This wild contest between the bulls and the bears continued until noon. The price of Erie at that time had risen to eighty-three dollars a share. Then, while excitement was at its peak, Jim sent word to the brokers who held his fifty thousand shares, which had cost him sixty dollars a share, to sell it. The transactions up to this point had involved only comparatively small lots of stock. Suddenly Jim's secret agents began to offer it in blocks of five hundred and a thousand shares. At first the offerings were snapped up by the Vanderbilt and Drew brokers, but in a few minutes the mob realized what was happening and an icy thrill of doubt silenced the yelling. Almost immediately it was discovered that the apparently unlimited supply of Erie stock, that had suddenly appeared when the available supply seemed to have been all but exhausted, consisted of bright new certificates that had been issued to James Fisk, Jr.

Up to this moment, the bears had been scrambling to buy stock enough to let them get out alive. In five minutes they turned about and sold for what it would bring the stock they had just bought and as much more short stock as the panic-stricken bulls would take. The pandemonium broke loose worse than ever, only it was bear instead of bull. In two hours the price of Erie fell to seventy-one dollars a share. Of course Uncle Dan'l didn't have to be told that Jim had thrown his stock on the market. He was able to get back some of the money he had lost. Vanderbilt's brokers ran to him with pale faces to tell him what had happened and to ask what they should do.

'Do?' he roared, his silver mane bristling with rage. 'Buy all the stock the sons-of-bitches offer to sell! They think they can pick my pocket, do they? Well, by God, I'll show 'em that there's such a thing as law in this State!' What he meant was that the conversion of Erie bonds into the Fisk stock was in violation of the injunction issued by Justice Barnard. He didn't know that the bonds had been stolen and the conversion made by a person who had not been enjoined. Of course, it was illegal for Jim to steal the bonds; but the Erie alone could make complaint and he had no fear that it would while he and Uncle Dan'l and Gould controlled it.

Nobody let any grass grow under their feet. Jim and Gould and Uncle Dan'l collected their money from the men who had bought their stock, and most of it was Vanderbilt money, about five million dollars or thereabouts. The Commodore sent his lawyers to tell Justice Barnard how his orders had been disregarded and to ask for warrants for the arrest of all the officers and directors of the Erie for contempt of court. They also wanted a receiver appointed to take possession of the road in the Commodore's interest. These moves were not unforeseen by us.

The truth was that the resolution of the board of directors which gave the executive committee power, by issuing convertible bonds, to borrow whatever money might be needed for the completion and operation of the road was passed in accordance with a general provision of the Railroad Law of the state, and the Commodore had done exactly the same thing when he wanted money for his railroads. But he raised a row when Uncle Dan'l did it, on the ground that the law did not apply to the Erie at all, since there were other and special laws that did apply. He also made a plea that the bonds were not really bonds at all, but actually stock, because they were converted into stock as soon as they were issued and had been issued for the express purpose of being so converted.

Jim's stock compelled the Commodore to give up his plan of buying control of the road. He could no longer afford it. So he went again to Justice Barnard. This time he was mad clear through. He asked Barnard to make his son-in-law, George A. Osgood, receiver for the eight million dollars proceeds of the ten millions of bonds that had been converted into stock and sold. In other words, he asked that his son-in-law be put in possession of the money he had paid for the new stock.

When Jim and Gould had word that Justice Barnard proposed to take the Erie away from them and hand it over to the enemy, they called Uncle Dan'l into a hasty council of war. David Dudley Field and Thomas G. Shearman felt certain that Barnard's action could be met and nullified in the courts; but Jim maintained that the wisest thing to do under the circumstances would be to beat a retreat.

'When the Commodore gets his claws on a thing, possession isn't nine points of the law with him – it's all ten points,' he argued. 'The thing to do is to get out of the jurisdiction, and take the assets along with us. How would Taylor's Hotel in Jersey City suit a band of Erie exiles?'

'I don't hardly think it's necessary,' Uncle Dan'l, remonstrated. 'The Commodore'll allus listen to reason. I've known him a whole lot longer than you boys have. I think mebbe I could bring him round.'

'Not this time, Uncle Dan'l,' said Jim. 'He swears he'll never dicker with you again. He says you cheated him once too often and that he's going to put you in jail for the rest of your natural life if it's the last thing he ever does. You come along with us. You ain't safe here.' Whether the Commodore actually said that, or whether Jim made it up, poor old Uncle Dan'l was scared to death. He said not another word but began to bundle up his records and papers.

Exiled to Jersey

This was early on March 11. Our exodus was hastened by a report that myrmidons from Justice Barnard, armed with notices, warrants, and writs, were on their way. In a remarkably short time everything needed to continue the business of the Erie in Jersey had been gathered up. Jim and Gould personally emptied the safes and crammed six million dollars in greenbacks into a hack. This was money that the Commodore had paid for the latest issue of Erie stock and it was practically all the Erie had. There was barely time to catch the ferry, but we made it on a dead run and got aboard. Most of the others were already there, with a bodyguard of Erie porters and railroad detectives that had been hastily assembled. It was a close call, for deputies were out after us to arrest us for contempt.

When we got aboard, we looked anxiously back for signs of pursuit. We didn't begin to enjoy life again until the boat was out in the river. 'Are we across yet Rabbits?' Jim asked. He meant the line between New York and New Jersey. I told him we were, whereupon he turned toward the receding shore, put his thumb to the end of his nose, and waggled his fingers in derision. We disembarked on the Jersey wharf in full command of the Erie. We had literally snatched it from the Commodore's maw.

———♦———

We went to Taylor's hotel and took possession. It was much the same as it is now, though it seemed then far more commodious and more comfortable. Our business offices were in the Erie depot, which had been the terminal ever since the abandonment of the terminal at Piermont, just north of the Jersey state line, in 1854. Stragglers kept coming in all day and until late at night.

The news of our hasty retreat spread quickly through the city, and it wasn't long before newspaper reporters were on hand looking for interviews with Drew, Gould, and Jim. Jim gave them audience at my request in the Ladies' Parlor of the hotel. He could manage them better than Gould could. In his replies to the questions put to him, Jim treated the exodus to Jersey City from the humorous point of view.

'The Commodore owns New York,' he said. 'The Stock Exchange, the streets, the railroads, and most of the steamboats there belong to him. As ambitious young men, we saw there was no chance for us there to expand, and so we came over here to grow up with the country. Uncle Dan'l says he feels like a two-year-old now that he's taken the plunge. Is the *Tribune* man here? Yes – well, please tell Mr. Greeley from us that we're sorry now that we didn't take his advice sooner – about going West. If we feel so much improvement after just crossing the river, the Lord knows how we'd feel if we went further!'

'How long shall you stay?' asked Norvel of the *Times*.

'We haven't decided that yet,' Jim replied. 'It depends somewhat on how they treat us here. We've had nothing so far to complain of.'

'What are your plans?' inquired Crouch, of the *Herald*.

'Well, we've established the Erie offices here, and the first thing will be to make the Erie a Jersey corporation. It's a bad thing to keep a railroad too long in one state; it does 'em good to move around now and then – keeps 'em from getting flabby and stiff in the joints.'

'What do you think is going to be the result of this move?'

Jim's face became serious as he replied. 'We think it's going to prevent the Commodore from setting up a monopoly in all the railroads that tie New York up with the West,' he said. 'The Commodore can't get it out of his noodle – this monopoly hope. He never'll be quite happy unless he owns all the railroads and can charge whatever he darn pleases for the freight that comes into New York. He don't care a cuss how much the people of the City pay for their bacon and eggs, not a bit, provided they pay it to him. Well, he isn't going to get hold of the Erie – at least, not as long as the Erie Exiles are patrolling the quarterdeck. We know what to do with pirates when we see one!' The newspaper men finally left in good humor with themselves and with Jim. On the whole, the stories they wrote didn't do us any harm.

November, 1867, was a great month for Uncle Dan'l. The dedication of the Drew Theological Seminary, in Madison, New Jersey, took place then. The old man was the central figure in a concourse of religious men and women, who praised and lauded him to his heart's content. The institution still endures and flourishes; but not on Uncle Dan'l's money. He gave the site and the original buildings, and also twenty-five thousand dollars for a library and two hundred and fifty thousand dollars for endowment. But it was characteristic of Uncle Dan'l that he should try to get the better of God. He didn't give real money for the library and endowment gifts, but only his notes.

Josie Mansfield

Association with bohemian companions who made Pfaff's their hang-out was not conducive to the practice of virtue. Sometimes we went to Harry Hill's or McGlory's and contented ourselves with dancing and drinking with the girls we found there. Sometimes we went over to the Bowery, where the breaking of commandments and of heads was carried out without the mild restraints that prevailed further west along Broadway. Sometimes we went uptown, where we were known at discreet establishments in which a certain degree of luxury and suppression of coarseness was practiced. One of these places was Annie Wood's, in West Twenty-fourth Street.

Of course, my relationship to Jim was known wherever I went. One night in October 1867, we managed to win almost a hundred dollars at a faro bank in Mercer Street, and somebody suggested that it had been a long time since we paid our respects to Annie Wood and that we couldn't do better than invest our winnings in champagne under her roof.

Annie Wood was a woman of varied experience. She wasn't troubled by prejudices. Her acquaintance was wide and it included Washington, where she was known to scores of officials. Newspaper men in those days used to get especial favor from all classes of public characters, and women such as Annie, who was a semi-public person. The reason for this was that they all depended for success upon public favor and they regarded editors and reporters, not wrongly, as able to give them a good send-off if they would. Annie was an advanced thinker. Annie wanted women to be as emancipated in their relations with men as men are in their relations with women. This was carrying things altogether too far. She was always spoken of in polite circles as 'the notorious Annie Wood.' Anyhow, she welcomed us that October night with cordiality despite the fact that we didn't get up to West Twenty-fourth Street until half past one o'clock in the morning. There were several handsome young women there and they played the piano for us while we sang, 'opened wine' and talked until almost daylight. In the course of events, Annie took me into a small reception room, saying she wanted to ask me something.

'What sort of a man is Mr. Fisk?' she inquired. 'I mean, does he care anything about women? I hear he's married, but doesn't live with his wife.'

'What do you want to know for?' I asked.

'Never mind; I'll tell you later.'

'Well, he's married and he's very fond of his wife. The reason he doesn't live with her is that he looks on himself as a Boston man and not a New Yorker. He hasn't got any home here, you know. He thinks he's just here on business, temporarily. He's got a house in Boston and his wife lives there. He goes over to see her whenever he can get away.'

'Have they got any children?'

'No.'

'Is he good to her?'

'Gives her everything in the world she wants.'

'Why doesn't she come here? What sort of a woman is she?'

I described Lucy as well as I could and Annie listened with attention. 'I see how it is – she's one of the cold-blooded kind,' she said when I finished. 'Maybe he's the same sort.'

'He never troubles his head much about women, that's a fact,' I said. 'He's so busy with all the things he does that he hasn't any time for 'em. As to being cold-blooded, I don't know. Perhaps he is.'

'Perhaps nobody ever tried to find out,' she said.

'Nobody ever has that I know of,' I told her. 'Now what's all this about?'

'I'll tell you.' She smiled at me with her hazel eyes and lighted a cigarette with a flashing of diamonds on the fingers that held the match. 'I know a girl who wants to know him and I think he'd like her. I thought you might bring him up here some evening and he could see what he thought of her. If he shouldn't like her, no harm done, you know.'

'What sort of a girl is this friend of yours?'

'Her name's Helen Josephine Mansfield. She's twenty years old. She's a Bostonian – born there – and she's been married. I've seen a good many women and I know something about 'em. I have never seen one that could beat her for – well, charm.'

'Who'd she marry?'

'An Albany actor named Frank Lawlor. I don't think her mother's a woman of much judgment. She took Josie to California when she was sixteen years old, and her husband was killed there. She met a man named Warren in San Francisco and married him. I don't think he was any good from what Josie tells me. She married Lawlor, she says, to get away from him. But Lawlor wasn't much improvement and Josie divorced him in Boston. They were married when she was sixteen, you know.'

'What does she think Jim could do for her?'

'She's thinking of going on the stage and she wants to talk with him about it. Will you speak to him about it and let me know? I'll arrange to have her here whenever you say.' I didn't see any harm in telling Jim what she wanted and I promised to do it. I got a chance a day or two later. He was interested right away and asked a lot of questions about Josie. Jim was getting interested in theatricals. He kept looking back to his circus days. He must have enjoyed them.

'You fix up an appointment for some night next week, Rabbits – let's say Tuesday night – and we'll go up there.' I began to feel a little uneasy, having brought about the meeting. 'We don't want to get ourselves into trouble, Jim,' I suggested. 'Don't worry about that,' he replied. 'I wasn't born yesterday, Rabbits. We don't have to do a darn thing we don't want to, you know. No harm in looking her over.'

The next Tuesday night we drove up to Annie's. It was the first time Jim had ever been there. Annie had set the stage for him. She had a small company of women – all paragons – in attendance, and one or two men, one of them George Butler, United States Minister to Egypt, and Jim was impressed, as she intended him to be.

But these trimmings, as Jim called them, were not necessary. Josie needed no allies. In the arts of strategy, attack, retreat, delay, and manoeuvre she was a female Napoleon. I may as well confess that, in spite of all she did, I've always kept a sneaking admiration for Josie. Nature made her a woman talented in matters of love. To men she was a magnet, even Uncle Dan'l. I've seen his cold eyes grow less cold and his mournful wrinkles relax at sight of her smile.

Though she had been married and divorced and had passed through other experiences when we first saw her, she was hardly yet out of girlhood. She was a little better than medium height, with a rounded figure, feminine in every soft curve. Her thick, abundant hair was glossy black. Her eyes were blue-gray, with black brows and long black lashes. Her features were regular and handsome. Her lips were full and red. She had beautiful, small ears. The color came and went under her warm, clear skin with every change of mood and when she was amorously interested a soft flush overspread her face from forehead to chin. Jim was thirty-three years old; she was twenty-eight.

♦

Annie introduced us to her guests, and to Josie with the others. In a few minutes she explained that Miss Mansfield wanted to consult Mr. Fisk on some business matters and suggested that they talk in the little reception room. She led them to it and shut the door on them. An hour passed and the second was well begun before they finished what they had to say. The delicate flush on Josie's young face and the increased brightness of her eyes indicated that the interview had been satisfactory. Jim's unusual animation confirmed this impression.

It was late, but Jim insisted on walking down to the Grand Central Hotel. He wanted to talk about Miss Mansfield. It appeared she wasn't any ordinary girl. I had seen that already. He'd never known any other girl like her. I thought that probable. She was a good girl. I had my doubts, but I didn't express them. 'She's had hard luck, Rabbits,' Jim confided to me, and then he went on to tell of a dissolute mother, a step-father who, according to Jim, was probably even worse, the girl's marriage with an actor, Lawlor, who appeared to have tried to blackmail another beau, and the flight of the defenseless Josie and her drunken, jealous husband eastward. 'And she was only sixteen or seventeen years old at the time – just a child! She's not much more now,' Jim concluded.

Later, I heard other versions of Josie's early biography, which I shall set down in due season; they were somewhat different from this first story of Jim's. When I asked what she was doing then and what plans she had for supporting herself, Jim revealed the extent of his infatuation. He told me that Josie was living in a cheap furnished room in Lexington Avenue and that she'd been trying to get a stage engagement. She had learned something about theatricals from Lawlor, it seemed, but all the managers to whom she had applied had made such advances that she'd almost come to the conclusion that the surrender of her virtue was necessary before she could hope to be considered. She wouldn't do what they wanted – had too much self-respect – would rather starve than give herself to a man she didn't love – and there you were! But she'd been told that she had a fair voice – 'You heard it yourself, Rabbits; you know how sweet it is' –

and that if she could take some lessons in music, and maybe some instruction in theatricals – stage deportment and that sort of thing – she'd get an engagement at Tony Pastor's without any trouble. But she was down to her last cent and so she had applied to Jim.

'She doesn't ask me to give her anything, you understand,' he told me. 'What she wants is that I should advance enough to get her started and let her pay it back out of her salary when she's got one. The poor girl's sure she'll be able to take care of herself as soon as she's learned the ropes a little. Of course it's a big risk and one that I don't suppose many men would be fool enough to take for a minute; but I believe she knows what she can do and that she's right about it.'

'So you're going to let her have the money?'

'Well, I haven't told her so, yet. I want to make a few inquiries first. I know something about the stage myself.' We were crossing Fourteenth Street and I looked along its gas-lit pavements where painted women, bedecked in poor finery, were soliciting the passers-by, drunk and sober. The piles of bricks that were being used to build the new Wigwam of Tammany Hall on the north side of the street near Third Avenue, loomed up in black masses.

Jim told me he had promised Miss Mansfield to think it over and that, meanwhile, he had advanced her fifty dollars to pay her board bill and get herself some things she needed. He was going to see her in Lexington Avenue and have another talk with her; but he didn't think that was a good place for her to live and he was going to get rooms for her in the American Club Hotel, if she'd let him. She could be more comfortable there, he thought, and it would be more convenient for him to see her there when they wanted to talk business.

♦

Jim didn't seem to have much difficulty in persuading Josie to move to the American Club Hotel. He got a parlor, bedroom, and bath for her there and she seemed more than contented. I believe Jim meant to be only a big brother to the little minx; but his flesh was no more immune from the common weaknesses than any other. I knew his conscience was troubling him. Josie had only one thing to give in return for what he was doing for her and she gave it. These attacks of conscience didn't last long. Within a few weeks Jim was head over heels in love with Josie. It was altogether a different kind of love from what he felt for Lucy. For her he had a tender affection; he had a passion for Josie. He had no more idea than the rest of us had how strong a passion it was. We didn't find that out until later.

I must say that Josie was as sweet as any bride could be. She didn't begin by wanting much. 'They think I'm a fool for not getting more out of Sardines,' she confided to me one day. Jim had taken me with him when he went to dine with her at the hotel. He was so proud of her that he couldn't keep his happiness to himself. 'Sardines' was one of her pet names for him, because he was fond of them; and 'they' were female acquaintances of hers. Jim called her Dolly; he liked that name better than Josie.

The beginnings of their romance were interrupted by our flight to Jersey City. When we found that our residence there was likely to be prolonged, Jim determined to bring Josie over. He couldn't get along without seeing her. He arranged to put her in a comfortable room which opened into the same bathroom with which his room connected and he asked me to fetch her for him. She had been reading in the papers about our exodus and she was much excited about it. She thought it was 'just like California.'

Of course her appearance in Taylor's Hotel revealed her existence in a way that Jim had not expected at first, any more than he had expected to fall in love with her. Gould looked at her and through her with his piercing black eyes and stroked his beard, but made no comment. Uncle Dan'l permitted his wrinkles to crease themselves into a smile. To him she was a happy little girl.

The newspaper reporters gradually learned about Josie, but they never said a word. When Jim got used to other people seeing her, I think he enjoyed the abandonment of secrecy about her. The plain language that was sometimes used in speaking of her and of him didn't reach his ears and therefore he wasn't disturbed by it.

♦

For the next few days after our arrival in Jersey City we were busy getting settled. It was decided to move the Erie offices into the Erie building on Long Wharf, and of course that was a big job. We had been there five days when Masterson, the Erie chief of detectives, got a hint from somewhere that it would be wise to delay the move we were about to make and keep under cover for a while. Uncle Dan'l was scared almost to death, and Jim had a lot of fun with the old man telling him what they would do with him if they ever got him. He finally locked himself up in his own room in the hotel and insisted that two armed men should guard the door. The newspapers had adopted the name that Jim had given us when he talked with them and we were known as the Erie Exiles. Jim organized the defensive force and he did it with his usual thorough attention to details. He even had cigars and drinks served to the guards to keep up their courage.

About four o'clock in the afternoon we got word that a bunch of forty toughs had landed from the Pavonia ferry. Some of them went to the hotel and looked it over; but when they saw the guards they understood that it would be no use to try anything there and they finally quit. We heard afterwards that they would have received fifty thousand dollars if they had succeeded in kidnapping the Erie officers.

This lesson taught us caution. Jim arranged for a permanent guard with a room in the hotel, and it remained on duty for as long as we were in Jersey. The hotel was christened Fort Taylor because of these martial precautions. Gould took charge of getting recognition and protection from the New Jersey legislature. He had no trouble in persuading it to pass a law giving the Erie all the rights of a Jersey corporation. That made us feel at home.

Gould Goes to Albany

It seemed clear that the quickest and best way to disarm the Commodore would be to have the New York Legislature validate the ten million dollar bond issue of the Erie that Uncle Daniel and Jim had unloaded on him so effectually after they had converted it into stock. Gould had a bill introduced in Albany for this and other purposes, and he hired lawyers and lobbyists to look after it.

They had it hot and heavy in the arguments for and against the bill before the Assembly Railroads Committee. Our side charged that the Commodore was trying to set up a monopoly, and they accused us of having issued the bonds for stock-jobbing purposes. There was some truth on both sides; but the public was mostly with us. Gould made a sworn statement of what had taken place before the Erie election in October, 1868. It was dated March 25.

———♦———

This statement of Gould's was the first that revealed the inside of the deal between the Commodore and Uncle Dan'l, which had saved Drew from being dropped from the board of directors and there was a lot of interest in it. He went on to say that the Commodore's program had three main points. First, that the new Erie board should guarantee four millions of Boston, Hartford and Erie Railroad bonds; second, that all the expenses of the canvass for votes against Drew should be paid and Gould's bond cancelled; third, that the new Erie board should include Vanderbilt, Drew, Horace Clark, James H. Banker, Augustus Schell, 'Willie' Vanderbilt, John S. Eldridge, Henry Thompson, Jay Gould, J. C. Bancroft Davis, and General Diven.

Gould swore that he and Eldridge refused to agree to the second and third proposals on the ground that they couldn't honorably change front and vote for Drew. They had a debate in which there was some plain speaking on both sides and in the end he and Eldridge left to think it over, as they told the Commodore. They went straight up to Uncle Daniel's house, and they hadn't been there more than a few minutes when in came the Commodore and had a talk with Drew in the back while they waited in the front parlor. Drew told them later that the Commodore wanted to know whether General Diven could be depended upon and suggested that, if he could be, the old Erie board might be re-elected. It was finally agreed that Levi Underwood should be put on the board in order to enable Gould to keep his promises to stockholders from whom he had obtained proxies, and should then drop out so that Drew might be reinstated. The election was put through on that basis.

Then Gould told how a bull pool was formed to buy nine millions of Erie stock, with Uncle Dan'l as pool manager. He said that besides the Commodore and Drew, Richard Schell, John Steward, and James H. Banker were in it. This pool operated until toward the end of January, 1868, and when the profits of it had been distributed, Schell made a row, accusing Uncle Dan'l of having cheated. As a result of this row, Work filed his complaint before Justice Barnard, praying for Drew's removal from the Erie board and asking for the repayment of the fifty-eight thousand shares of stock that had been given to him as collateral for his loan to the road.

This suit, the statement said, had been brought for revenge. Gould added that Schell had told General Diven he would withdraw it if Drew would buy fifty-five thousand shares of Erie from him at seventy-five dollars a share, or give twenty thousand dollars to the poor of the city.

Gould admitted that he had voted to guarantee the interest on the Boston, Hartford and Erie bonds so as to enable that company to get three millions out of the Massachusetts Legislature; but he had done it, he declared, because the Commodore wanted him to and because the old Erie board had agreed to it. He insisted that he himself never had had a dollar's worth of the bonds or stock of the Boston road, but that Schell got a thousand shares of its stock in return for his vote for the bond guarantee. In other words, Gould swore that the Vanderbilt crowd had insisted upon the things that they now went to court to complain about.

♦

This detailed statement was made by Gould under oath on March 25 in the hope of refuting the false stories that were being circulated in Albany for the purpose of beating the Erie legalization bill. It was too late. The bill went to defeat in the Assembly on an adverse committee report two days later, on March 27, by a vote of eighty-three for the adverse report and only thirty-two against it.

This was a heavy blow. Our agents reported that they had been swamped by Vanderbilt money – that the votes they had counted on didn't stay bought. Quick action was necessary to save the day. It was decided that Gould should go to Albany to take charge there. President Eldridge gave him five hundred thousand dollars for his expenses in rounding up votes. I went up with him to act as his lieutenant there and to carry confidential messages to Jersey City if necessary. We went up on March 30.

Although the Erie bill had been beaten in the lower branch of the Legislature, as I have said, the Senate had not yet taken action. Instead, it had appointed an investigating committee of five senators to report on the facts. The members of this Committee were James F. Pierce, John C. Bradley, A. C. Mattoon, G. W. Chapin, and W. J. Humphrey. Mattoon knew an opportunity when he saw one and wasn't content to do his investigating with the rest of the committee, but carried on a personal investigation of his own.

He called on Drew at his house at the corner of Seventeenth Street and Broadway. Drew said the Senator gave him to understand that he would accept money if it was offered to him. Senator Mattoon said that Drew had asked him to call for the purpose of finding out how his neighbor, Senator Bradley, who was also a member of the committee, stood. The second time he called he said his purpose was to help his son serve a subpoena for the committee on Uncle Dan'l. When he rang the bell, the maid told him that Mr. Drew was not at home. This seemed strange to him because he could see the old man quite plainly, sitting at the front window. But Mattoon couldn't get in, although he stood outside for quite a while in the hope that the old fox might come out.

We all knew that the committee was divided two and two, as to whether it would report for or against the Erie. Bradley was one of the Tammany senators from New York and of course he would be against us. Boss Tweed sat in the Senate with Thomas J. Creamer and they kept a sharp eye on their colleague. Tweed was strongly committed at that stage of the game to the Commodore and he was a powerful factor in the fight over the Erie bill. It was natural that Senator Pierce should stand with him; but we felt that we could count on the other three members of the committee, who were all up-State men.

The main point was whether a law should be passed to forbid the sale by railroads of bonds convertible into stock, thus increasing the stock total without consulting the stockholders. Senator Mattoon held the balance between the two sides and he left nothing undone to inform himself fully regarding the relative merits of the arguments. Gould very kindly furnished him with a printed copy of the kind of report he would make if he were in the Senator's place – fair to all, of course. O yes. He added such substantial arguments as he thought would most strongly appeal to the Senator.

The report that Gould suggested gave full approval to what the Erie had done to help the Boston, Hartford and Erie road by guaranteeing its bonds for four millions and it also commended the issue of ten millions of convertible bonds for the purpose of pushing its line into Chicago through agreement with the Michigan Southern and Northern Indiana Railroads. In issuing the convertible bonds, this proposed report pointed out, the Erie had done only what the New York Central, the Hudson River, and other roads had done. It recommended legalization of the Erie bonds and its contracts with the Western roads and legislation that would forbid in future the short selling of railroad stock and the election of Vanderbilt directors for the Erie.

Mattoon assured Gould that this report, which had the approval of Senator Chapin and Senator Humphrey, suited him, and that he disapproved the report favored by Senator Pierce, of Brooklyn, and Senator Bradley, who lived near Uncle Dan'l in New York. Their report accused Drew of having used the ten millions of Erie bonds for speculative purposes and said that Eldridge, Fisk, and Gould were probably interested in his corrupt proceedings. It referred to other matters of a highly reprehensible character that involved the Erie board, and denounced its dealings with the Boston, Hartford and Erie and with the Western roads. In short, it was such a report as the Commodore might have written. Maybe he had written it. We congratulated ourselves that Senator Mattoon had been persuaded to support our side rather than uphold such injurious views. But in matters of legislation, you never can tell.

The committee presented its two reports to the Senate on April 1, and, to our grief and surprise, it turned out that Senator Mattoon had signed the Vanderbilt report. We realized that the enemy had been able to furnish him with arguments more potent than the ones we had given him. Gould was deeply chagrined. Jim called Mattoon a 'thieving son-of-a-bitch.' Uncle Dan'l looked a trifle sadder than usual but he said nothing.

———♦———

On this same day, April 1, the spirit moved the Member of Assembly from Wayne County, E. M. K. Glenn, to hand the Speaker a document in which he had written

'1. I charge that the report on the Erie Railroad bill was bought.

'2. I charge that a portion of the vote on the floor, in adopting said report, was bought.

'3. I charge that members of this House were engaged in buying their fellow members.

'4. I charge that a portion of the vote on the Harlem milk bill was bought.

'5. I charge that some of the Committees of this House charge for reports.

'6. I charge corruption, deep, dark and damning, in a portion of this House.'

The report to which the Wayne member referred was not the famous Mattoon report in the Senate, but a report made by the Assembly Railroads Committee against our Erie bill. It was the adoption of this report on March 27, by a vote of eighty-three to thirty-two, that killed the bill in the lower branch of the Legislature.

'Hush!' said Jim, when he read the charges made by Glenn, 'the plot thickens! The Commodore's strong when it comes to the purchase of committees and such, but just you keep your eyes on Gould – that is, if you can; it takes a damn smart man to do it all the time!'

Glenn asked for a committee of five to investigate the charges he had made and he requested that three of them should be members who had voted against the Vanderbilt report of the Railroad Committee against the Erie bill and two should be members who had voted for the report. He refused to serve on the committee himself, saying that his health would not permit. He was a very nervous, conscientious old man, of strong religious leanings. He said that a fellow member had offered him five hundred dollars for his vote and that he knew of another case where twelve hundred dollars had been offered.

The Committee made an investigation. It had to. But it didn't find anything. It didn't dare to. To get around the offer that Glenn said had been made for his vote it was whispered about the Capitol that his mind was affected; in fact, that he was crazy. That took care of that.

♦

David Dudley Field, brother of Cyrus who laid the cable, was the foremost lawyer in the country. He and his brother came from the Bennington region. They were born in western Massachusetts. Jim and Gould had placed him at the head of their legal staff, with little Thomas G. Shearman, of Beecher's Plymouth Church Sunday school, as his chief lieutenant. Field's tall and dignified figure, in his long black frock coat, was an interesting contrast to that of his colleague, who was a small man, sharp as a razor and full of animation.

Before Gould went to Albany, Field saw Sheriff Jimmy O'Brien about an attachment that Justice Barnard had issued. This required the sheriff to produce Gould in Court on April 4. Field promised to have Gould there, and the sheriff in return promised not to bother him before that day. So Gould left Jersey City for Albany on March 30 to get the Erie fat out of the fire if he could, letting it be known meanwhile for publication that he had gone West to complete arrangements with the Michigan Southern and the Northern Indiana Railroad Company for laying eighty-seven miles of broad-gauge track for the Erie between Akron and Toledo, so that it could get into Chicago.

The Vanderbilt scouts had sharp eyes. Barely had Gould reached Albany and opened his headquarters in the Delavan House before they knew all about him. They didn't intend to let him undo what they'd done to the Erie bill. They lost no time in getting word to Justice Barnard, who was equally prompt in sending instructions to

Sheriff Parr, of Albany County, to arrest Gould. The Albany sheriff got his orders at one o'clock in the morning of Tuesday, March 31, and he made all haste to the Delavan House, where he took Gould into custody.

The plot seemed to be about as thick as it could be made. Gould was surprised and indignant. He sent me out to rouse Hamilton Harris who, in turn, woke up Erastus Corning, who gave bail for Gould's appearance in Justice Barnard's court on April 4. This gave Gould a few days in which to devote himself to the business in hand. The outlook for us and the Erie looked dark to me, with the heavy vote against us in the Assembly and the adverse Committee report in the Senate, with the powerful Vanderbilt lobby on the ground working for our defeat and the machinery of the courts, directed by Tammany, obstructing us at every turn. But Gould wasn't a man who got discouraged at anything. The greater the odds against him, the more formidable he became. The fact that our opponents didn't know this was a point in our favor. Another was that they had gone rather too far. The legislature, as a whole, was as crooked as a ram's horn, but the state wasn't and they forgot this. Glenn's outbreak in the assembly, although it was suppressed and smoothed over, aroused echoes all over the state. The New York *Tribune* came out with the charge that Mattoon had received twenty thousand dollars from the Vanderbilt crowd for changing his vote on the Erie report. I showed this to Gould, who read it and handed the paper back to me without a word.

———♦———

After all was said and done, perhaps the two chief factors in our favor were first, the hatred that existed in the public mind of Vanderbilt monopoly and of Vanderbilt's bulldozing methods, and, second, the five hundred thousand dollars that Gould had in his pocket.

The first gleam of hope for our side came when the Senate refused to accept offhand the Mattoon report condemning the Erie. Perhaps it heard rumblings of wrath at home that warned it to be careful. Perhaps it smelled the half million that Gould carried. Anyhow, after a long debate it referred both the majority and minority reports to the

Committee of the Whole for further consideration. The Vanderbilt lobby took notice of this check and warned its chief to get Gould out of the way.

A vigorous attempt was made to bottle him up when he went to New York in the custody of Sheriff Jimmy, who came up to Albany on purpose to get him. I didn't go to New York with Gould. He told me he'd be back again right away and he instructed me to take charge of his quarters in the Delavan and not to go outside the rooms on any account. In particular he unlocked a closet across the door of which he had placed his bed and showed me a black satchel. 'There are papers there that would ruin us if anybody should get hold of them,' he said. 'I trust you with them. Don't go outside this room until I come back, day or night. Have you got a revolver?' he asked. 'No.'

'Well, go and get one – not a toy, but one that will do some damage.' While he completed his arrangements, I hurried out to a hardware store in Broadway and bought a big revolver, with a box of cartridges. I showed them to him and he nodded. 'Don't use it unless you have to,' he said. 'Not unless they try to break in there,' and he nodded toward the closet door. 'If you have any trouble of any kind, send for Harris,' he said. 'Don't wait. Day or night, send for him at once.' With this final injunction he left me.

♦

The enemy believed they had won their battle when they got him to New York. Justice Barnard was primed to make short work of him in a fashion that would so cripple the Erie that a victory in the Legislature wouldn't save us even if he could win one there. He intended to compel the restitution of all the proceeds of the ten million dollar bond issue on the ground that the bonds had been issued in violation of his order. That would have bankrupted the road almost at once. But bold as he was, he wavered when he faced the array of counsel that Gould had called to his aid. They were headed by David Dudley Field and included, among others, Judge Pierrepont and James T. Brady. They showed him that he was proceeding contrary to law and to practice, and although the Vanderbilt lawyers, who were there in force, attempted to buck him up, he finally decided to adjourn the case until April 8, four days later; but he raised Gould's bail to fifty thousand dollars and demanded two sureties, and he gave warning of his intention to compel a refund of the money from the bond issue.

Gould left Barnard's court still in custody of Sheriff O'Brien, but they were scarcely outside before an order of habeas corpus was served on the Sheriff, commanding him to produce Gould forthwith before Judge Barrett, in the Court of Common Pleas. Thither the company proceeded and the eminent counsel on both sides began an argument over whether Gould should be set free or not. They talked until six o'clock, when Judge Barrett adjourned the hearing until April 7, the day before Gould was to appear again before Justice Barnard, and meantime ordered that the Sheriff should turn the prisoner over to James A. Oliver, an officer of his own court. This was the same Oliver who later became known as 'Paradise Jimmy' because, as a Member of Assembly, he got a bill passed creating a park in the crowded East Side district that elected him. He took charge at once.

'Where do you want to go, Mr. Gould?' he asked deferentially. He was deferential by nature.

'Back to Albany,' said Gould promptly.

'O you can't do that; you're in my custody, you know,' said Jimmy.

'All right, come along with me. I shall still be in your custody,' the prisoner replied.

'Can I do it, Mr. Field?' Jimmy asked.

'Certainly you can,' Field assured him. 'Nothing illegal about it. Go ahead.'

This satisfied Jimmy and they came back to Albany on a night train over Vanderbilt's New York Central. The judicial attack had been temporarily repelled. That won the second victory in the preliminary skirmishing.

Gould complained of illness as soon as he reached the hotel. He had Dr. Julian T. Williams, who had been a member of the Assembly from Chautauqua County, come in to see him and when he came out, he looked grave and told us that Mr. Gould must have quiet and rest and that on no account could he do any more traveling. It might kill him! 'But he's got to go to New York again day after to-morrow,' I said, 'to appear before Judge Barrett and perhaps Justice Barnard. Do you think he'll be well enough to go?'

Dr. Williams shook his head. 'I don't think there's a chance of it,' he said. 'He won't be able to travel for some time – probably weeks.'

'Then what will happen?' I asked.

'They'll have to wait,' he replied calmly.

♦

In spite of his illness, Gould began sending all over the state for men who might have influence with senators and assemblymen whose votes it was necessary for him to get. What we were doing the other side was doing, too. Each party had a certain number of votes that could be counted on at the start; the struggle was to gather in the doubtful votes in sufficient numbers to get a majority. The legislative atmosphere was thick with rumors of how much this senator or that assemblyman was getting for his vote. If the Vanderbilt party thought that Gould was an amateur who could easily be disposed of they soon found that they were mistaken. He developed qualities as a fighter that had never before shown in Albany, and he proved to be so persistent, resourceful, daring, plausible, and cunning that our campaign exceeded in intensity of interest all other contests either before or since.

Gould saw a good many members of the legislature. They were brought to him by his underlings and he talked with them alone in his bedroom. I thought of that black bag in the closet behind his bed. When the time came to leave for New York, Dr. Williams said he couldn't go and so Jimmy wired Judge Barrett that the prisoner was sick abed and couldn't come to court. This was the first Judge Barrett knew about the return to Albany and he postponed further proceedings for another three days, until April 10. When that day arrived, Oliver knocked on Gould's door and found him in bed in consultation with Hamilton Harris and Dr. Williams. The Doctor told Jimmy that Gould was still too sick to be moved and Harris advised Gould, as his counsel, to stay where he was. So Jimmy went to New York all by himself and gave Judge Barrett an affidavit, in which he related what Dr. Williams and Hamilton Harris had said, adding, however, that Gould wasn't so sick that he couldn't visit the legislature now and then and that he was doing business in his room with numerous men. Gould had locked the door against him – Oliver – and that was why he had been obliged to come to court without his prisoner. Judge Barrett expressed indignation and took steps to have both Gould and Harris brought before him at the end of another four days, on April 14.

Harris did appear then and he managed to convince the Judge that he had intended no contempt of court in advising Gould to stay away. But Gould, instead of showing himself in court, sent an affidavit in which he denied Oliver's allegations about doing business, insisted that he was still too ill to travel, and explained that his reason for locking his door against Jimmy was to prevent him from telling Tweed, his Tammany boss, and Senator Creamer, who his callers were and all that was going on. Judge Barrett listened to the remarks of able counsel and again deferred proceedings against Gould for a further period of four days, fixing April 18 as the fatal day when he must appear.

Uncle Dan'l Weakens

While Gould was doing his best in Albany under great difficulties, harassed as he was by the courts and threatened by investigations, there was something going on in Jersey City, too. I found out about it when I went down there to carry important letters from Gould.

Jim by this time was comfortably settled with Josie in Castle Erie and was as happy as I ever saw him. It was easy to see that he was more in love with her than ever. He had a good dinner sent up to their rooms in the hotel. Just the three of us were there and they two were in fine spirits, Josie flirting with him all the time without concealment. Jim was as pleased as Punch to have Josie pay him so much attention. After the waiter had finally pocketed his tip and gone out, and Josie had retired, he told me that he had found out more from her about her history.

'I thought her mother was a widow when they went to California,' he said, 'but that was a mistake. The poor girl has had more of a tragic history than I thought at first.' He went on to say that her father was Joseph Mansfield. He had been a printer on the *Boston Journal* until he took his wife and daughter to California in 1852 and settled with them in Stockton where he went to work on the *Stockton Journal*. John Tabor bought the *Journal* two years later and conducted it as a Whig party organ. Mansfield then started the *San Joaquin Republican* as an opposition Democratic mouthpiece.

'It seems there was a lot of politics to the square inch out there then,' Jim told me. 'They had a hot old fight for governor, with George S. Waldo the Whig candidate and John Bigler for the Democrats. Finally Mansfield and Tabor began to abuse each other instead of their candidates and they got so mad over it that they had to fight a duel, and Mansfield got shot through the heart. Josie was only a girl then, but those things hurt. He must have been a damn fool.

'Mrs. Mansfield went to San Francisco the next year and settled there next door to James D. Carter, a young truckman who had made a lot of money. He wanted to marry Josie, but she was only fifteen years old then and her mother said she was too young. Carter proposed to send Josie to Notre Dame Convent in San Jose and promised to pay her expenses there until she was old enough to marry. The mother agreed to that and Josie went to the convent. Then her mother married Warren. Then Lawlor came along, acting in Maguire's Opera House in San Jose. He got acquainted with Josie, ran away with her after ten days, and married her.

'She was just a romantic schoolgirl,' said Jim. It didn't seem tactful to remind him that Lucy was also a romantic schoolgirl in Brattleboro when he married her. 'Lawlor brought Josie East and they got here in 1864. Josie got her divorce from Lawlor in 1866 and he didn't oppose it. That was the whole story.' I didn't ask how she had managed to get along until she met him.

Jim read Gould's letters and listened to what I told him about how we were rounding up the Legislature in Albany. 'Leave it to Gould!' he commented. 'That man's a wonder. Whatever he sets out to do, he'll do it. I don't like this man Barnard, though. If it wasn't for him, we'd have clear sailin'. He does whatever the Commodore wants.'

'Well, tell me what's been going on here,' I suggested. 'Gould will want to know all about everything.'

'I'm sorry to say, Rabbits,' said Jim, 'that your Uncle Dan'l's a treacherous old skunk.'

'What's he been up to now?'

'I'll tell you. He's been in the habit of sneaking off across the river late on Saturday night. I thought he wanted to get home in time to get fixed up for church. You know he always passes the plate. Well, I can't say what it was that started me thinking. I began to suspect that he was up to some deviltry, and I said to myself, 'No harm in having him watched; if it turns out that he's playing straight, it'll be the first time in his life.' So I told Sam to take a couple of men and not let the old rascal out of their sight next time he went over, until he was back here again.

'They went with him on the boat and followed him home. He spent the night there. They made sure of that. Next morning, a little before church time, he came out and got into his carriage. Sam had a hack waiting and he jumped into that and trailed him. What do you think? The old hellion went to see the Commodore and they spent more than an hour together!

'Sam brought me the good news as soon as he could get back here and I was pretty well scared. It looked to me as though Uncle Daniel was playing us for first-class suckers and I didn't like it. It struck me that it might be a good idea to take a look at our money and, sure enough, when the safe where we put it was opened, the money wasn't there!

'If he'd been there, probably I wouldn't have been able to prevent myself from knocking him on the head with anything that came handy. But he didn't come back until Monday night, too late to discuss serious topics. So I waited until Tuesday and then I went in to see him. "Good morning, Uncle Daniel," says I, "how did you leave the Commodore?" "What do you mean?" he asked, looking gray around the gills. "You know damn well what I mean," I says, "and furthermore I want to know what you've done with our money, you sniveling old hypocrite! Where is it?" He began to whine and told me he'd taken it back to New York so it would be safe. "It's a big sum," he says, "an' I'm the one that's responsible for it." "Maybe you are and maybe you ain't," says I. "Anyhow, you bring that money right back here, every damn cent of it, or you'll be sorry." He began to look real worried. "I'm the treasurer, you know," he says. "I know that," says I, "and I want to tell you I feel a damn sight more uneasy about that money than you ever did. I want that money back on this side of the river and I want it quick – right now." He looked at me as mournful as a cow that's lost her calf and I could see he wasn't going to do it. "So that we shouldn't be left penniless," I told him, "in case the Commodore got his paws on our cash while it was over there, I've got an attachment on your account in the bank over here. You can't touch a penny of it until you bring back our working capital." You see, I knew he had a lot of money there and I took the precaution.'

'What did he say to that?'

'His mouth fell right open he was so surprised. There wasn't anything he could say. He saw his goose was cooked. He brought back the money and he won't take it away again – trust me.'

'What did he go to see the Commodore for when we're fighting him up there in Albany?'

'I asked him that, and he told me he was an old man and was tired of being kept from his home and his family. He'd known the Commodore so many years, he thought he might be able to arrange things so the Commodore'd call off Judge Barnard and we could go back. I told him we didn't want to go back, that we liked Jersey and expected to spend the rest of our lives here. I told him Gould felt the same way about it as I did. But the old man wouldn't promise to stop dickerin'. I don't feel at all satisfied with the way he's actin'.'

From this time on, poor old Uncle Dan'l was watched as carefully as though he were an open enemy. Jim read all letters and telegrams of his that he could get hold of and he had him surrounded by detectives. The old man's passion for secrecy was balked at every turn. He didn't dare complain because he stood in such fear of Jim, who threatened to punch his head if he caught him in any more tricks. But in spite of everything he kept on going to New York and seeing the Commodore.

Jim instructed me to tell Gould all about Uncle Daniel's double dealing. 'But you can say that he needn't lose any sleep,' Jim added. 'I'll make myself responsible for the Erie treasury. It won't get away again. Do you know what I think, Rabbits? I think the old cuss intended to give back the money that we got out of the Commodore when we sold him that last lot of Erie stock. It would put us on our uppers to pay back that money. We'd have to go into bankruptcy.'

He sat looking out of the window for a moment turning something over in his mind. 'There's another thing I want you to tell Gould,' he said in a low voice to make sure he wasn't overheard. 'Uncle Daniel's scheme to make it up with the Commodore put it into my mind. It isn't the Commodore that's giving us trouble – it's Tammany. If we had the Wigwam with us, we'd have Judge Barnard and all the other judges, and you know what that would mean to us. A hell of a lot! We'd have Tammany's votes in the Legislature and there'd be no more trouble for us up there. I want you to tell Gould that I'm going to see Boss Tweed and find out whether I can't get him to come with us.'

I told him I'd deliver the message but urged him to make the alliance with Tammany apply only to himself and Gould. 'If you can get Tammany with you,' I reasoned, 'you'll have everything your own way. You won't have to worry about the Commodore, Uncle Daniel, or anybody else. The Erie will be all yours.'

'Rabbits!' said Jim solemnly, putting his hand on my shoulder, 'That's my idea to a T. I've been thinking about it and I've got a letter of introduction from Hugh Hastings. I'm going to take it to Boss Tweed.'

♦

The next day was Sunday, and I went with Jim across the river. Writs couldn't be served on Sunday or arrests made in civil cases so we knew we were safe. Jim and I drove down to Duane Street. We stopped in front of a dingy sign on which was inscribed 'William M. Tweed, Counsellor at Law.' I was surprised to find the powerful Boss of Tammany occupying such quarters.

The Boss was in his outer office in his shirt sleeves. He was a big man. There seemed something formidable and menacing about his bulk. You could see from his face that he was a fighter. The leader of Tammany Hall has to be if he expects to keep his job. Jim had sent word that we were coming, and a conference that Tweed had been holding was just breaking up when we entered the outer office. The Boss introduced Jim to his friends. One of them was Peter B. Sweeney, the 'Squire,' who had just been made receiver of the Erie in place of Osgood, Vanderbilt's son-in-law, by Justice Barnard, who later allowed him $150,000 for doing nothing at all. With him were two other men. One was Richard B. Connolly, who looked like a financier, with smooth face and high, narrow forehead, but who was really only an ignorant, shrewd Irish bookkeeper. He and Sweeney after shaking hands with us went out together. They left A. Oakey Hall, who then was district attorney and who was elected mayor of the city at the next election, in November, when Connolly was made comptroller. Hall was a lawyer and a cultivated, versatile, charming man.

'Well, Senator,' said Jim to Tweed, 'I'd like to have a few minutes' talk with you. I hope it won't do you any harm even if I am an exile of Erie instead of Erin.'

'Come in here,' said Tweed in a businesslike way, and he took Jim into a private office where Hall and I could not overhear what was said. We sat down to await results, and Hall told me Tweed had started as a chairmaker, a business his father had when he died. He failed in that. But he had been rising in the Tammany organization through fifteen years of close application to the business of politics. His big frame, his quickness to act, his willingness to fight, and his merciless harshness in putting down revolts against his authority, had made him supreme. No man understood the city better than he did. He was proud of it. He had been born in it.

Hall chatted with me for half an hour, until the conference inside broke up and Jim came out, jovial and smiling, followed by the bulk of the Tammany Boss. 'I've started it, Rabbits!' Jim said as we drove away. 'You can tell Gould I hardly think he'll have much more trouble up there – that he can get the Tammany vote if he needs it. Tweed wants to carry out his contracts with the Commodore if we can get our bill through without him. Tell him that I haven't done anything final, and won't until he gets through up there. Tweed's a man I can do business with – I understand him. I believe we're goin' to get out of the woods now before very long. Of course, we shall have to talk some more before things are settled for good.'

♦

These talks took place, and the net result of them was that Tweed came over to our side and we carried him along with us. He was elected a director of Erie later on and still later a director of Gould's Tenth National Bank. He made money when we did and so it was to his advantage to help us along and not hinder us, as he had been doing until then.

That was the year, 1868, when the Democratic National Convention was held in the new Wigwam of Tammany Hall in Fourteenth Street, which was opened for the first time in July. Tweed made Horatio Seymour the candidate for president and General Grant beat him; but his candidates for governor of the state and mayor of the city, John T. Hoffman, and my friend A. Oakey Hall, were elected. This was done partly by the votes of twenty or thirty thousand new citizens naturalized that year by the Tammany-controlled courts, and partly by wholesale ballot-box stuffing and election frauds. It made our new ally, Boss Tweed, supreme in New York City and State and a big man in the nation.

♦

I took the train back to Albany after we came up from Duane Street and found Gould waiting for me. He took me into his bedroom and listened intently to the report I made to him about the treachery of Uncle Dan'l and Jim's approach to Boss Tweed. He looked grave and serious, as usual, and he asked few questions. When I had finished he seemed thoughtful, but he didn't make any comment. I got the impression somehow that he didn't relish Drew's negotiations with the Commodore. I asked him how things were getting on in the campaign for the Erie bill. 'All right,' he said. 'I think we've got them beaten; but we have to deal with so many rascals that it's hard to tell.'

♦

That next week was one of extreme activity. It gave me a respect for Gould that I hadn't had until then. One by one, the votes he needed were obtained. His experience with Senator Mattoon had taught him not to rely on a slender majority that might be bought away from him at the last moment. Every vote that could be won, he got. His agents scoured the state. If any senator or assemblyman hesitated, he soon found himself caught in coils of irresistible pressure. Everything about him was ferretted out.

Gould's intensity, his thoroughness, his complete devotion to the task in hand, and his fertility of resource were a surprise to Albany. That we should be able to carry the day against the Commodore's opposition and in spite of the adverse action that had already been taken in both houses of the Legislature seemed impossible, yet Gould did it. When the vote was finally taken, on April 18, we had seventeen ayes and Vanderbilt could only count twelve noes. Even Mattoon the elusive, who had signed the committee report denouncing us, voted for our bill.

Tweed's votes were cast against us. We didn't need them. If we had, probably we could have had them, but as things were, Tammany lived up to its Vanderbilt bargain. Our victory in the Assembly, where a hostile committee report on our bill had so lately been sustained by a vote of eighty-three to thirty-two, was even more astounding. The bill that came over from the Senate was passed by a vote of one hundred and one ayes to only six noes!

Even then the Commodore didn't give up the ship. His lawyers made an elaborate appeal to Governor Fenton to veto the bill. But Hamilton Harris had laid his plans so well that the arguments of the opposition proved unavailing. We had packed up and were on our way down the river back to Jersey City on the night boat when the Governor signed the bill. All the questionable acts of the Erie directors to date were now legalized and officially sanctioned. It was a great victory for our cause and an astonishing triumph for Gould.

That fight hasn't been forgotten yet in Albany. Everybody believed that votes had been bought by both sides and that money had been spent by the bagful. So it was, and the reputation of the Legislature has never recovered.

———♦———

Uncle Dan'l was beginning to get on Jim's nerves with his secret comings and goings by the time Gould got back from Albany. The old man knew that Jim and Gould hated the thought of any truce with the Commodore now that he was licked. But he kept Eldridge, our president, informed of his progress with the Commodore, swearing him to secrecy.

By the time the battle of Albany had been won, the main features of a treaty of peace had been agreed upon by Uncle Dan'l and the Commodore. Gould guessed this, and he and Jim began to work on Eldridge in the hope of holding a majority of the board of directors. How they finally found out what Uncle Daniel had done, when it was too late to stop it, is an episode that was described by Jim when he was on the witness stand in a suit that he brought against the Commodore in the following year for the purpose of undoing what the treaty had done.

'When did you first meet Commodore Vanderbilt on business connected with the matters contained in this suit?' he was asked.

'I had one interview with the Commodore some time last summer,' he replied. 'It was pretty warm – not the interview but the weather. I remember that well because the Commodore was a little profane about it. (Laughter from the audience.) I can't exactly fix the date of the first interview, but I know it was after my return from Jersey. I had been absent in Jersey for a short lapse of time (laughter all over the court room, even the Judge relaxing into a broad smile), and when I got back, I thought I'd make the Commodore a friendly call.' (Laughter.) Jim didn't explain then that when the Commodore saw that things were coming his way, he let up on us and we were able to return freely to New York whenever we felt like it.

'Did you call on Mr. Vanderbilt?' he was asked.

'Most undoubtedly. The recollection thereof is vivid and the memory green!' (Laughter.) '

The interruptions by laughter noted by the court stenographer were due more to Jim's droll way of speaking and his expressive countenance than to what he actually said. 'What passed at the interview between you and Commodore Vanderbilt?' the examination continued.

'Well, the Commodore received me with the most distinguished courtesy,' said Jim, 'and overwhelmed me with a perfect abundance of good wishes for my health. When we sat down and got fairly quiet, we came plump up to the matter that was uppermost, and then we had it out. From the beginning I saw that Vanderbilt would try the gum game.'

'What do you mean by the "gum game," Mr. Fisk?'

'Well, it would take a long time to explain that. You see, it's a game that so many can play at (laughter); and every man has his own peculiar way in dealing, and cutting and working for points. What I mean is that I saw that Vanderbilt was cunning – not half as cunning as Drew though – and thought that p'raps I wouldn't stand much chance with him. He has the advantage of years on his side and a good deal of promiscuous experience.

'Well, he told me that several of the directors were trying to make a trade with him, and he would like to know who was the best man to trade with.

'Why,' said I, 'if the trade's a good, honest one, you'd better trade with me.' (Laughter.)

'Then he said that old man Drew was no better than a batter pudding (laughter) or words to that effect; that Eldridge was demoralized, and that our concern was without head or tail. (Laughter.) This wasn't overly complimentary; but after thinking a minute, I said I thought so too. (Laughter, in which the court was forced to join.)

'Then he became very earnest and said he had got his bloodhounds on us and would pursue us until we took that damned stock off his hands – he'd be damned if he'd keep it.

'I was grieved to hear him swear so (laughter), but being obliged to say something, I remarked quietly that I'd be damned if we'd take it back (great laughter) and that we'd sell him stock jest as long as he'd stand up and take it. (Great laughter.)

'Well, when I made this observation, the Commodore mellowed down a little (laughter) and said he thought it would be a great deal better for us to get together and arrange this matter. Then he began to tell tales. (Laughter.) He told me that Daniel Drew, when we were suffering in exile over in Jersey (laughter), used to slip off to New York at night, whenever he could get away from our vigilance; that Drew would come to his house – the Commodore's – and let out our little secrets. Then he wanted to know if a trade with Drew and Eldridge could be slipped through our Board, adding in a sort of a seductive way that if it could, we should all be landed safe in the haven of peace and harmony.' Here Jim paused as though reflecting sadly upon the imperfections of human nature.

'Well, what then, Mr. Fisk?' prompted his counsel.

Jim's face assumed a look of virtuous determination. 'Of course,' he said firmly, 'I told him I wouldn't agree to anything of the kind; that I wouldn't submit to a robbery of the road under any circumstances; and that I was dumbfounded, actually thunderstruck, to think that our directors, whom I had always esteemed as honorable men (great laughter), would have anything to do with such outrageous proceedings!'

'Is that all that was said?'

'I rather think not! (Laughter.) We talked about half an hour, and I think I could say a great deal more than that in half an hour!' (Laughter.)

'Where was Gould all this time?'

'He was in the front room – I suppose. I left him there and found him there, but I don't know where he may have been in the meantime.' (Laughter.)

'Where was your next interview with Mr. Vanderbilt?'

'The next interview was at the home of Mr. Pierrepont. Gould and I had an appointment with Eldridge at the Fifth Avenue Hotel, and as we didn't find him there, we went out to see if we could find him.'

'Can you give the date of that meeting?'

'No, sir.'

'Can you give the week?'

'No, sir.'

'Can you give the month?'

'No, sir.'

'Can you give the year?'

'No, sir; not without reference.' Jim said this in such a way that everybody laughed.

'What reference do you want?'

'Well, I shall have to refer back to the various events of my life to see just where that day comes in. The almighty robbery committed by this man Vanderbilt against the Erie Railway was the most impressive event in my life. (Laughter.) The meeting at Pierrepont's was a week or ten days after the first interview with Vanderbilt. Gould and I went there about nine o'clock. We stepped into the hall together. We asked if Mr. Pierrepont was in. The servant said he'd see. When the servant went into the drawing room, I was very careful to keep on a line with the door, so I could see in. (Laughter.)

'Presently Mr. Pierrepont stepped into the hall, resembling a man who wasn't in much. (Laughter.) I asked him if our president was there. After some thoughtfulness on his part, he said he thought he was. (Laughter.) During this time I had moved along towards the drawing room door, Mr. Pierrepont having neglected to invite us in!' (Laughter.)

'Where was Gould?'

'Oh he was just behind me. He's always right behind at such times (laughter), and while he entertained Pierrepont, I opened the door and stepped in (laughter) and found most of our directors there!

'I stepped up to Mr. Eldridge and told him we had been to the Fifth Avenue Hotel and did not find him. He said he knew he wasn't there. (Laughter.) I asked what was going on and everybody seemed to wait for somebody else to answer. (Laughter.)

'Being better acquainted with Drew than any of the rest of them, though perhaps having less confidence in him (laughter), I asked him what under heavens was up. He said they were arranging the suits. I told him they ought to adopt a very different manner of doing it than being there in the night; that no settlement could be made without requiring the money of the corporation.

'He began to picture his miseries to me – told me how he had suffered during his pilgrimage, saying he was worn out and kept away from his family, and wanted to settle matters up; that he'd done everything he could, and saw no other way out, either for himself or the company.

'I told him I guessed he was more particular about himself than the company. He said, well, he was (laughter); that he was an old man and wanted to get out of the fight; that he was much older in such affairs than we were – I was very glad to hear that – (laughter) and that it was no uncommon thing for a great corporation to make arrangements of this sort. I told him, if that was the case, I thought our state prisons ought to be enlarged! (Laughter.)

'Then Eldridge, he took hold of me. He talked about his great exertions – what he had done and consummated – that there were only two dissenting voices in the board, Gould and myself, and that if we came into the matter tomorrow, the company would be free and clear of litigation and everything would be all right, as he had got the Commodore and Work and Schell to settle on a price.

'I told him I couldn't see it. I had fought that position for seven months, night and day, and for seven weeks in Jersey. I had hardly taken off my clothes, fighting to keep the money of the company from being robbed; and I could see no reason why we shouldn't fight on still.

'He said he didn't want to go into it, but had tried to do the best he could with Gould and myself and could do nothing; and now an arrangement had been made with Vanderbilt and it was all right and must go through that night. I said I didn't believe it was legal; these lawyers were all on one side and I wanted to see my lawyers. He said that was no good. (Laughter.)

'Then Mr. Pierrepont argued with me. He said he didn't think there was anyone present who wasn't going to derive benefit from it. Rapallo was writing at a table. Schell was buzzing around (laughter), interested in getting his share of the plunder. Work was sitting on a sofa. I had nothing to say to him (laughter) as we were not on very good terms.

'Gould and I had a conversation together and not till twelve o'clock at night did we give our consent. I told him I didn't believe the proceedings were legal; that we had no lawyers; that the lawyers were sold to Eldridge – hook, line, and sinker! (Laughter.) Gould said Eldridge had paid William M. Evarts ten thousand dollars for an opinion that it was all right, and Dorman Eaton had been paid fifteen thousand dollars for an opinion, and said it was legal. I told him I thought it a queer way of classifying opinions. (Laughter.)

'Gould consented first. He said he had made up his mind to do so as the best way to get out of the matter. I told him I would consent if he did. Drew came to me with tears in his eyes and asked me to consent, and I consented!

'Then there was some paper drawn up and passed around for us to sign. I don't know what it contained. I didn't read it. I don't think I noticed a word of it. I don't know the contents, and I've always been glad I didn't! (Laughter.)

'I don't know what other documents I signed. I signed everything that was put before me! (Laughter.) After the devil once got hold of me, I kept on signing! (Laughter.) I didn't read any of them and I've no idea what they were. Don't know how many I signed. I went with the robbers then and I've been with them ever since! (Laughter.) After signing all the papers, I took my hat and left at once in disgust! (Laughter.) I don't know whether we sat down or not. I know we didn't have anything to eat!' (Laughter.)

'Didn't you have a glass of wine or something of that sort?'

'I don't remember.'

'Wouldn't that have made an impression on you?' (Laughter.)

'No, sir; I never drink! (Laughter.) I think I left at once as soon as I had done signing. As we went out I said to Gould we had sold ourselves to the devil. (Laughter.) He agreed to that and said he thought so too. (Laughter.) I remember Mr. White, the cashier, coming in with the check book under his arm, and as he came in I said to him that he was bearing in the balance of the remains of our corporation to put into Vanderbilt's tomb!' (Laughter.)

'When was the next interview?'

'The next interview with Vanderbilt was several days after.'

'Was Gould with you?'

'Yes, sir; we never parted during that war! (Laughter.) We went to his office one morning and found his man Friday in the front room. (Laughter.) I don't know his name; it was the same man I had seen a hundred times before when I had been there with Drew.

'We found the Commodore in the back room. I asked him how he was getting on. He said: 'First rate.' (Laughter.) That he had got the thing all arranged, and the only question now was whether it could be slipped through our board. I told him that after what I had seen the other night, I thought anything could be slipped through! (Laughter.) He said he would have to manage it carefully. I told him I didn't think so – that they would be careful to go it blind. (Laughter.) He said the trade had been consummated at Pierrepont's house. I said I had no doubt of it. He said it ought not to have been carried out – that Schell had got the lion's share and that some of the lawyers on the other side might have to go hungry. (Laughter.)

'He asked if we were conversant with the rest of the trade. I said I had no doubt the whole thing had been cooked up in such a manner that it could be put through. (Laughter.) He spoke about putting Banker and Stewart into our Board, and said it would help both him and us to carry our stock, as people would say we had amalgamated, and Vanderbilt's men coming into the Erie Board would strengthen the market. That was admitted; but it worked rather different from what we expected. (Laughter.)

'I next saw him a day or two before the prosecution was closed up. Gould thought the Commodore's losses had not been so large as represented, and he asked to see his brokers' account. The Commodore said he never showed anything and we must take his word. He reiterated his losses and said they were so large because, when they had got him to give his order to sustain the market, the skunks had run and sold out on him! (Laughter.) As we were coming away, he said: "Boys, you're young and if you carry out this settlement, there'll be peace and harmony between the two roads."'

'When were you made a director of the company?'

'I became a director of the Erie Railway on the thirteenth of October, 1867.'

'You remember that date?'

'I do – well! It forms an episode in my life!'

'What fixes it in your mind so well?'

'I had no gray hairs then.' (Laughter.)

'You have gray hairs now?'

'Plenty of them! And I saw more robbery during the next year than I ever dreamed of as possible!'

'You saw it, did you?'

'I didn't see it, but I knew it was going on!'

♦

The treaty of peace that Uncle Dan'l and President Eldridge had worked out with the Commodore, and that raised Jim and Gould to the boiling point, covered everything up to date. The Commodore was to withdraw all suits against the Exiles of Erie and allow them to come back to New York unmolested. In return, the Erie Railroad was to take off his hands fifty thousand shares of Erie stock for which it would pay him two million, five hundred thousand dollars in ready money, and one million, two hundred and fifty thousand dollars in bonds of the Boston, Hartford and Erie Railroad at the rate of eighty cents on the dollar. Besides that, he was to get a million dollars more from the Erie in cash for giving an option to the Erie on fifty thousand additional shares of Erie stock. This million was usually referred to as a 'bonus.' That bonus made a lot of explaining for the Commodore to do later, as you will see. The Commodore thought he'd like to keep the stock for a while, so that he could still have a big finger in the pie in case of need. That made four million, seven hundred and fifty thousand dollars for him, all out of the Erie treasury. The old man always insisted, though, that he hadn't had any dealings with the Erie Railway in this settlement. I remember he wrote to the *Times* to say so when we had been accused of looting the road.

The treaty gave Vanderbilt the right to nominate two members of the Erie board of directors. He had that provision in mind when he told Jim and Gould what a nice thing it was going to be to have Banker and Stewart in the board as 'Vanderbilt's men.'

Eldridge was to get out of the Erie Railroad four million dollars of Erie acceptances in return for five million dollars' worth of Boston, Hartford and Erie bonds at eighty cents on the dollar. That would fix things so he could get the three millions that the Massachusetts Legislature had promised as a reward if the Boston crowd could find another sucker.

As for Uncle Dan'l, he had already got his. The treaty permitted him to keep it, provided he would pay back to the Erie five hundred and forty thousand dollars in settlement of all the claims the company had against him.

There was nothing in the treaty for Jim and Gould. That was natural enough. They hadn't had any hand in making it. But they refused to sign it unless Drew and Eldridge would agree to get out of Erie. Eldridge agreed. He had got what he was after and he didn't want to stay anyway. Uncle Dan'l hesitated a little, but he was so anxious to get out of the scrape he had got himself into with the Commodore that he finally consented, too. He had been in the management almost twenty years, most of the time in absolute control. He left the Erie treasury empty and the road itself practically a decrepit wreck.

'There ain't nothin' more in Airy, C'neel,' Drew remarked to Vanderbilt at this stage of the proceedings.

'Don't ye be too damn sure o' that, Dan'l,' the Commodore replied.

3
Fame

The Credit Mobilier

We came back from Jersey City after the Commodore had been convinced that the Erie board of directors would dip into the company's treasury to buy him off. He let us return on April 22, 1868, although the treaty wasn't actually signed until the following July and the terms of it couldn't be fully carried out until the new board of directors was elected in October.

Release from exile gave Jim a chance to show Josie what a hold she had gained over his affections. He took her with him secretly to Boston for two weeks, to make a little triumphant visit to her mother and other relatives while he visited Lucy. When they came back, he put her in the Clarendon Hotel for a while and finally he rented a house for her at No. 18 West Twenty-fourth Street, close to the Fifth Avenue Hotel where he was living at that time. She was delighted. She was loving and responsive and she didn't miss an opportunity to show Jim that he was making no mistake in being good to her.

By that time the relationship between them had become known to Jim's intimates. Gould didn't like it. So many people had found out about Jim and Josie that he hardly tried to make a secret of it any longer. He'd been afraid at first that the newspapers would make a stink about it; but the newspapers don't talk about such things unless they get into court. When Jim saw that there wasn't anything about Josie in the papers, though all the reporters knew she was there, he began to gain confidence.

Jim was devoted to Josie. The house he hired for her was furnished, but he bought pretty things she wanted to make it more attractive and he gave her a good deal of money to spend on herself. Gradually he built up a household with Josie at its center but he had to look after the details of it himself at first. In the course of time she learned how to do her own ordering from the butcher and baker, and how to get along with servants.

Jim used to make the house his headquarters, although he kept his room at the Grand Central. He had to spend a good part of his time there, anyway, to see that the establishment didn't fall to pieces. He almost always ate dinner there when he was in the city and now and then he had friends there to dine with them. Josie didn't know much about keeping house, but she knew how to entertain a party of men. Of course, Jim would order the dinner on such occasions and attend to all the fixings.

The men used to play poker at the house and one night one of them proposed that all the winnings that evening should go to their hostess. All hands agreed and Josie made about twenty-five hundred dollars out of it. Belden, Jim's partner, was one of the party. Jim advised Josie to let him take the money and buy Erie stock with it on margin. He knew it was going up. In fact, he and Gould were going to put it up to make the brokers for the English stockholders pay for selling it short. Belden ran the twenty-five hundred dollars up to fifteen thousand in three days. Jim bought Government bonds for her with the money.

♦

It was in April, 1868, that Jim laid the foundation for our treaty with Tammany Hall, when we went to see Boss Tweed while Gould was working in Albany to make the Legislature validate the Erie convertible bonds.

There have been few scandals in the history of this country that could compare with the scandals that attended the building of the Union Pacific. It was Jim who dug up what was going on among the silk hat and kid glove people who were up to their necks in it and he told the country about it. I don't mean to say that he was actuated by concern for the public welfare when he did this; I'm afraid that wouldn't be strictly true. The truth was that he had found a particularly good thing in the way of large and quick profits, and he wanted to buy or beat his way in. The man who owned this good thing tricked him out of the stock that he subscribed for and Jim let out a roar in the courts. It didn't do him any good. The respectable capitalists and financiers didn't care to divide with Jim. They wanted to keep all they were getting and they did; but Jim's suit, which they called 'blackmail' made the facts known in Congress where the opposition took them up. It was too soon after the war to shake the Republicans out, but not so very long afterward the Union Pacific scandal was a powerful factor in the defeat of the Republican candidate for president, James G. Blaine, and the election of Grover Cleveland. Jim did it.

At the same time, the standing and respectability of the men that Jim attacked gave credence to the stories they spread about him and they did their share to tag him. They were great at that sort of thing. They had always hated Jim anyhow as an upstart, and they hated him a thousand times worse for interfering with their plans.

In the legal proceedings, Tammany, which means Boss Tweed, was of great assistance to Jim. It turned the courts over to us, at least those presided over by Justices Barnard and Cardozo. David Dudley Field was in charge of the legal fireworks, and the Union Pacific Ring attacked him just as it attacked Jim. But Field was not so easily blackened. After it was all over a dozen lawyers of national reputation wrote commending him for the part he took in conducting Jim's 'blackmailing' case. It was a great contest, with Samuel J. Tilden defending the Union Pacific gang. All this happened before Tilden rose to political power as the champion of justice through the overthrow of the Tammany Ring. He didn't get anything out of his defense of the Union Pacific Ring except his fee.

♦

The government paid, and paid well, by bond issues and land grants, for the building of the railroad. The work had hardly begun before its enormous profits revealed themselves to the insiders. They decided that it was possible to keep all these profits for themselves and their friends. To do this they bought for a song the Pennsylvania Fiscal Agency, a worthless Pennsylvania company, and gave it a new and high-sounding name – the Credit Mobilier of America. Then they made a contract with this company to build the road.

This was actually making a contract with themselves. The chief owners of the Credit Mobilier were Oliver Ames, president of the Union Pacific, his brother, Oakes Ames, Thomas C. Durant, John J. Cisco, Henry S. McComb, Sidney Dillon, Benjamin E. Bates, Josiah Bardwell, John B. Alley, Charles A. Lambard, Ebenezer Cook, and John Duff. All except Oakes Ames were Union Pacific directors.

Under its agreement with the Union Pacific, the Credit Mobilier sublet contracts for the real building of the road at prices much lower than the government allowance; but it got the full government payment of bonds and pocketed the difference. Not only that, but the Union Pacific issued its own bonds equal in amount to the Union Pacific bonds issued by the government and these – all clear profit – were mostly turned over to the Credit Mobilier. Finally, large amounts of Union Pacific stock were authorized and offered for subscription.

I never knew exactly what started Jim after the Credit Mobilier. I always suspected that the man behind him was Thomas C. Durant, vice-president of the Union Pacific and also a large stockholder and president of the Credit Mobilier. It was Durant, I believe, who first thought of the plan of buying the worthless Pennsylvania Fiscal Agency, changing its name to the Credit Mobilier, and using it as an instrument for milking the railroad. It was copied after a French company of the same name that made a big scandal in France.

The United States government empowered the railroad to issue its own bonds in case of emergency; that is to say, the supposition was that they would be issued only in case of emergency. It was this permission that opened the way.

Durant acquired the Pennsylvania concern because it was a state company and beyond the reach of Congress. Its charter also limited the liability of its officers. It had a capital of two and a half millions and it bought the whole capital stock of the Union Pacific.

A man named H. M. Hoxie, a figurehead only, made a contract with the railroad in the spring of 1864 to build a hundred miles of track. He immediately assigned this contract to the Credit Mobilier. Of course the Credit Mobilier made what profit there was, about five million dollars, which meant that the big stockholders in the railroad made it, because they owned the Credit Mobilier. This contract cost the railroad thirteen million dollars.

The Ames brothers were making the shovels with which the

grading was being done. The Durant idea was to make the Union Pacific stock an attractive investment by giving its holders a profit out of the construction of the road. It had not occurred to Durant, so far as I know, that the government might be made to pay for building the road and then be shut out of its money by the sale of prior mortgage bonds covering the entire outfit.

Durant, after the Hoxie contract, made a contract with a man named Boomer to build a hundred miles of road at not more than twenty-two thousand five hundred dollars a mile. Boomer went ahead, but Durant got into a row with the Ameses and they dropped him out of the Credit Mobilier. This was in 1866. The directors of the railroad under the Ames influence, refused to approve the Boomer contract, although Boomer had built fifty-eight miles of road. The happy idea of including this section in the Hoxie contract and paying for it at the rate of fifty thousand dollars a mile captured the imagination of the directors in January, 1867; but Durant got out an injunction and stopped it. Later on, when he had made peace, he allowed the Boomer road to be paid for at forty-two thousand dollars a mile.

Congress had stipulated that the stock of the Union Pacific should not be sold for less than a hundred dollars a share. To get around this, the railroad paid the Credit Mobilier by check, and the Credit Mobilier used these checks to buy stock, which it then sold for whatever it could get, on the average about thirty dollars a share. That was regarded as a neat way of chasing the devil round the stump.

The Ameses didn't let the grass grow under their feet when they got control. Oliver was made president of the Union Pacific and Oakes of the Credit Mobilier. The subterfuge of having an outsider bid on contracts was dropped as tiresome. Oliver and the rest of them made a direct contract with brother Oakes to build six hundred and sixty-seven miles of railroad for forty-seven million dollars, or at the rate of from forty-two thousand to ninety-six thousand dollars a mile. When this contract was made it carried an agreement that brother Oakes should assign it to seven trustees, extensive stockholders in both the Credit Mobilier and the Union Pacific, and that they should divide the profits among the stockholders of the Credit Mobilier.

Brother Oakes charged the railroad a great deal more than the liberal estimate made by the government engineers for building the line. Brother Oliver approved. At first blush this looks like a waste of money. If you think so, you don't know much about finance. The high cost of brother Oakes not only absorbed the modest allowance of government bonds, but called for much more.

———♦———

The next step was to fix things in Congress so that there would be little or nothing to fear from that quarter. 'There's no difficulty in getting men to look after their own property,' said Oakes Ames sagely. So the thing to do was to give members of Congress a personal interest to look out for. With this in view, the capital of the Credit Mobilier was increased by one half and the new stock was divided between Durant and Oakes to be distributed where it would do the most good, mainly in the pockets of Senators and Representatives in Congress. Oakes had himself elected a member of the House and he tried to get the stock into the hands of men of unquestioned honesty, such as Senator Dawes, of Massachusetts, and Senator Bayard, of Delaware. They were both lucky enough to escape, and so was Speaker James G. Blaine but a lot of members, both Republicans and Democrats, innocently or otherwise, took some of the stock. Of course they paid for it – a hundred dollars a share, with accrued interest from the preceding June first. A plain and ordinary business transaction in all details – of course.

The Oakes Ames contract was paid for in stock and by the issue of Union Pacific bonds, which under the law were a first lien on the property, leaving the government outside the door with a second mortagage, to whistle if it wanted to. The Credit Mobilier didn't lose any money on brother Oakes' contract. It paid its stockholders, including the members of Congress who had to come in, a dividend of eighty per cent in January, 1868, and another one of sixty per cent in June of the same year! This was what made Jim's mouth water.

———♦———

His operations began in 1867 when he got his friend, Justice McCunn, of the Supreme Court, to hold up the Union Pacific election of that year by enjoining everybody so that neither the Ames faction nor the Durant crowd could vote. Somebody sent for Benjamin F. Butler, the hero of New Orleans, who knew McCunn. After looking the situation over, General Butler saw the justice and got him to let the Ames faction vote, but not the other side. He stopped over a day or two to explain to the Ames brothers and their associates that the contract with Oakes was illegal because it was in fact a contract made by the owners of the railroad with themselves in contravention of the laws in such cases made and provided. He showed them a legal hocus pocus by which they might get out of the hole they had put themselves in, and then went back to Boston and sent in a bill for six thousand dollars, five for his fee and one for expenses. The bill didn't mention Justice McCunn, however. Ben got his money, but he had to threaten suit before they would pay it.

Jim knew a good man when he saw one and he sent Ben a check for five thousand dollars to retain him. The other side had Tilden and Judge Jere Black and Charles Tracy. But Ben wouldn't take it. Maybe he thought the other side would keep him on, but they didn't. They had plenty of courage but very little imagination. The Ameses made peace with Durant in August, 1867. If Durant was really behind Jim, as I suspected, this left Jim up in the air, but it didn't stop him.

♦

Jim had six thousand shares of stock that he had picked up somewhere. Just before the annual meeting of the Union Pacific in 1868 he walked into the office of the company and subscribed for five thousand shares more. He handed over checks for two hundred and seventy-five thousand dollars, which was fifty-five per cent of the par value of the stock. The printed invitation to subscribers gave them this privilege. Cisco wouldn't let Jim have the shares. As treasurer of the company, he refused to accept the checks. Jim took them, left the office, and in a little while came back and repeated the offer, subscribing for five thousand shares more and offering the same checks as before. He was refused, and he did it again, making a total of fifteen thousand shares he had subscribed for in New York. He telegraphed to

Chicago, too, and had an agent there subscribe for still another five thousand shares. Then he asked Field to take charge and brought suit before Justice Barnard for twenty thousand shares of stock on the ground that his subscription had been illegally and unjustly refused. 'Now you'll see 'em flutter!' said Jim; and we did.

The Credit Mobilier's fabulous dividends on its stock were attracting attention. 'That money ought to come to the Union Pacific,' Jim declared. 'Damned rascals – they're stealing it right under our noses!' Whereupon he asked, in legal form, for the twenty thousand shares of stock he had tried to buy; also that the Union Pacific be restrained from paying out any money; also that its contract with the Credit Mobilier be declared a fraud and the money paid under it be refunded; also that all contracts be set aside and all securities returned to the Union Pacific; and finally that the Credit Mobilier be forbidden to make any payments. Justice Barnard granted Jim's prayer temporarily and ordered a hearing on July 21 as to making the injunction permanent.

Of course this proceeding aroused a great outcry among the Better Element. They had suspected that Jim was a rogue, for hadn't he been a tin peddler in his youth? His exposure of the Credit Mobilier added some dozens to the already long list of his enemies and detractors. Nevertheless, the immediate result of the suit was an exodus of the defendants from the state so that they couldn't be haled before Justice Barnard. Such a situation couldn't continue and plans were made to get the tell-tale books and records of the Credit Mobilier out of the state.

Jim tried to stop this move by obtaining an order from Justice Albert Cardozo, on July 17, enjoining the removal of the records. Meanwhile, we couldn't get at them. Nobody seemed to know the combination of the safe in which they were supposed to be kept. The office of the Credit Mobilier suddenly vanished. Nobody could tell under oath what had become of it. The men who did know were away, either in Jersey, or Washington, or Europe, or somewhere else outside New York. Everything was delightfully vague. If by chance a subpoena was served on a witness and he obeyed it, he refused to answer questions on the advice of his counsel. But Jim clung to their coat-tails and they loathed him more and more. He had David Dudley Field exhaust all the powers of the Tammany Justices of the Supreme Court before he finally resorted to violent methods to get at the elusive records of the Credit Mobilier. The dodging patriots were desperately trying to squirm out of the New York State courts and into the Federal courts, where they knew the boot would be on the other leg. Jim had got Justice Barnard to appoint William M. Tweed, Jr., receiver for the Credit Mobilier and started him on the liveliest kind of a hunt for assets. They couldn't get hold of any. All the officials of the company were roosting high in Jersey and elsewhere. At last the receiver, after telling his troubles, got an order to break open the safe.

♦

Jim knew how to make the most of this authorization so as to attract attention to what was going on in the affairs of the Union Pacific. He went down to the Union Pacific offices in Nassau Street where the safe was, with a band of twenty husky mechanics armed with sledge hammers, cold chisels, and other burglarious tools. He and young Tweed showed Barnard's order and gave the word to begin the assault on the big safe, while the railroad employees in the office looked helplessly on. Their banging and clattering attracted a crowd and it wasn't long before half of Wall Street had jammed into the offices and was looking on, while Jim in his shirt sleeves supervised the work. The men kept at it until at last they ripped the safe open. There wasn't much in it, as far as that went, but the business made a lot of noise and the subsequent flight of the company to Boston helped to convince people that it was afraid and that maybe what Jim said about the rascality of it was true. How could Congress very well help investigating after that? It couldn't and it didn't.

♦

The breaking open of the safe aroused an almost fanatical outburst of indignation in New England, or at least, parts of it. There was a meeting of stockholders in the Fifth Avenue Hotel in the early winter of 1867, to consider the increase in the Credit Mobilier stock that had been agreed on to provide Oakes Ames and Durant with enough shares to implicate their friends in Congress and elsewhere. McComb promptly grasped the opportunity to demand some of the new stock and he made a row about it. He didn't get it; but before he finished, he gave some of Oakes Ames's letters to the *Sun* and the whole business had an airing in the national campaign of 1872. An investigating committee recommended the expulsion of Oakes Ames from the House but he finally got off with a reprimand – and died in three months.

Investigations by committees of the House showed that the Union Pacific directors had paid themselves – as stockholders of the Credit Mobilier – ninety-three million dollars to build the road, and that – as contractors – they had built it for fifty millions, leaving them with a face-value profit of some forty-three millions. The government couldn't get any of it back, and Jim didn't succeed in getting any of it either. You can say what you like about that crowd, but you can't truthfully say they didn't know how to keep what they got!

The exposure of a broadcloth conspiracy arouses protest. People couldn't believe that the Union Pacific gang were crooks. To tell the truth, I don't think the Ameses believed it. All their lives they had boasted of their honesty, and they were hurt and astounded when they found themselves accused.

The Tweed Ring got away with some hundred millions of public money by charging the city more than things cost and pocketing the difference. I never could see why the operations of the Union Pacific crowd were very much different, if any. They charged the government more for building the road than it cost and distributed the difference among themselves in the form of dividends.

Tammany Politics

Our new friends in Tammany Hall were deep in politics all this time. That year a candidate for president had to be nominated and after that, candidates for governor and mayor. Of course we were interested. We found Boss Tweed a powerful and necessary ally, so much so that Gould and Jim were more than willing to pay him well for his services. He and Peter B. Sweeney were elected that year directors of the Erie Railroad, and when the board was reorganized in 1869 under the Classification Act, Tweed was put in for the longest term with Gould and Jim. Boss Tweed could deliver anything that the mayor and aldermen, the legislature, or the courts had to give. No wonder we were interested in politics; and there was plenty of it to be interested in.

The hatreds and passions of the Civil War were still burning hot. They were kept so by men who knew how to turn them to their own profit. General Grant was nominated for president by the Republicans in Chicago in May, 1868.

———♦———

Tweed had just finished a new Wigwam for Tammany Hall in Fourteenth Street and he got the Democrats to hold their national convention there on the Fourth of July. Horatio Seymour presided and the galleries were filled with shouting Tammany braves. There was a long list of candidates. The convention took seven ballots on each of three days. Seymour got nine votes on the fourth ballot. He immediately declared himself out, saying he couldn't accept if he was nominated. 'Your candidate I cannot be!' shouted Seymour from the platform – and then the convention nominated him unanimously!

It was a great feather in Tweed's hat to have bagged the nomination for New York. Jim was smart but he didn't know much about politics. Wall Street and that crowd usually don't. Jim believed Seymour had a chance of being elected. He talked about it all the time.

Tweed nominated Mayor John T. Hoffman for governor, and my genial and eloquent young friend, District Attorney A. Oakey Hall, for Hoffman's place. The Boss didn't make such a bad showing on election day, considering. Hall beat Fred A. Conkling, the Republican candidate for mayor, getting seventy-five thousand votes out of ninety thousand cast; Hoffman beat John Griswold, of Troy, by almost twenty-eight thousand votes, and Seymour carried the state by ten thousand, although Grant was elected by over three hundred thousand votes in a total of five million seven hundred thousand cast. The Democratic states of Virginia, Mississippi, and Texas were not allowed to vote. They hadn't yet been readmitted into the Union. Of course, there were a good many fraudulent votes that year. 'Who ever saw an honest election in New York?' Tweed asked; but the result was an approximation of the truth. Samuel J. Tilden, who became the

Democratic hope as candidate for president himself some years later, was chairman of the Democratic state committee that year. A circular signed with his name was sent out all over the state telling Democrats to wire to Boss Tweed as soon as the polls closed telling him about what the result had been as nearly as they could guess at it. This gave the Boss a fair idea of the Republican vote in the upstate counties and he was able to make the city returns large enough to overcome it. He also kept the telegraph wires so busy that the Republicans couldn't use them to do the same. It was a great trick. Oakey Hall was secretary of the Democratic state executive committee. 'We would have put the Bible on the wire if we had had to,' he said.

Jim took an active but silent part in the political proceedings that led to the nomination of Seymour. His interest in politics didn't prevent him from attending to business. All that summer of 1868, he kept after the Credit Mobilier crowd.

♦

Now and then we did a stroke of business with the city, such as furnishing stone from our Pennsylvania quarries for building operations on public works. We collected good prices for such material; but the bills we rendered the city were substantially larger than the receipts that reached us. Jim told me confidentially that the Boss was getting a rakeoff on all money that the city paid out. I didn't pay much attention to it at the time. I liked Boss Tweed, and so did a good many other people – good people, I mean – then.

When he went to the State Senate in 1868, he got a bill through that allowed the city comptroller to adjust claims against the city and pay them. This enabled him to put into effect a plan by which creditors got thirty-five dollars out of each hundred dollars paid out by the city and the Ring got the rest. The logical development of this scheme of larceny was to compel everybody who wanted to sell anything to the city to add on enough so that his bill, when it was paid, would leave him his profit after sixty-five per cent of its total had been first subtracted.

The Erie Citadel Captured

All that remained after the Erie treaty had been signed in the early part of June was to execute it. Accordingly, on June 12, one of the Commodore's lawyers, Charles A. Rapello, moved dismissal of the various charges that had been made against us by the Commodore and his agents. The slate was wiped clean. Then, on June 30, Justice Barnard disposed of his contempt proceedings, which had driven us to Jersey, by imposing nominal fines on some of the directors and letting Uncle Dan'l, Jim, and Gould go scot free.

Finally on July 2, a million dollars in cash and bonds were paid out of the Erie funds to the Commodore and fifty thousand shares of Erie stock were taken off his hands at seventy dollars a share, involving a further payment of three and a half million dollars. Richard Schell and Frank Work got four hundred and twenty-nine thousand two hundred and fifty dollars in cash to make up their losses when they attempted to speculate in Erie with Uncle Dan'l and found he held a longer spoon than they did.

Peter B. Sweeney, as Tammany receiver, got one hundred and fifty thousand dollars for nothing, and that was the only payment that Jim and Gould didn't begrudge. Eldridge resigned the office of president of the Erie, and he also got out of the board. Uncle Dan'l gave up the treasurership and he, too, resigned from the board. Gould was then elected president to succeed Eldridge, and Jim stepped into Uncle Dan'l's shoes with the title of Comptroller and Managing Director. We were now, for the time being, in full and undisputed control of the Erie. The retiring directors thought they had squeezed all they could out of the road. The Commodore knew better. Jim and Gould proved that he was right.

Interest in the fortunes of Erie continued. Wall Street was filled all summer with rumors about the road. Having got the stock where they wanted it, Gould and Fisk closed the stock transfer books for the October election that year on August 19, a month earlier than usual. This enabled them, without risking their control, to go ahead and issue more convertible bonds and transform them into stock so as to provide the money needed to operate and extend the road.

♦

We really worked hard to build up the business of the road. Jim and Gould were young men with hope in the future. Jim was thirty-four years old and Gould was thirty-two. They leased the Paterson and New York Railroad which gave the Erie a large Western traffic; they made connections with the coal fields in Pennsylvania and they built yards, warehouses, and elevators to handle the new traffic.

For some reason a foreign demand for American railroad stocks occurred that year and a great deal of the twenty millions of new Erie stock that was issued to finance this expansion was bought in England. It didn't appear at first in the New York market.

The new board of directors elected on October 13, 1868, consisted of Jay Gould, Alexander S. Diven, James Fisk, Jr., Frederick A. Lane, J. C. Bancroft Davis, William M. Tweed, Peter B. Sweeney, Daniel S. Miller, Jr., Homer Ramsdell, John Hilton, George M. Graves, John Ganson, Charles G. Sisson, O. W. Chapman, Henry Thompson, William B. Skidmore, and George M. Diven. As soon as it had been chosen, the new board reelected Gould president.

The Commodore had no representatives on the board. I never knew exactly why this part of the famous treaty settlement was not carried out. The advent of Tweed and Sweeney, otherwise Tammany Hall, in the board was regarded as a shrewd stroke. Within three years their names became forever synonymous with thievery and corruption; but at that time they meant important political power.

The election of the new board didn't put Erie into the class of housebroken railroads as far as Wall Street was concerned. The stock market began to be agitated by rumors of large new issues of stock since Eldridge and Drew retired, and the price of it was cut in two before the end of October. A Stock Exchange committee went to ask Gould about the new stock and he made no bones of it. He told them that the Erie had already issued ten millions, or rather bonds that were convertible into stock, and that it might have to issue more.

Uncle Dan'l's Waterloo

Uncle Dan'l, with his Erie connections, had discovered this new financing and he had formed a big bear pool. The drop in the value of the shares demoralized the market in the last week of October. Money was scarce and interest rates were high. Scores of men went broke. The stock fell to thirty-five dollars a share; but Uncle Dan'l made the fatal mistake of thinking it would go lower, and he and his friends hung on.

There was no real reason why the Erie shouldn't have remained in its West Street building. The location was convenient and the accommodations were ample. But Jim's active and adventurous mind had been turning toward the theatrical stage. It occurred to him that he might as well conquer the opera and the drama. His ignorance of that vexed and vexatious field of endeavor was sufficiently shown by his entering it. I didn't know very much about it myself, but I knew enough to know that he was foolhardy to attempt it and I told him so. He paid no attention to what I said.

Pike's Opera House hadn't been built long before there was a chance to buy it. The temptation was too strong for Jim. Gould fell in with him, but he was thinking of something else. They bought the Opera House with Erie money, but in their own names, and then leased it to the Erie for the main offices of the company, which were moved up from West Street in 1869, as soon as changes had been made in the building to accommodate them. An Erie ferry from the terminal in Jersey City to the foot of West Twenty-third Street was started. The railroad was thus up to its ears in the social swim.

Uncle Dan'l was out of 'Airy,' as he always called the railroad that had been a gold mine for him for many years. It is hard to tell how much he had made out of the road, first and last, but it must have been a good many millions. In the Great Robbery, as Jim characterized the Vanderbilt agreement, Drew's part of the spoil was a full discharge from liability for all that had happened in the past. He had to pay five hundred and fifty thousand dollars from his release, but it was well worth the money.

When we got full swing, with Gould as president and treasurer of the road, and Jim as comptroller of accounts to audit Gould's financing, it was easy to raise money. During the next four months, twenty-three million five hundred thousand dollars' worth of convertible bonds were issued. The financial district was filled with rumors and alarms.

♦

Money always gets scarce in the fall. It is withdrawn from Wall Street for the purpose of 'moving the crops' – that is, paying the farmers for their wheat, corn, and cotton. The rate of interest goes up and consequently the value of stocks goes down, since it isn't so easy to borrow money to buy them with. Gould and Jim and a few others saw a chance that fall to make some money in the bear side of the market in Erie. They formed a big bear pool and took in Uncle Dan'l, who agreed to furnish four million dollars capital for the contemplated operations. New Erie stock, into which the new bonds were transformed, was thrown on the market until the price fell to thirty-five dollars a share. The English holders got scared and began selling their stock for whatever they could get for it. The sales were made here and the stock was mailed from England for delivery to buyers. It took ten days to get it here.

Wall Street was demoralized by the squeeze the bear pool gave it. The speculators sweated gold into the pockets of the manipulators. As usual, they uttered loud wails of distress. They even appealed to Washington to make money more plentiful by issuing more greenbacks. This was contrary to the policy of the Secretary of the Treasury, Hugh McCulloch, who was aiming to get back on to the gold basis by making the greenbacks redeemable in gold and who therefore wanted fewer greenbacks rather than more.

Uncle Dan'l began to feel afraid and he made up his mind to desert the pool. He had put in only one of the four millions that he had promised. He took this out and retired to see what would happen. Betrayal of his associates didn't trouble him in the least; never did. But he wasn't indispensable any more in the management of bear pools in Erie. This one got along very well without him until it received a warning from Washington to quit or face a flood of greenbacks. They quit. They wound up their bear operations and then switched around. They began to devote themselves to putting up the price of Erie stock of which they had bought heavily at the lowest price. The bears who didn't know were pinched as badly as the bulls had been the week before.

Uncle Dan'l, no longer a member of the pool, miscalculated the pool's ability to boost the price. From a low mark of thirty-five dollars a share on October 30, it ran up to fifty-two dollars a share on November 15. Drew was a bear by nature. On its way up, he began selling the stock short, expecting to buy it back later at a lower price and pocket the difference. He looked to see the price go down pretty soon; but it didn't. It kept on up, and he kept selling more stock short until finally he had sold seventy thousand shares of it, in all, at an average price of thirty-eight dollars a share. He began to understand how his victims of former years had felt when he had turned the screws from inside that forced them to settle. He found himself as helpless as they had been. If he had to settle by delivering the stock at fifty-four dollars a share that he'd sold for thirty-eight dollars a share, he stood to lose more than a million dollars. The thought was agony to him. To be robbed in his old age by mere boys he had set up in business! He was seventy, but straight as an arrow, and he had hardly a gray hair in his head. He'd show 'em yet!

He wasn't on the inside any longer, but he knew what was there and his information, if properly used in court would blow things sky-high! Of course, Uncle Dan'l wasn't the only speculator who'd been caught in the upward rush of Erie. He compared notes with his fellow-sufferers. He showed himself ready to help them. If he did, they figured that they could take the Erie away from Gould and Jim by getting a receiver appointed – the same old game that the Commodore had played with so much success. They didn't realize that there was a difference. The Commodore had aimed at Uncle Dan'l, who quaked at his own shadow. There were no quaking hearts any longer in Erie; quite the contrary.

♦

Among Uncle Dan'l's associate sufferers was August Belmont, from Germany. He was the agent of the Rothschilds, famous in Europe then for their wealth and their loans to kings. His firm was one of the most important in the city. On a Saturday in the middle of November, he went to talk things over with Uncle Dan'l – he and some other Erie bears. He'd been selling Erie for foreigners. They agreed that they were being unfairly treated. They were convinced that the Erie was being robbed by Gould and Fisk so that its resources might be used against them. They decided to appeal to the courts. Uncle Dan'l knew a thing or two about the Erie and how it had been robbed in his day. Would he make an affidavit? Yes, he was ready to do his part.

They decided to ask Justice Josiah S. Sutherland, of the Supreme Court, on Monday for an order restraining Gould, Fisk, and the other officers of Erie, including the directors, from doing anything further in their official capacity, and then to ask for the appointment of a receiver. They helped Uncle Dan'l prepare an affidavit to serve as the basis of the application. But he didn't sign it just then. He said he wanted to look it over to make sure it was all right. He took it away with him.

♦

When he thought it over, he found he didn't like his new associates. He never cared for 'furriners' much. Perhaps there might be a safer way. He wasn't eager to confess his own stealings from the Erie, as he had been obliged to do in the affidavit so as to make out a case for a receiver. Perhaps Fisk and Gould would be willing to let him out of the trap he was in if he refused to sign. He went to his Methodist Church in Madison Avenue Sunday morning and in the afternoon he called on Jim at the Opera House. I was there when he came in and so was Josie, who was talking with Jim about some plans that somebody had put into her head. 'Run along, Dolly; we'll talk about this some other time,' Jim said, when the hall man told him Mr. Drew wanted to see him. 'I've got to attend a funeral now.'

His old face was impassive as usual when he came in, but his brown bony hand trembled a little as he carefully set his tall, stovepipe hat down on the floor beside the chair to which Jim invited him and drew a red bandanna handkerchief out of its crown.

'Well, Uncle Dan'l, what's the matter with your old tin stove today?' Jim asked. Uncle Dan'l blew his nose noisily and dropped the handkerchief back into the tall hat.

'Jeems,' he said, 'I'm an old man.'

'Old enough to know better, Uncle Dan'l.'

'You an' Jay be drivin' me inter my grave!'

'Gammon! What's your trouble? Out with it!'

'I wish ye to loan me some o' your Airy.'

'How much do you want?'

'Jeems, I won't lie to ye; I'll tell ye the hull truth. I'm short thirty thousand sheers an' if you an' Jay don't let me have it for a few days, I don't know what I kin do. I've come here to throw myself on your mercy. When I was in church this mornin' the Lord pointed the way to me. I know ye' won't fail an old man.'

'I know you're short thirty thousand shares of Erie, Uncle Dan'l; but that ain't the worst of it. Besides those thirty thousand, you're short forty thousand calls. Isn't that the truth, now?'

'I won't deny it. Ye kin see, Jeems, that if I don't git that there stock for a few days I'll be ruined.'

'Too bad!' said Jim, smiling at the supplicant. 'You'd ought to have stayed in the pool with us.'

'I know it, Jeems, but I was skeered of what the gover'ment was a-goin' to do. I ain't so young as I was once, ye know. Ye'll let me have the stock, won't ye, Jeems? I expec' to pay ye sunthin' for the use on't.'

'I won't beat around the bush, Uncle Dan'l; Gould and I haven't got any stock to lend you.' The old man's jaw dropped and for an instant he stared at Jim as though he didn't believe his ears. He stooped down and fumbled for his handkerchief and a whine of self pity crept into his voice. 'Jeems,' he said, 'ye can't mean to say ye'd refuse an old man that started ye fust off here in N'York? Ye can't mean that!'

'That's exactly what I mean.'

'Don't ye be hasty now, Jeems. There's somethin' goin' on ye don't know nothin' about.'

'What kind of somethin' do you mean?'

'I mean law suits.'

'We ain't afraid of law suits; you know that, Uncle Dan'l.'

'You'd ought to be afeered o' this one.'

'Why? Who's in it?'

'I can't tell ye who's in it, but they're goin' to Jedge Sutherland in the mornin' to git a receiver for the Airy.'

'What can they say?'

'There's a plenty, Jeems; they're goin' to say that I took twenty-eight thousand shares of Airy for loan collateral back in '66 an' never give none on't back.'

'You denied that when the Commodore sued us, didn't you?'

'Mebbe I did, Jeems; mebbe so. An' then they say we put out ten millions o' bonds last Spring an' turned 'em into stock, an' that I bargained to pay ye half o' what we got over an' above seventy-two cents on the dollar for 'em. Them was the bonds you an' Jay sold for seventy-nine an' eighty, ye know.'

'Seems to me they know a hell of a lot!'

'An' then they're goin to say that ye cheated the Airy when ye let me settle for them twenty-eight thousand sheers o' stock I had for a million dollars an' my resignin' out o' the Airy treasury. They're a-goin' to say that was dishonest of ye, Jeems.'

'What else?'

'Then they're goin' to tell the Jedge that ye bought Eldridge off by givin' him five millions of Airy money fer the Boston an' Hartford, so's't Jay c'd git to be president, stid of Eldridge.'

'Well? Anything more?'

'Yes; they'll say that ye two hev got everythin' your own way now in the Airy an' that ye've gone an' spent a mint o' money fer reel estate an' hed it put in ye're own names.'

'Perhaps they'll tell how you helped us in the pool when we locked up money to put prices down, and how you put in a million!'

'I think likely they'll do that.'

'How are you going to prove all this?'

'Jeems, they're pesterin' me to swear to it. They want me to sign a paper.

'I suppose you'll do it unless we loan you seventy thousand shares of Erie stock, hey?'

'I don't want to do it, Jeems; I've never signed no paper like that in my life an' I'm an old man now.'

'Uncle Dan'l, you're a damned old hypocrite! You've always sold your friends. You sold us out to the Commodore when we had him licked. You sold us out to Eldridge. You sold out the pool – or tried to. You're an old scalawag, that's what you are! You can sign anything you've a damned mind to! We shan't lend you a share of Erie stock – not a share, do you understand?'

Drew hesitated and blew his nose again. At last he asked to see Gould. 'He isn't here. He won't be here before to-night some time,' Jim told him. 'What do you mean by laying the things to us that you did yourself in Erie?'

'Jeems, I'm bein' ruined! What kin I do?'

'You know this whole thing's a piece of blackmail, you old sinner!' Jim cried, banging the desk with his fist as he got warmed up. 'You know damn well that there don't any of you care a damn how much the Erie's robbed if you can get out of the market with whole hides!'

'What kin I do?' Uncle Dan'l whined again.

'Hang yourself, for all I care!'

'Jeems, I shall have to see Jay; I've got somethin' to tell him.'

'Who's in this thing with you?'

'Wal, there's Frank Work; he's in it.'

'Who else?'

'Schell's in it, an' so be Lane an' Thompson. They're all short, same as me.'

'I suppose they'd all quit if we'd let 'em have some stock, wouldn't they?'

'Jeems, I don't know and I can't tell ye; but I think likely they would.'

'Are they the ones that are bringing this suit you talk about?'

'No, 'tain't them. I ain't a-goin' to tell ye who 'tis, not onless ye let me see Jay fust.'

'Uncle Dan'l, you can talk until you're blue in the face. This whole thing's just one of your tricks. You're the last man on earth to whine about being caught in Erie after all the times you've done exactly what we're doing. Did you ever loan stock to the shorts when you were squeezing 'em? Not by a long shot, you didn't! We ain't going to do it, either. It was you that taught us!'

Uncle Dan'l sighed deeply, but he made no reply except to insist that he must see Gould. 'Ye're too suddin, Jeems,' he said. 'Jay's got a longer head than ye have. When is he a-goin' to be here?'

'If you must see him, he'll be here, I expect, about nine o'clock; but it won't do you any good to see him. It won't do you any good, either, to sign affidavits; you'd ought to know that by this time without my having to tell you. The best thing you can do, Uncle Dan'l, is to pay up an' get out of Wall Street while you've got a dollar left to your name.'

'I'll be back here to see Jay at nine o'clock,' the old man said as he picked up his hat and transferred the bandanna to his coat-tail pocket.

'You'd better see him right now, if you're bound to do it,' said Jim and he turned to me. 'Rabbits, tell him, will you?' I went to the room where Gould was working and told him that Uncle Dan'l was there begging for stock and wouldn't go away. He asked what Jim had said to him and nodded his head when I told him.

Uncle Dan'l went over the same story about the law suit and the affidavit that he had already told Jim. At last he told who it was that was asking for a receiver – August Belmont and another man. Gould listened to him until he had finished and then told him that he agreed with Jim and that they wouldn't lend him any Erie stock on any account whatever. This answer was too much for Uncle Dan'l. He seemed to go all to pieces. He begged and pleaded for the stock and kept saying the same things over and over, until at last Jim got up and put on his hat.

'It's no use, Uncle Dan'l,' he said. 'You could talk till doomsday and it wouldn't make any difference. Our eyes are sot! You can't get any stock from us.' Still the old man clung to his last hope of buying his own release by betraying his accomplices to Jim and Gould. He insisted that he must see them again and finally, to get rid of him without resorting to force, Jim told him to come back at ten o'clock.

He took me to dinner with him at Josie's, where there were some actresses and one or two men. We talked and laughed and smoked Jim's cigars and drank his wine until it got to be ten o'clock and I reminded Jim that Uncle Dan'l would be waiting for him. 'Let him wait a while,' Jim replied to my reminder. 'It will make the agony shorter.'

♦

We went over to the Opera House at eleven o'clock and there was Uncle Dan'l waiting for us. He'd been waiting since nine o'clock, the hall man said. He told the same old story, begging for the loan of thirty or forty thousand shares of Erie for fifteen days, and declaring over and over that he'd be ruined if Jim refused him. He offered three per cent for the stock, or about a hundred thousand dollars.

Jim kept telling him that he was wasting his time; but he kept on arguing and at last he began to threaten. He said that he and his associates would do everything they could to ruin Jim and Gould and drive them out of Erie, if they didn't loan the stock. He went on to describe all the injurious things that he could do and the great resources that Belmont and the rest could command, meaning the millions of Vanderbilt and the Rothschilds. He made out such a strong case that I confess I'd have given in if only for the sake of peace; but Jim this time had a heart of stone. Nothing could move him. At last, realizing that all his efforts were in vain, at one o'clock in the morning Uncle Dan'l gave up. He rose from his chair with a resumption of dignity in his thin, tall form, and turning to Jim, sitting at his desk, he said: 'I will bid you good-night!'

With that, he went out. 'His goose is cooked,' said Jim, 'but it's a mighty tough one!'

Litigation

Uncle Dan'l fought hard, but his goose was cooked, as Jim had said. August Belmont presented to Justice Sutherland on Tuesday, November 17, a petition for the appointment of the Commodore's son-in-law, Osgood, as receiver for the Erie, basing his request on an affidavit signed by Daniel Drew. This affidavit had practically everything in it that Uncle Dan'l had warned Jim and Gould he would say if they forced him to sign by refusing to loan him the stock he wanted. Gould and Jim and the other Erie officers against whom the action was directed appeared in court represented by new attorneys, the law firm of Brown, Hall and Vanderpoel, who said they represented Charles McIntosh, superintendent of the Erie ferry between New York and Jersey City. Rapallo and Spencer asked Justice Sutherland, who was a high-minded man, by the way, to make Osgood receiver. Whereupon the other side laid before the court an order that Justice Barnard had signed on November 16, the previous day, making Gould receiver and restraining Belmont and the Vanderbilt faction, as well as the officers of the road, from issuing any orders or exercising any official powers until the legal right of the Erie to issue the stock that it had issued had been decided. This McIntosh application was supported by an affidavit that Jim signed, in which he said that he had no doubt of the legality of the stock that had been issued and that other speculators in Wall Street had been threatening by appeals to the courts to depress the value of the stock. This was the result of the warning that Uncle Daniel had given. The discovery that Gould had stolen a march on them and that he occupied the ground that they had intended to occupy, showed them that they would have to get up early in the morning if they intended to get the better of him.

♦

The application to Justice Sutherland on Tuesday was intended, as Jim had informed the court, to depress the price of Erie stock. With this in view, Uncle Dan'l, who was short seventy thousand shares, cast doubt upon the legality of the issue of two hundred thousand shares – which was all the stock available for speculative uses. Gould thereupon went to Justice Barnard and asked for authority, as receiver, to buy for the Erie at any cost up to one hundred dollars a share, this stock that Drew objected to and that the Erie had issued and sold for forty dollars a share. Justice Barnard, on November 18, gave the consent Gould asked for. By this simple device, the value of all the Erie stock that was by any means to be had before the arrival of the stock that had been sold by the panic-stricken Britishers, was fixed at more than double the price at which Uncle Dan'l and the other bears had sold short.

They had got themselves into a fine fix. They were helpless to avert their fate. They had to step up and settle. Uncle Daniel squared up at a loss of a million and a half. The Erie crowd had only to hold up the price of the stock to empty all the bear pocketbooks in Wall Street. But sixty-two dollars a share was too tempting. From all quarters an army of small stockholders suddenly came pouring into the Street, eager to sell their stock at the high price. The bulls, who had already bought up almost the entire floating supply, had to buy this also or the bears would get it and take away from them all they had won. They preferred to hand over their cash to the stockholders and so they bought from them. But when they got through, they had paid out almost all the money that the bears had paid them. As soon as the market closed and deliveries had been made of the real stock that had been sold, the price slid down to forty-two dollars a share. The bulls found themselves loaded up with stock that had cost them all the way up to twenty dollars a share more than that. For once, the public had got away with the money.

♦

The lawyers, once they get into a case like that, don't like to let go until they have to and the motion before Justice Sutherland was followed by a series of snappy court skirmishes. All these legal proceedings were dry stuff that the average man didn't pretend to understand. I know I didn't at the time. But Judge Davies gave us a little variety. As soon as he had been appointed receiver, he set out in innocent good faith to execute his mandate. He took Dorman B. Eaton with him as counsel, and ex-Judge Noah Davis. He was met at the outer gate by a gang of guards, recruited from Five Points and the Bowery by Tommy Lynch, their Captain and Chief.

'What do youse want here?' Tommy demanded.

'I have been appointed receiver of the Erie and I want to come in,' said Judge Davies.

'Well, youse can't come in here; g'wan away now!' said Tommy.

'I have a court order to come in,' said Judge Davies, showing the paper.

'What the hell do I care fer papers? Do youse t'ink I'm a dom fool? Youse can go to the divil with your papers!' says Tommy.

At this juncture an Erie clerk happened to come along and he saw Eaton through the bars of the gate. Eaton had been acting on our side until these new proceedings began and this clerk – his name was Billings – thought he was still with us.

'O, Billings! Come here a minute, will you?' Eaton called out to him. 'These men here don't know us. They won't let us in.' Billings came forward and shook hands. Eaton explained things to him carefully, leaving him under the impression that they were Erie men. 'Let 'em come in,' Billings said to Tom, 'They're all right.' Whereupon Tommy swung back the iron gate and in they all marched. The citadel had been taken without a struggle.

Gould and Jim were conferring with their lawyers in Gould's office when the door opened and Judge Davies, with his lawyers, calmly walked into the room. They took us by surprise; I can't deny that. Gould never changed a hair, but I thought Jim would burst then and there. 'How are you, gentlemen?' said Eaton with an easy smile. 'I want to introduce Judge Davies and Judge Davis.'

'You've introduced 'em! How in the deuce did you do it?' Jim demanded. Eaton smiled again but he didn't answer Jim. Instead he proceeded to explain why Judge Davies had come. Jim didn't wait to hear him but slipped out of the room. He was back before Eaton had finished and he held the door open when he came in. He had found out how the enemy had managed to enter. He was madder than ever. 'Eaton, you and your friends have got no business here!' he shouted. 'You can't get into this circus by crawling under the tent; you've got to pay admission. Get out!'

Eaton continued to smile, but Judge Davies protested that he had been made receiver and had a right to be there. 'Right or no right!' shouted Jim, 'I don't give a damn! Get out or you'll be thrown out. Here Tom!' Tom Lynch and half a dozen strong-arm toughs showed themselves in the doorway, ready for action. 'Will you go?' Jim demanded. But this drastic method didn't suit Gould's game. 'Don't get het up, Jim; this is a business for the courts to settle,' he said. 'You see, Fisk isn't a lawyer and perhaps he doesn't always appreciate the duty of obedience to the courts,' he apologized to Judge Davies.

While he was speaking, our lawyers pressed around Jim and remonstrated with him, warning him that Justice Sutherland might lock us all up for contempt if he wasn't careful and urging him to call off the guards. 'All right,' said Jim at last. 'Have it your own way,' and he signed to Tom to fall back. But he wouldn't trust himself to stay and he disappeared with them.

Justice Davies thereupon served written notice that he had taken possession, and the lawyers persuaded him that everything would be in better shape if he would give the Erie staff until Friday to prepare for him. He and Gould, both duly appointed receivers, shook hands and he was led out amid a deluge of kind words. He never did get back in again. When he returned on Friday, Tom and the plug-uglies had forgotten him and no persuasions or threats moved them.

♦

Gould, as receiver in possession, and Jim, as immune comptroller and managing director, continued to run the affairs of the company under the protection of cohorts of railroad guards and city police, assigned to duty there by order of Tweed.

The other side tried to break in by going before Judge Nelson of the United States Court, on Saturday, November 28, and asking for the removal of Gould as receiver under Judge Blatchford's order. At the same time, Judge Davies asked to be put in possession. Judge Nelson issued an order to show cause on Monday, November 30, why these requests should not be granted.

All concerned filed detailed affidavits with Judge Nelson on November 30. The most interesting was a statement made by Gould himself, denying the charges brought against him by our enemies and justifying his acts. The hearing was postponed. All these suits and countersuits were enough to give a man heart failure. You never could tell what was going to happen next. The attitude of Justice Sutherland, who had general respect, and of Judge Nelson, seemed discouraging from our side of the fence.

To shake off Justice Sutherland, our lawyers on November 30 applied to Justice Cardozo, also of the State Supreme Court, for an order vacating the appointment of Davies as receiver. Justice Cardozo set down the hearing for December 7. He would have succeeded Justice Sutherland by that time and of course he himself would hold the hearing on the application. But Justice Sutherland announced a hearing on December 2, on why Justice Cardozo's order shouldn't be vacated. Argument was to begin at eleven o'clock. Justice Cardozo gave notice that at ten o'clock – an hour earlier – on the same day he would hear anybody who didn't think he ought to set aside Justice Sutherland's order. This petty judicial squabbling was too much for Justice Sutherland. He threw up the sponge and abandoned the entire mess to Justice Cardozo. That left only Judge Nelson to be disposed of.

———♦———

While matters were in this position, on December 10, 1868, Jim brought suit against the Commodore in the name of the Erie, to get back the million paid to him in cash as a bonus, under the treaty, and the three and a half millions given to him to redeem fifty thousand shares of Erie stock. He and Shearman first went and demanded the money of the Commodore, at the same time offering the stock. Of course they didn't get it.

The Commodore denied he'd had any such dealings with the Erie. In fact, he wrote to the *Times* about it, saying: 'I have had no dealings with the Erie Railway Company, nor have I ever sold that company any stock or received from them any bonus.' That wasn't true and Jim proved it wasn't by publishing copies of two Erie checks calling for a million dollars, endorsed to the Commodore by the Erie treasurer, and paid on the Commodore's order. He added that the Erie had a document in the Commodore's writing which said that he, the Commodore, had placed fifty thousand shares of Erie in certain hands to be surrendered on payment of three and a half millions, and he declared the money had been paid.

The complicated litigation of the fall of 1868, including the suit that Jim brought in the name of the Erie to get back the millions that had been extorted by the Commodore before he would allow Uncle Dan'l to come back from Jersey City, had been entirely forgotten when this action against the Commodore was called for trial before Justice Barnard a year later, on November 20, 1869. The Commodore was a witness and David Dudley Field examined him. Although he had denied in the *Times* that he had received the money that Jim swore had been paid to him, he now admitted that he had taken it; but he insisted that he hadn't done any business with the Erie. It was with Uncle Dan'l that he'd been dealing.

Judge Nelson disposed of himself on December 15 by deciding that Judge Blatchford ought not to have made Gould receiver of the Erie, because the case was one for the State and not the Federal courts. Therefore he removed Gould and sent the case back to the courts of the State, which meant that it would come before Justice Cardozo. 'Now we're all hunky-dory,' said Jim, when he heard what Judge Nelson had done.

Jim was right. Justice Cardozo decided, on February 10, 1869, that there had never been any good reason for appointing a receiver, because the directors had a perfect right to issue the convertible bonds and turn them into stock, as they had done. That left Gould and Jim monarchs of all they surveyed and they made the most of their time. They went to work with all the energy that was in them to build up the Erie and make it a real rival to the Commodore's New York

Central to the north of them and the fast extending Pennsylvania combination to the south.

♦

Uncle Dan'l Drew's loss really marked the end of his career as a character to be reckoned with in the financial or business world. He continued to speculate in a picayune way for a while longer; but in 1875, when he was seventy-eight years old, he retired altogether. He died in September, at the age of eighty-two, four years later, a pensioner on his family. Though his life ended in failure, he was no common man, Uncle Dan'l. His schools for ministers over in Jersey and for young women up in Carmel will keep his name from being forgotten.

The Grand Opera House

The building then known as Pike's Opera House is still standing on the northwest corner of Twenty-third Street and Eighth Avenue. It's dingy and decrepit-looking now, but when the Erie occupied it there was no dispute about its splendor. Jim fitted the place up and he spread himself when he did it. A grand staircase led up to the second floor and to huge doors of carved oak.

On the second floor were the offices of Jim, Comptroller of the Erie, President Gould, and Secretary Otis; and there was a large room for meetings of the board of directors. These apartments were impressive, to say the least. On this second floor were a lot more offices of railroad executives and their staffs. The quarters of the general freight agent and the passenger agent were on the third floor. On the fourth were the auditor's and the engineering departments, and also kitchens, pantries, store-rooms, and rooms for the porters, cooks, and servants. In the basement were a complete printing plant, a telegraph office with wires reaching from Jim to every department, and a steam plant. There was a dining room for the executives, and another for the help, connected with the kitchens by dumbwaiters which reached all the floors.

He and Gould bought the building in December, 1868. They had the title recorded in their own names; but they paid for the property out of the Erie treasury and then leased it to the Erie at a rental of seventy-five thousand. They had also the income from the rent of stores on the ground floor of the building.

Although Jim and Gould seemed as close together after they got control of the Erie as they ever had been, as a matter of fact, their interests began to draw apart. Jim liked adventure and variety. Then there was Josie, whose fascination had taken full possession of him. He began to dabble in theatricals, with the stage of the Grand Opera House, into which Pike's had been transformed with the change of ownership, as a basis. He was absorbed in the steamship lines to Fall River and Long Branch which he had acquired. And all the while he was gambling in Wall Street. But everybody was doing that.

Jim bought all the houses behind the Opera House between Twenty-third and Twenty-fourth Streets halfway back to Ninth Avenue. In one of these, three doors from the Opera House on Twenty-third Street, he had two rooms on the second floor simply fitted up, and that's where he lived. It was generally supposed that Jim spent a large income on himself after he and Gould got hold of the Erie. Nothing of the kind. No man could work so hard as he did, and permit himself the dissipations that were credited to him by scandalmongers and sensational preachers.

Behind the intervening houses Jim arranged a passage so that he could get into the Opera House from the rear of his own without going into the street. All his business was done in the Opera House, or in his Broad Street office, although he did little down-town after the summer of 1868. He dissolved the firm of Fisk and Belden as soon as he could in that year after he became managing director of the Erie. He ate in the restaurant for executives that he had installed in the Opera House.

Here is an unprejudiced estimate of Jim as a business man that was printed in the *New York World*, a newspaper that later was bought by Gould:

'The *World* concedes that the business qualifications of Colonel Fisk were of the highest order. He possessed prodigious executive capacity, indomitable pluck and clearness of perception in forecasting results which was truly remarkable. In fertility of resource, he was in no sense the equal of Jay Gould, and he seldom entered upon any really important enterprise without first taking the advice of that astute and wily deviser of the great campaigns which have marked the present Erie management; but in power to execute difficult undertakings he was altogether the superior of the latter. His daily round of duties embraced an amount of work which no man of less natural exuberance and elasticity of temper could possibly have carried through. From nine o'clock in the morning until four o'dock in the afternoon of each working day, he was constantly employed, literally never having a spare moment. At times as many as forty or fifty persons would be found in the anterooms waiting to bring before him matters of every sort and description, and to each he gave prompt, ready attention, deciding instantly upon the case presented.

'Often he was importuned by applicants for charity, women thronged to his presence begging for passes over some of the many lines of travel under his control, frequently disabled soldiers applied for situations, pleading their services in the Union cause as a reason why they should be favorably considered. It is said that none of the latter, who were able to bring credentials, was ever turned away without an order directing that a place be found for them somewhere in the Erie service, and he seldom if ever refused to extend the "courtesy of the road" to any person in actual need.

'One notable feature of Colonel Fisk's business policy was the directness and celerity with which he got at the heart of every subject coming up for consideration. He abominated "red tape," and required of everyone having business with him to state it without circumlocution, and then, when his answer was given, to depart without further words. He admitted no appeal from a decision once made upon the facts of the case.

'His good humor was unfailing and in the presence of the gravest emergency he was as jolly and cheerful as when all the world was smiling fair. Under other circumstances and in some other sphere, with his energies properly directed, he might have accomplished services for mankind of almost incalculable value, for, in his capacity to look on the bright side of life, and to utilize every resource in the prosecution of great enterprises, he had two at least of the qualifications essential to a successful leader.

'Colonel Fisk's relations with his subordinates were of the closest and most sympathetic nature. He was prompt to recognize faithful service, and to resent any ingratitude or wrong to anyone to whom he was attached. About a year ago he handed a check for ten thousand dollars to a clerk, who having been charged with the management of a special interest, carried it through with an unexpected degree of success.'

♦

Jim's private and personal surroundings were plain enough, but he let himself loose when it came to furnishing and decorating the settings in which he made public appearances, such as his boats, his turnouts, and the Opera House.

In 1869 Jim put a new ferryboat on the North River. It was the biggest of all ferryboats, and he named it the *James Fisk, Jr.* At each end of this boat was a large portrait of himself, surrounded by the national colors and the coat of arms. The panels in the cabin were painted a delicate green, with pearl trimmings. Large and handsome mirrors everywhere reflected travelers. This boat made such a hit that he put on another like it and named it the *Jay Gould.*

Jim was equally lavish in his stables, which were in Twenty-fourth Street, behind the Opera House. In them he kept fifteen horses, black and white. His vehicles included a big barouche sleigh and a very large phaeton, for driving in Central Park winter and summer. He had four drags and, for fashionable uses, two clarences. These were covered carriages with curved glass fronts, like a coupe in general appearance. One of these clarences was built to order for Jim and it was partly lined with gold cloth.

Jim had learned to drive when he was working for Van Amberg and he had perfected himself in the art when he drove his four-in-hand peddler's wagon in New England. It was his custom to drive six-in-hand through Central Park. When Jim drove out in state, his pairs were harnessed, a black horse and a white one together, with two black coachmen in white livery in front and two white boys in black livery in the rear. 'There goes Jim Fisk!' the observers said to one another. Some of them smiled and some frowned, according to the way they were made; but Jim didn't care what impression he made so long as he made one.

He also had an elaborate music box made with a working model of the Sound steamer *Providence* in solid gold and silver on it. This cost twenty-five hundred dollars. The upkeep of his stable amounted to about ten thousand dollars a year.

Any quantity of examples of Jim's private philanthropies might be given. His chief method of enjoying his money was to spend it for poor and unfortunate people. Half a dozen poor families, who, for one good reason or another, couldn't support themselves, were wholly dependent on his generosity. Never a day but he helped some casual applicant. One day a boy got in to see him. He was a humpback.

'Are you Mr. Fisk?' he inquired.

'That's what they call me, sonny; what's the matter?' said Jim.

'I'm a newsboy. My name's Mike Ryan and I'm tryin' to get me a stand where I can sell papers.'

'Father and mother?'

'I got only my mother and two sisters. I have to take care of 'em.'

'Run over to the drugstore on the corner and ask the man there to let you put a stand in front of his place. Then come back and tell me what he says.' Pretty soon the boy came back and told Jim the druggist wouldn't do it. 'You come along with me, Deacon, and we'll see what we can find,' says Jim.

He went out with the boy and I went along. We tried a dozen places, but Jim couldn't get the boy permission to put up his stand until we got around to Broadway and Twenty-ninth Street. He got a haberdasher to let him locate there and gave the boy five dollars towards the stand. He used to go up there every now and then to see how Mike was getting along. The boy did well there.

Jim was entitled to fifteen dollars in gold for every meeting of the Erie board of directors that he attended. They all got it, but Jim never used his. He always handed it over to Comer, his secretary, and told him to put it away for him until some deserving request for help came along.

It always came. There was one day, I remember, when a thin woman, with a shawl over her head, came in and tried to tell him what the trouble was. At first, she couldn't get it out, but he told her he wasn't going to eat her – that he'd had breakfast already – and finally she managed to tell him that her husband, who was a mechanic, had broken his leg and that they didn't have a cent in the house or a thing to eat, and five small children.

'Well, well, we must look into this,' said Jim, and he called one of the Erie detectives into his office. 'Here, you go along with him and show him where you live,' he told the woman, 'and then we'll see what can be done.' It wasn't long before the pair came back and the detective reported that the story the woman had told was true. 'All right,' said Jim. 'Here, Comer, give her twenty-five dollars for me and the same every week until her man gets well.' The payments were kept up until the husband was able to go back to work. Jim got a lot of pleasure out of cases like this. He could see where his money went and how it was helping.

♦

His generosity wasn't confined to the poor. He had a friend named Morse, who went bathing in New Orleans in Lake Pontchartrain and broke his neck diving in shallow water. He left his widow and two daughters and her mother with nothing to support them. Jim told him before he died that he'd take care of them, and he did. He even sent the whole family to Europe one winter so that Mrs. Morse could be treated for some trouble with her eyes.

♦

The trustees of the Congregational Church in Brattleboro were getting subscriptions for improvements to the cemetery. They asked Jim for a hundred dollars. 'What do you want to do with it?' he asked. 'We want to put up a new fence,' they told him. 'I don't see what you want any fence around the cemetery for,' he remarked. 'Those that are in there can't get out, and those that are out, don't want to get in!' But he gave them the money.

♦

The National Savings Bank got into trouble and the president of it, Henry Smith, came to Jim with Thurlow Weed to appeal for help in the crisis. Weed was the Republican boss of the state. It was Saturday afternoon and the bank had to have forty thousand dollars when it opened Monday morning. Jim promised to subscribe five thousand dollars, toward what was needed to rescue the bank. 'A lot of poor people have got their money in it,' he remarked. 'It would be a damn shame to have 'em lose it.'

Smith made the rounds of his friends but he couldn't raise any more money. He had got about all he could hope for from them before he applied to Jim. He was ready to throw up the sponge Sunday morning. Weed sent a man to the Grand Opera House to tell Jim how things stood. Jim drove over to Tweed's Metropolitan Hotel, where Smith and Weed were. They went over the situation in the bank and finally Jim asked whether they could get in there and look at the securities and the books. Smith said yes, and Jim sent his clarence for Bingham, one of the Erie lawyers, telling him to find Comer and bring him along, with a first-class accountant. When they came, Fisk told them to go to the bank with Smith and get the securities out of the vault.

'You stay there with the accountant, Comer, and look over the books with him. Check 'em up and let me know what you find.' When the securities were brought up to the hotel, Jim sat down with Smith, Weed, and Bingham to examine them. 'Some of this stuff ain't worth a damn, Smith,' Jim said when they finished, 'but I guess there's enough here to go ahead on if the books are all right.'

Comer reported that there was no hitch in the books and Jim instructed him then and there to get forty thousand dollars and give it to Smith before banking hours next morning. Smith couldn't find words to thank Jim for saving the bank, and Weed was greatly impressed. He put his arm across Jim's shoulders. 'This is a noble act,' he said to Jim. 'If I ever hear a man speak ill of you again, I shall knock him down!' Thurlow Weed was a pretty good friend to have in those days. The bank got through all right.

♦

Jim wasn't averse to making useful friends through his charity when he could just as well as not. When he first moved to Twenty-third Street, he met Police Captain Killalee, of the Sixteenth Precinct, in which the Grand Opera House was situated. He had never seen him before. 'If that's your own cap you've got on, you must be Captain of this Precinct,' he said.

'That's what I am,' said Captain Killalee.

'I'm Jim Fisk. I wish you'd come and see me.'

'Thanks, Mr. Fisk; I will one of these days.'

'Come in right now; I want you to help me about something. There must be a good many poor people here in the precinct – widows and orphans. You probably know who they are better than anybody else. Whenever you come across a family that's really hard up and that a barrel of flour or a ton of coal would do a lot of good to, I want you to send 'em to me. Just send along a note with 'em so I'll know it's all right.'

'That's handsome of you, Colonel; I'll do it.'

They had some further talk about the ward and the condition of the poor in it and the Captain got up to go. 'Another thing,' said Jim as he shook hands with him, 'If you come across any poor people who'd like to go West and haven't got the money, send 'em to me and I'll pass 'em out over the Erie.' Captain Killalee sent more than twenty poor widows to Jim and he gave each of them an order for flour or coal, and sometimes for both.

♦

Jim began to wax the points of his moustache not long after he fell in love with Josie. I don't know whether he got the idea from her or borrowed it from the French emperor. It was an improvement – made him look more up-to-date, though he was always careful about his personal appearance and his clothes. Altogether Jim was a striking figure. His appearance, the lavish decorations of his office in the Grand Opera House, his generosity, his high spirits, and his conspicuous turnouts, made people call him the Prince of Erie.

♦

Jim had his own modest home and his elaborate stable in the block west of the Grand Opera House. In the same block, a few hundred feet beyond the house in which he lived, he helped Josie to buy a much more imposing dwelling. This was No. 359 West Twenty-third Street. She paid forty thousand dollars for it. She put into it the fifteen thousand that she got out of the poker game and subsequent speculation in Erie stock, to which Jim added enough to bring the total up to twenty thousand and she borrowed twenty thousand dollars on a mortgage.

Jim had the house frescoed and decorated in Erie office style and furnished accordingly. It was a brownstone, four-story-and-basement building and it was one of the best houses in the block. This decorating and furnishing cost Jim ten thousand dollars or more.

Josie didn't have words to express her joy when she moved in. She was like a child with a plaything that she had long wished for but never dared hope to get. Jim helped her select her servants, made her a generous allowance for the household expenses, and kept her supplied with pocket money and credit. His love for her increased in proportion to what he did for her. It was an overmastering passion.

Erie Development

While Jim scattered his energies and had a good time, Gould focused all his remarkable powers of mind upon the railroad. He had seen the Commodore create the great New York Central system and he had an ambition to build up a system of his own. He knew what he could do and he went to work to rival the Commodore. When he got hold of the Erie, it virtually stopped in Buffalo and Dunkirk, its western terminals, both inside the borders of New York State.

In order to reach Chicago, the Erie had to transfer its passengers and freight either to the Lake Shore Railroad at Dunkirk or to lake boats at Buffalo. The New York Central on the north and the Pennsylvania Central on the south were both scheming to get into Chicago by lines of their own. They had been thinking about it for quite a while when they suddenly learned that Gould had made an agreement with the Columbus, Chicago and Indiana Central Railroad to lease that line, which would give the Erie a through route to Chicago, and that he was negotiating for a lease of the Chicago and Rock Island, which connected at Omaha with the Union Pacific, then approaching completion. The signing of this lease would then extend the Erie to San Francisco.

The powerful Pennsylvania drew on its bank account and persuaded the Columbus, Chicago and Indiana Central Railroad to repudiate its agreement with the Erie and to lease itself to the Pennsylvania for ninety-nine years. While they were chuckling over this fine stroke, Gould turned up as owner of a majority of the stock of the Pittsburgh, Fort Wayne and Chicago Railroad, which would give him an even better pathway to Chicago than the other line. The Pennsylvania's smile vanished. It began to understand the kind of railroad man that Gould was.

———♦———

Although blocked for the present in the West, the Erie, under Gould's driving, made progress nearer home. It bought a half interest in Abram S. Hewitt's Trenton Rolling Mills; it bought and built new locomotives, parlor and drawing-room cars; it made new and important connections in the Pennsylvania coal fields; it secured new docks on the Hudson in Weehawken; it secured connections with Newark and Newburgh; it built car shops in Buffalo; it substituted coal for wood as fuel; it had hopes of getting to Boston over the tracks of the Boston, Hartford and Erie; it made alliance with Jim's Narragansett Steamship Company, the Fall River Line, to carry Mississippi River cotton direct to the New England mills – and it increased its capital stock to the tune of fifty-three million, five hundred thousand dollars!

———♦———

The railroads that were competing for the freight that the West produced sometimes had rate wars that swallowed up all their profits, and more. The Commodore once tried to monopolize the cattle business by making a rate that was actually below the cost of carrying the cattle. When he found this out, Jim wired agents in Chicago to buy out the Stock Yards and ship the cattle east over the New York Central. He sold them in New York at a good fat profit. 'Business is business,' he remarked. 'If the Commodore wants to make me a present, I can't stop him. I always felt that he had a sort of sneaking fondness for me.' This was only one of the opportunities that he took advantage of for making money out of his connection with the Erie in ways that did not cost the road a dollar.

♦

Jim and Gould did their level best to make the Erie a real railroad instead of an excuse for stock-jobbing, as it had been under the guidance of the pessimistic and cunning Uncle Dan'l. The legal skirmishing with that professing Christian and his bear allies had hardly been wound up in 1869, when the Prince of Erie and his partner set out to capture the Albany and Susquehanna Railroad. This link between Binghamton and Albany, a distance of a hundred and forty miles through a hilly and difficult country, had been built almost single-handed by David H. Ramsay. He originated it and he was the whole thing – president, counsel, financial agent, and inspiration.

The Albany and Susquehanna Episode

If we could get the Susquehanna, it would give us an entrance into New England over the Boston and Albany line, and northward over the Rutland, and it would help us in the development of our coal fields south of the main line of the Erie in Pensylvania. There was a row in the Susquehanna board of directors when the road was finally finished in January, 1869. Half the board was against President Ramsay, God knows why, after all he had done to bring the work to completion.

The stock was quoted at about twenty-five dollars a share and there were twenty-eight thousand shares of it issued, out of a total of forty thousand shares authorized. The subscription books had never been closed, so that anybody was at liberty to buy the remaining twelve thousand shares. The directors owned some of the outstanding stock, some of it had been pledged by the company for loans, and the remainder belonged to towns along the line which had bought blocks of it under authority of the Legislature to help the good work along. To get control, we had to have a majority of the stock when the new board was elected in September, 1869.

———♦———

Both sides began buying stock in July and the price suddenly went up to forty and fifty dollars a share, and even to sixty-five. It wasn't long before the market was swept bare of stock. It then appeared that neither side had a majority, but that the stock owned by towns would decide the election. Jim and Gould and Shearman looked into the matter and they could see no way of getting hold of the town stock without paying the full price for it. 'It'll cost a lot of money,' Shearman said doubtfully. 'Damn the expense!' Jim retorted. 'We've got to have that stock, haven't we? All right, then we'll buy it, by Jimminy Crickets!'

He sent men up along the line with satchels full of cash to buy the town stock for a hundred dollars a share if they could get it right away. The other side heard of this move, and Ramsay sent out men to warn the town boards against selling. In spite of this, we got some stock – several hundred shares of it – but still we didn't have the majority we needed. Then the other side began to buy and prices got so high that some plan had to be found for getting the use of the stock on election day without actually buying it. It was Jay Gould who discovered how to do it. He knew that country.

We got the town boards that had hung on to their stock to come down to the Fifth Avenue Hotel one Sunday. After a lot of talk, Gould and Fisk told them that they would give their personal bonds to buy their stock at the prices they asked if the stock was voted with them at the September election of the new board. This offer was accepted by the towns, the bonds were handed over, and we went to bed that night believing that we were going to have everything our own way.

♦

But Ramsay was a fighter. He was Scotch. When he found out what had been done in New York, he saw that he was beaten unless he could vote more stock. He considered the twelve thousand shares in the company's treasury that had not yet been subscribed for. As a result of this consideration, he put the subscription books under his arm and carried them home with him. Then he called in a few friends, and amongst them they subscribed for nine thousand five hundred shares of the unissued stock. Ramsay promised to provide for a ten per cent payment and it was agreed that no further payments should be made until the board of directors called for them. Ramsay borrowed the ten per cent payment from David Groesbeck in New York. For this loan, Ramsay pledged securities from the Susquehanna treasury.

Each side had now got all the stock it could hope to get and the skirmishing was transferred to the courts. The object of the litigation was to prevent the enemy from voting on the stock that had been forfeited by subscribers and reissued for less than par. Ramsay came back at us with an injunction against the transfer of seven hundred shares of stock we had bought from the town of Oneonta. This move quickly brought on the crisis. We had the injunction dissolved immediately and at the same time we got an order enjoining Ramsay from acting any longer as president or a director of the railroad.

Shearman regarded this as a clever stroke because the board of directors was divided, seven to seven, and the removal of Ramsay gave us control. All we had to do now was to call a meeting of the board, throw out the treasurer, get at the books, and make such transfers of stock as would assure our control. When the meeting convened on the morning of August 6, the eleventh hour so to speak, the Ramsay lawyers served four injunctions on four of our directors forbidding them to act, and then nobody could do a thing. The four suspended directors took the first train for New York and a cab for the Grand Opera House, where we were waiting for them. Shearman questioned them and then gave it as his opinion that the management of the Susquehanna had been so shot to pieces that the immediate appointment of receivers was absolutely necessary.

'You'd better take this job yourself, Fisk,' Gould said.

'All right,' Jim assented.

'But it will look better if we put in somebody else with him – not quite so – so – one-sided,' Shearman suggested.

'Put Charlie Coulter in with me then,' said Jim.

While Shearman was drawing up the order, Jim invited the four restrained directors to dinner at Josie's. Before he left he sent a telegram to Poughkeepsie, where Justice Barnard had gone. Jim told him to hurry back to the city. I don't know whether he came; but at any rate his signature appeared on our order and we all took the eleven o'clock train that night for Albany. Jim carried along half a dozen Erie guards in case of emergency and Shearman came, too.

We thought this was rather quick work and we had no doubt that we were going to gobble up the Susquehanna in the morning; but that man Ramsay knew his business. He must have had word somehow of what was going on. Before we started he applied to Justice Rufus H. Peckham, of Albany, for the appointment of Robert C. Pruyn as receiver of the Susquehanna. We got into Albany at eight o'clock, and as soon as the train arrived we marched upon the offices of the Susquehanna. I noticed that there were more people than usual in Broadway and that they seemed to be watching us with more than an idle interest.

♦

The Susquehanna building down near the river was wide open and filled with activity when we got there. In the main office we found a sturdy-looking, dark man with strong features whom I recognized at once as John Van Valkenburg, Democratic leader of Columbia County. I shook hands with him, but Jim didn't ask for an introduction.

'Who are you?' he demanded.

'My name's John Van Valkenburg, and I'm superintendent of this railroad. I'm in charge here.'

'The hell you are! Who says so?'

'Robert C. Pruyn. He was made receiver yesterday by Judge Peckham. He took possession right off and he appointed me.'

'He did, hey?' snorted Jim, plumping himself down in a chair behind one of the desks. 'Well, I'm James Fisk, Jr., and I've been made receiver of the Susquehanna. You can go and tell Mister Pruyn that you've been fired!'

'Yes?' Van Valkenburg retorted. 'If you wait until I do that you'll wait till hell freezes over and thaws out again!'

'I've come up here to take charge under authority of the Court,' Jim insisted, 'and I'm going to do it if it takes millions of money and an unlimited number of men.' Jim turned to the entrance door and waved his hand to the scanty bodyguard of Erie men under command of Lynch, that he had brought up with him. 'Come in, boys!' he shouted. 'Make yourselves at home!'

Van Valkenburg was prepared for this move. He stepped back and opened a door, from which fifteen or twenty Susquehanna guards, filed in.

'Where are the books?' Jim demanded. 'I want 'em!'

'Then find 'em if you can, and take 'em if you're able!' Van Valkenburg challenged. Almost before we realized it, we were thrust out of the building amid the jeers and laughter of the watching Albanians. That was what they'd been waiting for!

'I'll be damned!' Jim exclaimed as he stood on the sidewalk looking up at the Susquehanna citadel. A policeman shouldered his way through the crowd. 'What's all the row about here?' he demanded. Instantly a chorus of bystanders accused us of having forced our way into the railroad offices. They pointed to Jim as the leader. 'Come along, then,' said the policeman, and he took Jim by the arm and led him away to the station amid a renewed burst of catcalls and witty comments from the crowd. Lynch and I trailed along, leaving Coulter and the others on guard. The policeman couldn't very well explain what he thought Jim had been guilty of. He hadn't seen him do anything himself. The sergeant ordered him to be turned loose.

When we got back to the river front we found that Coulter had gone to the Western Union office to telegraph the facts to New York.

'We can't do anything until we hear from Gould,' Jim said. 'We're in their bailiwick and they've got the best of us; but we'd better stay on the ground for a while.'

He led the way once more into the Susquehanna offices and I followed. He walked up to Van Valkenburg and put out his hand. 'Shake!' he said. 'I like your style. You're wasting your time up here; come down with me to New York and I'll make it worth your while.' He then shook hands with Pruyn and complimented him on the thoroughness of his preparations. 'I'm used to this sort of thing,' he said, 'and I know what I'm talking about.'

Ramsay came in while they were talking and Jim greeted him cordially. 'I suppose I'm about as welcome here as a skunk at a wedding,' he remarked, 'but I'll tell you how we can settle the whole thing in fifteen minutes and save ourselves and everybody else a lot of trouble.'

'How's that?' Ramsay inquired. He looked weary and careworn.

'I'll sit down here with you and we'll play a game of seven-up, the winner to take the railroad.' Ramsay smiled but shook his head. 'I've got other people to think about besides myself,' he said. Coulter came in before long and Jim introduced him all around. He and I then retired to the Delavan House for refreshments, leaving Coulter to represent our side.

———♦———

Several telegrams for Jim came while we were at luncheon. These caused Jim to engage rooms in the hotel and set up our headquarters there. We had hardly taken possession before several long telegrams arrived from Shearman. One of these was a copy of an order signed by Justice Barnard enjoining Pruyn, the police, the sheriff, and everybody else from interfering with Jim and Coulter, as receivers. Another was a writ of assistance by which the sheriff and his posse were put at the orders of the two receivers. These proceedings in New York had been taken by Justice Barnard on the strength of what had happened in Albany that morning as sworn to by telegraph.

Jim hustled around to the sheriff and found that he had received by wire copies of Justice Barnard's orders with instructions to execute them. Pruyn and Ramsay of course objected to the telegraphed orders and the upshot of the matter was that a sort of truce was patched up. Next day was Sunday, when the courts would be closed.

♦

We left Coulter in Albany and took the night boat for New York. Most of Sunday we spent in consultation. It was evident that the Albany atmosphere was hostile. Gould doubted whether we could do much there before the annual election of directors in September, when we intended to take control. Shearman thought that something might be accomplished through the writ of assistance. So it was decided that we should go back. There were fifteen of us in the party that went up on the night boat Sunday night.

Coulter had discouraging news for us when we got there. 'Judge Peckham has dissolved our injunction,' he told Jim, 'and he has restrained the sheriff and everybody else from interfering with Pruyn. That isn't the worst. He has asked a referee to consider whether you ought not to be held for contempt and you've got to appear on September 13 and show why you shouldn't be if you can.' Jim was silent for a minute. 'I think we've overlooked the fact that every railroad has two ends,' Jim said. 'There may be something in that,' the little lawyer replied.

Inquiry revealed the fact that copies of Justice Peckham's orders had been sent down the Susquehanna on the eight o'clock express that morning to be served on the sheriffs of all the counties on the line. But Jim and Shearman telegraphed Justice Barnard's injunction and writ of assistance to the sheriff of Broome County, in which Binghamton is located, and called upon him to put the division superintendent of the Erie in charge as the agent of the Barnard receivers to represent the 'Church party' in the Susquehanna, as the faction opposing Ramsay was called. Jim also sent the superintendent full instructions, directing him to get hold of all the rolling stock he could lay hands on.

Binghamton was as strongly with the Erie as Albany was against it. The Broome County sheriff grabbed the two o'clock train for Albany that was on the point of starting and he got two of the three locomotives in the place. He was just going to get the third, riding down upon it in one of the other locomotives, when the Susquehanna people turned a switch and shunted him off on a side-track while the locomotive slid past him down the grade, got up steam, and puffed away toward Albany.

News of what was being done at the Binghamton end was wired to Albany by both sides. Jim was highly pleased at the diversion. He had been once or twice in company with Shearman to the railroad offices to demand admittance, but the guard at the door refused to let him in. He went a third time when we heard from Binghamton that the southern terminal was in our possession, but he had no better luck then than before. In fact, while he was expressing his mind as usual to the guards, out came Coulter looking rather roughed up, with Van Valkenburg at his heels. 'Sorry to throw you out,' he said, standing in the doorway, 'but I'm too busy now for any more damn nonsense. This is our railroad and we're going to keep it. That's all. Goodbye!' He turned back into the building and, as we afterward learned, he sent an order down the line stopping every train where it happened to be until further instructions.

The express with Judge Peckham's order, which was scheduled to reach Binghamton at three o'clock, was halted at Harpersville, about twenty-five miles from Binghamton. Within fifteen minutes after he had stopped traffic on the road, Van Valkenburg sent out a special train from Albany loaded with a hundred and fifty men from the Susquehanna shops in charge of a master mechanic. Meanwhile the Broome County sheriff and twenty Erie men had got aboard a train in Binghamton and started north, serving the Barnard order and replacing all the station agents with Erie men as they went. They got as far as Afton, about thirty miles out of Binghamton, when a telegram from Albany was delivered to the Erie conductor in charge. It was from Van Valkenburg, who warned them that if they went any further, it would be at their own peril. Afton is about six miles from Bainbridge, where the Ramsay forces were concentrated. The special that Van Valkenburg had sent down from Albany stood there on a siding. There was a lot of hesitation and telegraphing for orders; but Jim told our train not to be bluffed and finally it went on. By then it was night, and the train ran cautiously to prevent accidents. It had received reinforcements from Binghamton, however, and did not fear an encounter.

It passed the Albany train on the siding and was just pulling into the Bainbridge station, when the engine ran off the track and it stopped with a jolt. The energetic Van Valkenburg had ordered a derailing frog to be put on the track and there the trainload of Erie-ites, with the sheriff of Broome County and his posse, stood helpless. While in this condition, the order issued by Judge Peckham, forbidding them to interfere with the Pruyn receivership, was served upon them. All that they had left to do was to wire the facts to their Binghamton base and to Jim's headquarters in Albany.

The Ramsay train, that had been waiting patiently on a siding, now slid out on the main track in the rear of the stalled train from Binghamton and rattled off toward that city, firing the brand new Erie station agents as it went and restoring their recently deposed predecessors. This process met no opposition until the avengers came to the long tunnel fifteen miles from Binghamton at about ten o'clock. There they found a mob of men from the Erie shops, armed with oak clubs that had been cut in the woods, lying in wait for them and they halted for orders. Reinforcements swelled the ranks of both sides during the night, and at seven o'clock in the morning our army contained about eight hundred men and the Ramsay troop numbered four hundred and fifty.

Jim, breathing slaughter in his Delavan Hotel headquarters in Albany, ordered an Erie train to advance through the tunnel. It was loaded accordingly with club-men and sent in. Most of the combatants were Irish and they were anxious for a scrimmage. The train crept through the tunnel and came safely out at the other end, where it had to pause to replace a rail that had been taken up. It then proceeded toward Albany, and its load of Erie employees yelled defiance until the hillsides echoed with their threats and boasts.

As the train glided down the grade from the tunnel around a curve, it encountered the Ramsey train, also loaded with men, puffing angrily up the hill. The conductor stopped the Erie train, jumped down, and began signalling wildly to the Ramsay train to stop. The only reply was a series of threatening toots and the Ramsay train continued to snort on up the grade with what speed it could make, which of course wasn't very much. 'Jump!' cried the Erie conductor to the men on his train when he saw that the other intended a collision. 'Back her!' he shouted to the engineer.

His orders caused the shopmen to pile out, clubs in hand, and the driving wheels of the Erie engine to reverse until the sparks flew from under them; but the grade was so sharp that the train hardly had begun to move before the other reached it amid a furious belch of steam and smoke, with bell ringing and whistle blowing, and bumped into it, head-on. There was a crash and a smash and the Albany locomotive rolled off the track and subsided, leaving the other without cowcatcher, headlight or smokestack.

With the shock of the collision, the Ramsay forces tumbled out of their train with a chorus of yells and a cracking of pistols, and made for the Erie army on the run. They were better armed than our side was. A good many had pistols, a few carried guns, and the rest had axes, shovels, pickaxes, and similar tools for which our green oak clubs were no match. Our men didn't wait. They put out for Binghamton as fast as they could go. A few went through the tunnel and a few stuck on the train; but most of them legged it up over the mountain, pursued by a scatter of shots and a shower of stones from the Ramsay men in their rear. At the same time, the Erie train at last got up enough reverse speed to reach the tunnel, into which it vanished, tail first.

The Ramsay detachment put forth superhuman efforts to get their locomotive back on the rails and in a short time their train was puffing after the Erie train, which it pursued into the tunnel and out on the other side. The Erie forces, invigorated by warlike messages from Jim in Albany, made a stand, yelling threats and imprecations, mingled with sacred and profane epithets of opprobrium, until they raised a terrible din. This caused the Ramsay troops to deliberate, and before they could make up their minds to attack, a sound that the Civil War had made familiar – the sound of drums – became audible from the direction of Binghamton. The sheriff had called upon the State for aid and the militia had been ordered out. The Ramsay crowd knew then that the game was up. They climbed into their train, which backed away with them into the tunnel, which they blocked with an upturned freight-car to check pursuit, and then retreated to Albany, bearing the signs of conflict.

The arrival of the Ramsay train was the signal for an outburst in Albany on the part of the Ramsay supporters, who were of course in a great majority there. The militant shopmen, smeared with grease and dirt, and some of them with black eyes or bruised faces, glowed to find themselves heroes.

♦

Governor Hoffman, informed by wire of the battle of Broome County, hurried back from his vacation and took charge. He ordered all sheriffs to recognize the Susquehanna employees who were in possession of any property of the railroad as rightfully so and not to call on the militia unless they had to. This left everything as it was, the Ramsay faction holding the Albany end of the road and the Erie faction the Binghamton end.

Jim decided to see whether he and Coulter couldn't get possession of the railroad office. He had received by telegraph another order from Justice Barnard which set aside the latest order issued by Justice Peckham. He and Coulter and I got into a hack and drove unobserved to the sheriff's office. There the sheriff joined us and we all drove to the Susquehanna building down on the river front across the New York Central tracks. Jim had an idea that Van Valkenburg might let the sheriff in. Nothing of the kind. The Superintendent was on edge from anxiety and lack of sleep and what he had to say to us was a caution. He'd be God-damned if he'd let us in, and he didn't, although Jim made him a handsome offer to win him over to our side.

♦

As we turned away to get back into the hack a policeman found us and arrested Jim and Coulter on a warrant issued by Jacob Clute, County Judge. We took the policeman into the hack with us and drove to Judge Clute's Court. He was a calm-looking man with a club foot and he remained unruffled under Jim's earnest language of protest. He and his fellow receiver could either go to jail for attempting to take possession of the railroad by force in the face of the

Governor's orders and Justice Peckham's injunction, or they could give bail. They finally gave bail and we all went back to the Delavan.

♦

Jim was mad clear through over his arrest because it humiliated him and he couldn't stand that. He sent off long telegrams telling Gould and Shearman all about it. These complaints sent David Dudley Field to Justice Barnard, who immediately issued an order for the arrest of Pruyn, Ramsay, and Van Valkenburg and their production before him on a charge of contempt of his court. This order was placed in the hands of the overworked Albany sheriff, who took the three culprits into custody in the State Executive Chamber, where they were waiting to see Governor Hoffman. Judge Clute then issued a writ of habeas corpus and next morning he ordered their release from arrest.

All these proceedings had aroused a lot of prejudice against us in Albany, which was hostile territory, anyway. Besides, the Governor had taken charge of the road and there was really nothing more for us to do there until the annual election of directors on September 7.

♦

Great preparations were made by all concerned for the annual election. On our side, everybody was there except Gould, who stayed in New York looking after his gold speculations and running the Erie. Jim was in command, backed by Field and Shearman, and he brought up a tough gang of bruisers from New York. We were also provided with a supply of warrants from Justice Barnard, issued at the request of our lawyers in the name of the Susquehanna road. They called for the arrest of Ramsay and Pruyn, and also of Phelps, secretary of the Susquehanna, and Henry Smith, its counsel. Without these men, the Ramsay faction could hardly hold an election. They were charged with having stolen the stock books.

As a matter of fact, the books were brought back on the night of September 6, the evening before the election. We had men on the watch for them; but Phelps and young Ramsay took them to the rear of the building and hoisted them up to the Susquehanna offices by using a basket tied to the end of a rope. That was one on us; but we had one on them in the shape of an order from Justice Clarke restraining the regular inspectors of election from acting on the ground that they were not holders of stock as the law required.

When the election was all over, Governor Hoffman's agents still kept control of the Susquehanna and Van Valkenburg continued to operate it. There had been no real change in the situation. There were already twenty-two separate legal actions pending. Governor Hoffman refused to surrender the road to either side until the courts decided who really owned it. He asked the State Attorney General to bring an action to settle all the disputed questions and the case was brought to trial before Justice E. Darwin Smith, in Rochester.

Gould and Jim were all tied up by their gold speculation and they proposed a compromise to settle the Susquehanna fight. But Ramsay wouldn't take it. He knew he'd get the decision from Justice Smith and so he did. The case was argued in November and the court found for Ramsay in January. Without waiting to give us another chance at him, Ramsay promptly leased the road in February to the Hudson and Delaware Canal Company in perpetuity and that was the end of the great Albany and Susquehanna campaign. Jim fought hard; I don't see what more he could have done; but the odds were too great. He hated to be licked.

Black Friday

Pop Fisk was still in the asylum at Brattleboro. His wife, Love, Jim's stepmother, stayed near him and Jim made liberal provision for the comfort of both of them. But when he began to make money in a large way, he moved his own residence to Boston and Lucy went down there to live. Jim bought in her name a fine house there, for which he paid seventy-five thousand dollars, and gave her a generous allowance. Besides the Boston property, he transferred to her some real estate that he bought on Main Street, in Brattleboro.

Jim always had a tender affection for Lucy, even when he was most infatuated with Josie. Whenever Lucy came to see him in New York,

Josie had to wait. Lucy always stood a long way first with Jim. Jim went frequently to Boston and Lucy came now and then to New York, but for seven years they lived actually apart.

♦

Jim's affair with Josie was unknown to Lucy during almost all its continuance. Toward the end, Jim confessed and she forgave him. He wrote to her every day and she to him. She always made allowances for him and always stood by him.

Ceda was very much worried by Jim's love affair with Josie. She continued to live in Brattleboro, but once in a while she came down for a visit to New York. She always went to the Lafayette Hotel because it was as different as possible from the Revere House in Brattleboro. She'd let me take her to dinner and to the theatre, but she didn't depend on me, as I wished she would.

Ceda asked a hundred questions about Josie. Finally she insisted that I should arrange things so she could see Josie and I took her to the theatre one night when I knew that Josie was going to be there. Ceda was quiet and thoughtful when we went for a welch rarebit at Martin's after the show. 'Well,' I asked after waiting for her to give her opinion, 'what do you think of her?'

'I'm sorry for Jim!' she said. 'I don't know that I could tell you why; but I am.' That's the best I could get out of her. The fact is, I began to feel the familiar symptoms that I knew were going to make me propose again to Ceda and my mind was diverted from Jim and Josie. My attention was absorbed by my own state of mind until Ceda let me kiss her goodnight at the door of her room, and I went home with my thoughts and pulses in a turmoil. Next morning she went back to Brattleboro.

♦

In 1869, Jim became half owner and president of the Narragansett Steamship Company – the Fall River Line – and thereby head of the finest fleet of steamers on Long Island Sound. He made them so. You should have seen Jim. Every afternoon about half an hour before the boat was due to sail he went into the offices of the line. In a few minutes out he came dressed in the full uniform of an admiral. He really did look splendid. Did he know it? Well! He stationed himself at the gangway, where all the passengers had to enter and issued orders as though he knew something about it. All bunkum. 'If Vanderbilt's a commodore, I guess I ought to rank as an admiral,' was the way he explained this pose. Jim stayed on the bridge, going through the motions of responsibility, until the boat had nosed her way around the southern end of Manhattan Island into the East River. There a tug was lying in wait to take him off and his carriage was ready on shore to carry him back to the point of departure, so that he might shed the uniform.

♦

The Narragansett Line was his plaything in 1869; but by the end of the summer it had grown stale and something new must be found. When the 1870 season opened he bought the *Plymouth Rock* from the Stonington Line for ninety-four thousand dollars and refitted her. The boat was in fact a floating hotel of the most luxurious sort. It went to Poughkeepsie, seventy-five miles, and back. On these occasions Jim was present in his admiral's uniform, smiling blandly upon everybody and playing the host.

In that same summer of 1869, when the Erie offices were moved to the Grand Opera House, Jim also established the new ferry service by land connection from the Erie depot in Jersey City, past the Grand Opera House, to the Fifth Avenue Hotel. The two boats of this ferry of course surpassed in elegance everything used in any of the other ferries. They were named *James Fisk, Jr.*, and *Jay Gould* and they were in entire keeping with the rest of Admiral Fisk's flotilla.

♦

Jim and his steamboats played a part in Gould's famous campaign to put up the price of gold. Gould and a few speculators were together in it at first. They made up a pool and they invited Jim to come in with them, but he wouldn't. 'The country's against you,' he told Gould.

'Folks don't want gold to go up; they want it to come down. It's too dangerous. Count me out.'

I don't think Gould liked this. They'd always been in together before then, share and share alike, win or lose. But he didn't say anything; that wasn't his way. He went on buying gold until he had too much to unload without losing a lot of money – all he had, in fact. He saw he had to do something and he did it.

We were building a horse railroad at that time over in Jersey and part of the right of way ran through a piece of land that belonged to Abel Rathbone Corbin, whose wife was a sister of Mrs. Grant, wife of the President, who had just taken office in March, 1869. Corbin was then an elderly man and he made a good deal of his relationship by marriage to Grant, who often stopped at his house when he was in New York. One day he met Gould in New Jersey and asked him whether he knew of a good investment.

'I think gold's going higher,' Gould told him.

The old man was interested at once. He asked a lot of questions. When Gould explained to him that the only danger to a bull movement in gold was the possibility that the Treasury might jump in and throw some government gold on the market, he saw a chance to make himself useful – and valuable. The upshot of it was that Gould bought some gold for him and carried it at his own risk, so as to keep the old man interested and active on the bull side. He had a million and a half for him before he got through.

They wanted to get an Assistant United States Treasurer in New York on whom they could depend to work with them and keep them informed. At first they thought of trying to have Robert B. Catherwood, whose wife was a daughter of Corbin's first wife, put in; but later they decided on General Daniel Butterfield and he was appointed.

Gould always denied that he and his friends had tried to corner gold. He insisted that he had only attempted to keep the price up so that the Western crops might be moved to the Atlantic coast for shipment to Europe. He contended that the wheat and other Western products couldn't be sold abroad at a profit unless gold was kept at a premium compared with greenbacks. If it couldn't be sold, it wouldn't be shipped, and the Erie wouldn't get the business.

♦

During the Civil War, the United States had issued millions of dollars of paper money. These bills greatly depreciated as compared with gold. Sometimes it took as much as $280 worth of them to buy a hundred dollars worth of gold, the value of which constantly fluctuated during the war.

The Gold Room was in Exchange Place between Broad Street and New Street. This room was provided because speculation in gold became so lively that it interfered with the regular transactions in stocks and so the Stock Exchange pushed it out into the Gold Room.

Parity between gold coin and the promises to pay issued by the government in the form of greenbacks could exist only when people were confident that the promises would be fulfilled whenever they asked. The government was keeping most of the gold that it took in, and this had reduced the free supply of gold outside the treasury available for commercial purposes, to about fifteen million dollars. The treasury had perhaps eighty or ninety millions more. If the government kept its gold, there was so little left outside the treasury that it might be bought up and a corner created in which the price might be put up indefintely. It looked to Gould like a good chance.

'Do you know what Gould has gone and done?' Fisk asked me one evening. 'No,' I said, 'what?'

'He's gone and bought a lot of gold, something like seven millions.' He paused a moment and then added, 'I think he's a damn fool because the government isn't goin' to let him get away with it. With gold scarce he thinks the price is too low and that it's bound to go up; but I told him that the government doesn't want it to go up and won't let it. If he doesn't look out, they'll turn his socks inside out for him.'

'Are you in it with him?'

'No, and I don't want to be. I'm too poor to indulge in such gaieties.'

♦

The general run of Wall Street took the view that Fisk had expressed, that the government wanted to complete deflation and that it wouldn't permit gold to go up very far. Gould had continued to buy and sell; but his purchases were much larger than his sales and his stock of gold was continually increasing. He was getting himself into a situation where he ran the risk of ruin unless he could manage to extricate himself. What he did to get himself out of his fix reveals his character, his energy, and his resourcefulness. He had to influence public opinion so that the average speculator would think the government was going to keep the gold it had in the Treasury and not dump it on the market. Then he had to furnish a plausible reason why the government should keep its gold and let the price go up.

An English financial authority, James McHenry, happened to be in this country. McHenry advanced the argument that a high price for gold would help to move the western crops. Since international transactions are settled in gold, his theory was that the higher the value of gold, the greater the return to the producer from sales paid for in gold, and the more ready he would be to sell. This seemed simple and reasonable enough. But why should Gould be trying to put up the price of gold? You couldn't make people believe he was doing it to increase the profits of Illinois and Iowa farmers. But the explanation was simple. If the crops didn't move, the Erie naturally wouldn't have the privilege of moving them out and its revenues would suffer. As president of the Erie, it was obviously Gould's duty to see that the crops moved.

Wall Street wasn't convinced. The explanation was too simple. Something more complicated was needed. The great point was to remove the fear that the government would sell gold if the price went up. To remove this fear, Gould determined to get President Grant committed to his policy for moving the crops, and at the same time to make people think that the President was speculating in gold for higher prices. It was with this in mind that he got Corbin interested and helped to have General Butterfield made Sub-Treasurer.

The hardest and most essential thing that Gould had to do was to find out for himself before anybody else knew excepting the President and the Secretary of the Treasury, whether the government was going to sell any of its gold, how much, and when. He depended on Corbin to get this information through General Butterfield and he cultivated the old man until Corbin became more enthusiastic about the speculation than even the members of the pool.

♦

The first thing was to find out how Grant felt about gold and to see that he got the right idea. There was going to be a great Peace Jubilee in Boston beginning on June 15 and the President came down from West Point to attend it. He went to Corbin's house, as usual. It had been arranged by Gould and Corbin that Grant should go to Boston on the *Providence* of the Narragansett line as a guest of the line, that is, of Jim and Gould. This would enable Gould to get at him and feel him out. It was quite natural that Corbin should have Gould come to his house to escort the President to the boat and this was done. Jim made all the boat arrangements on an elaborate scale.

About nine o'clock, we all went down to supper; all the good things to eat the market afforded; leave that to Jim. It wasn't long before the talk turned to business prospects and what effect the big crops in the West were going to have. This was Gould's cue. He explained that the crops would rot where they were and go to waste unless they could be sold in Europe. The farmers wouldn't sell unless it was made worth their while, that is, unless they could get good prices. In order to assure this, gold must be kept at a fair premium.

'What's that got to do with it?' somebody asked. Grant was sitting there, but he didn't say anything. Gould pointed out that a premium on gold was necessary because the crops that were sold abroad must be paid for in gold. If a gold dollar would buy only a greenback dollar, it wouldn't pay them to send their wheat and corn to market; but if it would buy a dollar and a half in greenbacks, they would sell, gold would flow in from abroad, and the replenishment of the supply would eventually wipe out the premium. Meantime the farmers would have money, the railroads would profit, and everybody would be happy.

'You see, General,' Jim remarked with careless frankness, 'Gould isn't entirely disinterested in this business. He and I have got the responsibility of running the Erie railroad. We've got about forty thousand wives to look after and we can't do it if our sidetracks are full of empties. If the farms send their wheat to Europe, we can keep the cars busy and the sidings clear. You see he's selfish about this gold premium; he's thinking about those wives and their children. I don't want you to get any wrong idea about his motives.' Grant nodded; but still he didn't say anything.

The talk went on, back and forth, until it got to be almost midnight. Finally Jim asked the President plump out what he thought. Grant took the cigar out of his mouth and hesitated a moment. 'Well,' he said slowly, 'it seems to me that there's a good deal of fiction in all this talk about prosperity. The bubble may as well be pricked one way as another.' This gave Gould quite a jolt. As the President was looking at him as the leading talker the other way, he made bold to remonstrate.

'If that policy is carried out,' he said in his quiet, soft voice, 'I think we shall see a great deal of distress among the poor. Wages will have to come down, and that will bring on strikes and unemployment. There will be riots and a state of things resembling civil warfare. I believe the government ought not to interfere with the price of gold – let it find its natural level. And if it does interfere at all, it ought to help the upward movement of the price.' It was plain that he was disappointed. Grant was a contractionist. But we had found out how the land lay and before long the party broke up.

As soon as the boat got in next morning Gould made tracks for the nearest Western Union office and wired his broker to sell some stocks that he was carrying. He found another member of his party there doing the same. He went back to New York, but Jim kept on with the Presidential party. The crowds waved and cheered and the President acknowledged it by taking off his hat and bowing. Jim, walking at his side, did the same. There was a lot of comment about it, all good-natured, and it was then and there that the name 'Jubilee Jim' was bestowed upon him. It was so appropriate that it stuck.

♦

We got back to New York on Thursday, June 17. Gould didn't give up. He kept at Corbin and a little later sold some of the gold he had bought for him and paid him twenty-five thousand dollars profit on account. Then he bought some more until he was carrying two millions for him. It was whispered around that this twenty-five thousand was to go to Mrs. Grant.

Gould saw the President again at Corbin's house, and he told Jim that he found Grant much more inclined to listen to reason about the price of gold. Gould reported that the President had expressed the belief that the harvest was going to be very big and that part of it would have to be sold abroad, and that he didn't think the government ought to do anything that would make money tight and hinder the movement of the crops. 'That's the first glimmer of sense that we've had out of Grant,' Jim said. 'But I wouldn't trust him around the corner; somebody else will get at him and then he'll change his mind again.'

♦

That gold fight was no place for gentlemen's sons. The financial articles in the *Times* were generally influential in those days. John Bigelow, who'd been Minister to France, had just been appointed editor-in-chief of the *Times*. He was a cultivated man, of diplomatic and guileless mind, and he was one of the President's friends. When Grant was in the city early in August, Bigelow saw him and afterward wrote for the *Times* two editorials which were accepted as having been inspired by the President. In these articles the financial plans of the administration were outlined. They attracted a lot of attention and gave people the impression that the *Times* spoke with authority when it discussed administration affairs.

Grant came through the city again on August 19 from Newport, and Gould got Corbin to fix up an article that expressed his own views, and Corbin's too, regarding the proper policy for the government to follow in regard to gold. It was so written that it could be printed as an editorial in the *Times*. The heading they put on it was 'Grant's Financial Policy,' and it was marked to be double-spaced as an article of unusual importance.

How to get it printed was the next question. They gave it to a personal friend of Bigelow's to take to the *Times* office. Bigelow rose to the bait and ordered the article to be put into type; but as it dealt with a financial subject, he gave instructions that the financial editor should see it before it was printed. The financial man of the *Times* was Caleb C. Norvell and he smelled a rat as soon as he read Corbin's production. He had the extra spacing taken out of the article and he trimmed off the last paragraph, which would have given the impression that the government didn't intend to sell any of its gold. In short, he hamstrung Jay's production. But enough remained to cause talk and the final outcome was that Bigelow soon afterward left the *Times*. The owners felt that he was too innocent to run a paper in the same town with Gould.

♦

Gould saw the President again later in the summer when he was arranging to give him a special Erie train to Correy, Pennsylvania. He reported then that Grant had told Corbin he had countermanded a Treasury plan to sell gold. Things looked safe up to then, at any rate; but Jim remained skeptical. 'I think it's all right,' Gould assured him. 'I told Corbin that Boutwell might take it into his head to sell some gold on his own hook, but he said no; that the President had written a letter to Boutwell, and that he had given it to Butterfield to deliver after the President left. Butterfield had told him that he gave the letter to Boutwell.'

'What was in it? Did he tell you that?'

'He didn't know exactly what was in it, but he felt certain the President had given instructions to Boutwell not to sell any Treasury gold, and Butterfield thinks so too.'

About this time gold began to rise. On September 6 it went above one hundred and thirty-seven. Gould continued to buy heavily, but his two associates in the pool got scared.

'Woodward and Kimber have quit,' I heard him tell Fisk in the Erie offices one night. 'They've deserted me like rats deserting a sinking ship. That isn't the worst of it. Kimber has not only sold out but he's gone short of gold.'

'Why don't you quit, old man, and take your loss while you can?' Fisk inquired.

'No,' Gould said in his soft voice. 'They'll never get me to show the white feather.'

General Butterfield was enlisted, or at least Gould supposed he had been, by a loan that Gould had made him. He felt it was necessary to have some bank that would certify checks so that the gold he was buying could be paid for. He invited Butterfield to join him in getting control of the Tenth National Bank. He told us, too, that in August and September, on General Butterfield's order, he had bought a million and a half of gold for him. These purchases, as well as those made for Corbin, had no margins nor any kind of security. His purpose in getting Butterfield in was so that he might have ample warning in case the government was going to sell. The order would naturally come from the secretary to the assistant treasurer in New York.

In spite of all these efforts the price of gold went down. Gould couldn't keep it above one hundred and thirty-five or one hundred and thirty-six up to the middle of September. He began to show the strain that he was under. After he had been deserted by Woodward and Kimber he again asked Jim to join him.

'I don't like it,' Fisk told him. 'The whole country's against you. Everybody wants gold to go down, not up. And if you do succeed in putting up the price, the Treasury'll sell.'

There was an investigating committee, as usual, after Black Friday had done its work. The Chairman of this Committee was Representative James R. Garfield, who was afterwards elected President and assassinated by Guiteau. The report of that committee was framed for the purpose of exculpating the President from complicity in the effort to advance the price of gold. Fisk, in spite of his better judgment and his remonstrances to Gould, did join him at this time.

———♦———

Gould came into the office looking pale and fragile and worried half to death. Jim got up in his hearty way and shook him by the hand and patted him on the back. Then he asked him: 'How much gold have you got? If we put it up, the Government is going to unload on us.'

'Oh, no, that's all fixed,' Gould replied. 'What is there that makes you think they will? Butterfield's all right and Corbin has got Grant fixed.'

'What do you mean by that?'

'I mean Grant is in it with Corbin.'

'The hell you say! I don't believe it!'

'Go and ask Corbin.'

'All right, I will; but give me a letter to him, so he'll talk to me.' Gould wrote the letter and Jim went to see Corbin. He told what had taken place.

'When I first met him he talked very shy,' he said. 'But finally he came right out and told me that Mrs. Grant had an interest. He said that five hundred thousand dollars worth of gold had been bought for her at thirty-one and thirty-two and that Gould had sold it at thirty-seven. He said that he held for himself about two million dollars worth of gold, of which five hundred thousand dollars was for Mrs. Grant, and five hundred thousand for General Porter. I told him that I hadn't had anything to do with this business at all, but that Gould and I were standing together and that we had no secrets from each other. I told him that he could make everything clear and straight. 'This looks like a pretty big thing,' I said, and I told him that Gould had lost, as things now stood, and that it looked as though it might be a serious business to come out alive. I showed him that everything depended on whether the government was going to unload on us.

'You needn't be afraid of that,' says he.

'What I want to know is whether Gould is telling me the truth,' I said, I want to know right out whether you have sent this twenty-five thousand dollars that he paid you to Washington.'

'Yes, I have sent it,' says he.

'Can you show me anything that goes further than your talk?' I asked.

'Oh, well, no, I can't show you anything,' he says, 'but it's all right. You can take my word for it.'

A few days later Corbin came around to the Erie offices in the Opera House and Jim had another talk with him. On that occasion, Gould went home with him, but Fisk didn't see Gould till the following afternoon. He had been over in Jersey. Gould told Jim that as a result of his talk with Corbin he was assured that everything was all right and that if Butterfield got any information from Washington we should have it in time to get out of the market. 'I may be able to tell you something later,' he said.

Putting this and that together, and looking over the details of what took place, I can't help believing that Gould misled Jim. I am pretty sure that Jim felt it. He knew men and he knew Gould. His asking Corbin whether Gould had told him the truth struck me as significant. I felt convinced that Gould must have induced him to believe what he himself didn't believe, which was that the President was implicated. If this were the fact, of course, we had nothing to fear. Jim didn't have much confidence in anybody's integrity and it wasn't very hard for him to believe that the President was gambling when the President's friends assured him that it was so. At any rate, Jim took off his coat and waded in to help Gould out of the hole he was in.

♦

The kind of co-operation that Jim was able to give in the bull campaign was soon made evident. Having been persuaded to join, he dashed into the business with enthusiasm, inspiring weak-kneed bulls by his expressions of exuberant confidence and filling the hearts of the bears with misgivings. If it had been only a Wall Street fight, he would surely have carried the day; but, as he himself pointed out to Gould, the whole country was arrayed against them on the bear side.

We had a feeling – that is, Fisk and Gould had – that the time for action had come. The plan of campaign was laid out and everything was guarded against so far as possible. Butterfield was to warn us as soon as the government ordered the sale of gold, or as soon as he had reason to think that it intended to sell; the bank would take up gold that short sellers might abandon to us when the price went up; we had a lot of brokers buying for us and a pool account known as the National Gold Account was opened to create the impression that national officials were in. Rumors were set afloat and carefully propagated that not only the President and all his Cabinet, but every office-holder of any consequence in the national service was in a gigantic conspiracy to make fortunes in gold on the long side.

Of course, the bears were active, too, and they had some pretty big men among them. They got up a demonstration by bringing Secretary Boutwell over for a dinner at the Union League Club. We had reason to believe, or thought we had, that they were going to put the screws on him to get him to sell gold. Gould didn't like the looks of things. He distrusted everybody, including Corbin, whom he saw always twice a day. He decided to go over Boutwell's head direct to President Grant and he used Corbin for the purpose. He was nursing a plan when he told Jim that afternoon that he might have something to tell him later. He had. When he got back to the Opera House between nine and ten o'clock, he came in quickly.

'We need a confidential messenger,' he said. 'Have you got a man you can trust absolutely?'

'Trust with what?' Jim asked.

'With a letter to Grant, from Corbin.'

Fisk whistled but he said at once: 'The man is W. O. Chapin. Will you get him here, Rabbits? This is no job for a telegraph boy.' While I was away, which wasn't long, they talked over their plan together. 'Can you get the eight o'clock train for Pittsburgh tomorrow morning?' Fisk asked Chapin as soon as we came in. 'I can try,' Chapin said smiling. I hadn't told him anything and he was curious to know why he had been sent for. 'All right, then, get it,' said Jim, 'but start early enough to call at Corbin's house on your way and take two letters that he'll hand you. One will be addressed to General Horace Porter and will ask him to see that you have a chance to hand the other to the President.'

'Whereabouts in Pittsburgh are they?' Chapin inquired. 'They're not in Pittsburgh at all,' Fisk said. 'When you get there, about midnight, you'll hire a good horse and buggy and drive at a good clip to Little Washington; that's thirty miles. Grant's there. You won't have any trouble finding him. As soon as you've delivered the letter to him, you hang around until you're sure he's read it. Wait for an answer, you know, or something of that sort. Then get to the nearest wire as quick as the Lord will let you, and send me this message –

'Letter delivered all right.' Send it to me here. Do you understand?'

'Yes, sir,' Chapin replied. 'It shall be done.'

As soon as he was gone, Jim turned to me. 'This is a mighty serious business, Rabbits,' he said. 'We've bought a lot of gold, God knows how much – forty or fifty millions. We've got to put up the price and we're going to put it up. We'll be all right if we can have a few days to turn around in and shake 'em down, and it will help us a lot to have Grant get that letter from his brother-in-law. He may get something different from Boutwell and we want him to be able to study both sides before he acts, if he does act, which God forbid! To make a long story short, if the Treasury sells any gold before we can get out, we're ruined.'

'What do you want me to do about it?'

'Nothing much; only wake up Chapin and get him out of bed at six o'clock to-morrow morning; and then go with him, and see that he doesn't forget to do everything I've told him to do. Can you do it?'

'Of course I can. I'll wake you up, too, so you'll know we're on the way, if you want me to.'

'That's kind, but unnecessary,' he replied.

All this time Gould sat without saying a word in his big, carved oak chair, his nervous fingers spread out on the arms of it, watching every move with his sad, deep eyes. He listened as intently as though his life depended upon what was being said. And, in a way, it did.

♦

I've always been able to wake without an alarm clock but that night I didn't sleep much for fear I might sleep too long. We rang Corbin's bell at a quarter after seven o'clock and the maid called him to the door in his dressing gown. He handed Chapin the two letters, sealed, one addressed to the President and the other to General Horace Porter.

It was a long, tedious ride to Pittsburgh. It was after midnight when we finally got there. We routed out a livery stable and hired a two-seated buggy, with a span of horses and a driver, to take us the rest of the way. It was breakfast time when we sighted Little Washington and we had breakfast before we did anything else. We couldn't get Grant out of bed. Then Chapin went off with his letters and I waited for him.

'The President and General Porter were playing croquet when I got there, and the secret service man took me into the parlor and told me to wait there,' he said when he got back. 'They came up before long and the President sat down on the porch while General Porter came in to see what I wanted. I gave him the letter addressed to him and when he had looked at it he called the President in and I handed him the other letter. The President took it out on the porch and General Porter went out of the room by another door, leaving me alone. I stayed there until I thought the President had time to read what was in his letter and then I went out to where he was sitting and asked him if there was any answer. He said there wasn't. It seemed to me that it wasn't the kind of a letter to cheer him up any. Well, he's got it anyway. Now let's telegraph.'

We walked to the telegraph office and wired the message that Fisk had ordered: 'Letter delivered all right.' Late next day we got back to New York and I reported to Jim with Chapin. We found him at the Opera House.

'You did a good job, boys!' he said, slapping Chapin on the back.

'You got my wire?' Chapin asked.

'Yes; here it is,' Jim replied and he picked it up from his desk.

'"Letter delivered. All right."'

'I didn't send it that way,' Chapin said. 'I sent: "Letter delivered all right."'

'Geehosophat!' Fisk exclaimed. 'I've bought about fifteen millions of gold on the strength of that extra period!' We were tired and he told us to go home and go to bed.

'Funny about that wire,' said Chapin as we reached the street. 'Do you think so?' I asked. 'Well – maybe not. Good-night!'

I must put in here something that I didn't learn about until later, but it will help to explain things that happened next. It seems that the

President didn't like Corbin's letter at all. In it the old man urged him not to let the Treasury sell any gold, no matter what happened. The President thought his brother-in-law was too darned anxious, and he asked Mrs. Grant to write to her sister and tell her to tell Corbin to get out of the market right away if he was in it.

Corbin showed this letter to Gould and it scared them both almost to death. Corbin wanted to get out right away. He asked Gould to give him a check for a hundred thousand dollars, which was his profit on the two millions of gold that Gould was carrying for him, and let him out so that he could write to the President that he wasn't in the market. Gould said he'd think it over and let him know in the morning. He was worried. 'If what's in this letter gets to be known, I'm a ruined man,' he told Corbin.

Of course Corbin promised not to say a word, and he didn't. The strange thing was that Gould didn't say a word either when he saw Jim next day. He didn't dare settle up entirely with Corbin and so lose his hold over him. 'Corbin's nervous about his gold,' he said to Jim. 'He wants a hundred thousand dollars. What do you think about giving it to him?'

'If he wants it to deal out to people, and it will help us hold the price up, we can afford to give him one hundred thousand or two hundred thousand,' Jim said. 'Well, use your own judgment,' said Gould. Not a word about the letter, you see! He was a deep one.

Jim, of course, thought Corbin wanted some money for the President, and Gould let him think so, just as he had let Corbin convince him that the President was in it. Perhaps Gould really thought he was for a while, but he couldn't have kept on thinking so after he read Mrs. Grant's letter. Anyhow, Jim went and got a check for a hundred thousand dollars for Corbin and gave it to Gould, who put it in his pocket. Corbin never got it.

♦

On this same day – Thursday, September 23 – the President ended his vacation and went back to Washington. We saw it in the papers. We knew then that we had no time to waste. This was the plan of campaign that we agreed upon:

Jim was to lead the buying. He got his old partner, William Belden, to give him a letter which authorized him to buy any amount of gold at Belden's risk and to issue any orders he thought fit to Belden's brokers. Belden gave Jim and Gould's firm – Smith, Gould, Martin and Company – as his principals in the business. E. K. Willard was assigned to attend to the loans of gold that were made to the shorts and to force the payment of all the money he could squeeze out of them. Albert Speyers was to bid up the market. Half a dozen others were to frighten the shorts into making private settlements. Gould was to keep in touch with the Treasury through his secret avenues of communication and give warning of any action on the part of Boutwell.

♦

Belden brought Speyers into his bank office the next morning and introduced him there to Jim, Gould, and Smith. He told him to take instructions from Jim; but Speyers got the idea that he was to act as broker for everybody there. 'Buy two million gold,' was his first order. Jim gave it carelessly, as though it were a matter of trifling importance. Speyers dashed into the Gold Room and bought the two million at the market. Then he dashed back to Belden's office. He liked to dash.

'I bought it!' he announced. 'What shall I do now?'

'Buy some more; and when you've got that, keep on buying,' Jim replied, with a benign smile. 'Well – but how much?' Speyers asked, rather taken aback by Jim's coolness.

'All you can get,' Jim replied. 'It's cheap at these prices. It'll go to two hundred – mark my words!' Speyers looked at him to see whether he was serious. 'I mean what I say,' Jim assured him. 'Come on; I'll go over with you and we'll give 'em something to talk about.'

He took the excited Speyers by the elbow and marched him back to the Gold Room. I trailed along to see what would happen, and it was well worth seeing. Gold was then changing hands at around 142. At first Jim attracted no attention. He stood at the door looking on with a smile at the struggling, yelling brokers. Speyers screeched hoarsely for a million gold at 142 and three-eighths. Then the traders saw Jim and a great shout went up as though somebody had touched off a powder magazine. Everyone wanted to hear what Fisk would say about the market.

'It'll go to two hundred,' he announced. 'Better get in out of the wet while you can, boys!' There was a yell of derision. 'I'll bet fifty thousand dollars it will go to two hundred!' Jim shouted. 'Fifty thousand, or any part of it, that gold goes to two hundred! Don't be bashful! Who'll take some of it?'

The yelling ceased and almost complete silence fell upon the crowd. The brokers looked at one another and at Jim with a sort of stupefaction. 'Who wants it?' Jim asked again; but nobody had the courage to take him up. Then men who had been selling looked scared; the brokers who were buying for the clique uttered a wild war whoop. Jim stood there cool, calm, and collected, chatting with acquaintances and explaining to them why gold was bound to go up out of sight, and what a blessing its high price would prove to the farmers of the West and to the railroads and the country in general.

A man edged his way up to Jim, making an obvious attempt to quiet himself down so that he would appear as cool as Jim was. 'What do you think of these reports about Washington, Mr. Fisk?' he asked.

'What reports?' Jim inquired quickly.

'Why, that they're all in on the bull side, from the President down.' I could see that Jim was relieved. 'I don't know anything about it – for certain,' he said cautiously. 'It isn't the sort of thing anybody would be likely to know about – for certain, I mean.'

'They say Corbin's in it.'

'I shouldn't wonder.'

'And Butterfield.'

'That wouldn't surprise me.'

'What do you really think?'

'I'm offering to bet fifty thousand that gold'll touch two hundred.' Jim replied.

'If Boutwell lets go of the gold he's got in the Treasury, you'll lose,' said the man.

'Do you want to take a piece of my bet or all of it?' Jim asked blandly, and the man went away. He was evidently under the impression that

Jim knew a lot he wouldn't tell and this was just the impression that Jim wanted to create. But I'm convinced that he himself thought Grant was in it. At any rate, he acted as though he did.

It was a terrible day, that Thursday. The transactions in the Gold Room amounted to two hundred and thirty-nine millions. All previous records were broken. Excitement was intense. The air was full of rumors and the newspapers printed a lot of them. Gold closed that night at one hundred and forty-five and the Treasury hadn't sold any.

Jim took me uptown that afternoon in his carriage. He was in high feather and he laughed at me when I tried to express my anxieties. 'Look here, Rabbits!' he said. 'We've got calls on a hundred millions of gold, or thereabouts, and there's only about fifteen millions outside of the Treasury. When we call it, they've got to settle, haven't they? Where are they going to get it except from us? Hey?'

'It seems all right,' I admitted, 'but suppose the worst comes to the worst. Suppose the Treasury sells – what then? The bottom will fall out, won't it?' Jim said nothing for a moment, but he didn't look a bit scared. Finally he pulled some letters out of his breast pocket and picked one out. 'Read it,' he said.

It was the Belden letter. People have said it wasn't written until afterward – that it was a fake. But I'm telling what happened. It was addressed to Jim and it had never been through the mail. I took it out of its envelope and read it while the carriage jolted over the pavement up Broadway. It authorized Jim to buy and sell gold for Belden's account and to use Belden's brokers to do it.

I saw at once that this letter might be used by Jim to protect himself if the worst happened. He could say he was acting for Belden and wasn't responsible himself for the gold he bought and sold. I gave the letter back and Jim put it away in his pocket with the greatest care.

'Satisfied now, Rabbits?' he asked.

'I don't know whether I am or not,' I replied. 'Perhaps they can't ruin you; but they may lynch you, if you don't look out.' This suggestion struck him as humorous. He laughed over it; but there was more real ground for my fears than either of us knew.

♦

We drove to Josie's. Jim had sent word to her to have supper ready – plenty of it, as he expected company. As soon as we got there, he went upstairs to put on his black velvet coat and a brilliant necktie. The company he expected turned out to be Belden, Speyers, and some others of the gold clique. Jim was in great spirits. We all took an appetizer and Belden took several before we sat down at the table, Jim laughing and joking was at one end, and Josie, buxom and smiling, in a pink silk dress, at the other. The talk was mostly about what had been done that day to put up the price of gold and of measures to put it up still further next morning.

We didn't stay long after supper. Josie followed us to the door to wish us good-night, and to have a whispered word with Jim. We walked across to the Opera House and went up to the Erie offices. It was still daylight, but the gas had been turned on inside and everything was brilliant. The outer office was filled with people and everybody turned to greet Jim when he entered, fresh and smiling, with a flower in his buttonhole. At once he was surrounded by a knot of men who had questions to ask or who wanted to hear his answers to questions asked by others.

'What's going to happen to-morrow?' asked a young fellow, a reporter from the *Herald*.

'God alone knows and he won't tell,' Jim replied. 'If he would, we'd all be rich. But if you bet that gold'll sell for two hundred, you won't be far wrong.'

'You're still a bull, then?' asked the *Sun* man.

'You can tell Mr. Dana not only that I'm still a bull, but that the pasture bars are down.'

'But why should it go up any further?'

'Why? Because a whole lot of people want to buy it. I suppose a thousand men right now are thinking how they're going to buy gold first thing tomorrow. You know that yourself, don't you?'

'Yes, I suppose that's true.'

'Well, where are they going to get it from? We've got all the gold there is, and I don't mind telling you, a whole lot more. We ain't selling it. We want it. If anybody's got any more gold to sell, we're here to buy it, and we don't care what we have to pay for it. That's the reason why I think gold's going to two hundred.'

'A lot of people will be ruined if it goes much higher – a lot are ruined already.'

'Their pastors and Uncle Dan'l Drew will tell 'em that it's wicked to gamble – unless it's on a sure thing, of course.' Jim replied. 'You have only to lose once to realize how wicked it really is. That's the reason I never gamble myself. But there's no need for anybody to be ruined. We don't want that for anybody.' He paused a moment and then added thoughtfully – 'Except maybe a few. If they can't afford to buy gold at the market, we're always ready to sell 'em a little for what they can afford to pay us for it, provided we don't lose money on it ourselves. I don't mind saying that we saved quite a good many from ruin today by settling with 'em way under the market. We'll do the same thing tomorrow if we can; but I'd advise the distressed brethren to come early so as to avoid the rush.'

The crowd was rather feverish, everybody talking at once in loud tones. I left Jim surrounded and slipped through the guarded door to the inner offices. It was quiet there. Belden had preceded me and with him were E. K. Willard, Henry M. Smith, Osborne, William Heath, and half a dozen more. They were talking in low voices, glancing now and then at Gould, who sat at his desk with a young man beside him, working away silently at a mass of railroad papers, reports, and correspondence that had accumulated during the day. He heard me as I entered and beckoned to me.

'Ask Jim to come in as soon as he can get away,' he said, and then bent his head again over his papers. I carried the message to Jim, who tore himself away from his admirers at last and came breezing into the quiet inner room. 'Gosh! What's going on in here – a funeral?' he inquired, looking around at the serious faces.

'You ought to know,' Willard replied. 'Is it?'

'It isn't mine, anyway, whatever it may be for others,' said Jim with emphasis, 'and I'm generous enough to say that my offer to bet any part of fifty thousand that gold's going to two hundred is open to all, without any invidious discriminations. Don't all speak at once!'

If Jim had any misgivings about the final result, he didn't betray them in the smallest particular. To tell the truth, I don't think he had any. He could make himself believe almost anything that he wanted to be so.

♦

It was a strange thing when you think of it that a Vermont tin peddler, a Yankee youth from the country, should have been the engineer of an episode that won't be forgotten in Wall Street as long as that happy hunting ground exists. The events of that day threw a light upon what speculation really is that the Street never will entirely shake off. Jim knew he had them where the hair was short. He had bought rights that enabled him to demand delivery to him of a hundred and ten millions of gold any time at the market price. This was a great deal more gold than was anywhere in sight. In fact it didn't exist, and Jim knew it. He himself called it 'phantom gold'. He knew well that it would fade away and vanish at a breath, and he knew that the Treasury might breathe that deadly breath at any moment. He and all of us knew that it was time to settle; that this was our last day. It was evident to the whole world that Jim and Gould had cornered gold. The shorts could get it only from them on their terms. They were not only willing but anxious to sell; the trouble was that the sellers didn't want to buy at their price. They wanted to wait a while until it had fallen. They believed it was too high at a hundred and forty-four and that they could buy it cheaper, perhaps for a hundred and thirty-four, if they only waited a little. Jim was scornful of this point of view. 'I don't know what makes 'em think I'm in this thing as a philanthropist,' he said. 'They need to wake up.'

Corbin wasn't the only anchor to windward that Gould had. He depended also on General Butterfield, whose appointment as Assistant Treasurer Corbin had accomplished. Gould and Butterfield were great friends. They saw each other constantly at each other's houses or the Union League Club. When Gould bought gold for Corbin, he also bought an equal amount for Butterfield and he carried it for both of them. He bought some of this gold up around a hundred and thirty-eight and some more several points lower, so that

Butterfield and Corbin each had a million and a half of gold that Gould was carrying for them without its costing them a cent.

Of course you would suppose that both men would be anxious to tip Gould off if they thought the Treasury was going to sell gold so that he could sell what he was carrying for them and save their profit. Corbin was frank enough when he showed Gould the letter from Mrs. Grant to his wife with the message to him to get out of the market if he was in it. This could be interpreted in two ways – either that the President didn't want his brother-in-law gambling in Wall Street in stocks whose value could be affected by official action, or that he had made up his mind to let the Treasury sell and didn't want Corbin to lose money. Corbin told what he knew and tried hard to get Gould to pay over his profit and let him out. He wrote a letter to the President assuring him that he had no interest in the market and telling him that he would be making a great mistake if he permitted the sale of gold just then. He showed this letter to Gould and asked for a hundred thousand dollars to close his account so that when he sent the letter, his assurance about not being in the market would be true.

Gould was too shrewd to bite on that. He may have believed the President knew Corbin was in the market and would be less likely to sell gold if he thought he was still in, or he may have wanted to keep Corbin in a position where it would be worth while for him to do all he could to prevent the sale of gold by the Treasury. But after seeing Mrs. Grant's letter to her sister, he knew it was more than likely that the order to sell gold would be given next day and he went to see Butterfield about it the first thing in the morning.

'The General tells me he hasn't heard anything; so we can go ahead,' he said to Jim.

'I'm glad to hear that,' Jim replied. 'Have you read the *Times* editorial?' He held out the paper, and Gould read the article. It said that the gold bulls in Wall Street were saying that everybody in Washington, from the President down, including Corbin and Boutwell, were mixed up in the gold business. Gould looked thoughtful. He handed the paper back to Jim without a word. 'It's likely to scare 'em silly down there,' Jim said. 'Of course it was written to be put on the wire and probably fifty men have wired it to the White House already.' Gould didn't reply. He went quietly over to a corner of the room and sat down there at a raised desk. He could sit there and see all that was going on and whisper into the ears of brokers, messengers, and anyone else who stood beside him. He could give instructions without being overheard. This was just what he liked. We all thought he was buying gold and it wasn't until after everything was over that we discovered he'd been selling all the time around a hundred and forty the gold he had bought around a hundred and thirty-five. While he was quiet and secret, Jim was just the other way. He wanted everybody to know that he was buying all he could get. His voice was loud. He didn't care who knew it; the more, the merrier.

The door of the room was guarded by a squad of half a dozen men Jim had brought down from the Erie office. 'We may want 'em before the day's over,' he explained. On that morning of Black Friday, gold was quoted before the market opened at a hundred and forty-three and a half. Speyers, proud of his conspicuous role, came in for orders. 'Buy all the gold you can at a hundred and forty-five, or under!' shouted Jim across the room. 'Right!' he shouted back and immediately dashed out to execute the order. A dozen camp-followers dashed out after him to buy gold at a hundred and forty-four so as to sell to Jim a point higher. Jim, of course, knew they would do this; he calculated upon it while they believed they were outwitting him. Gould didn't seem to be paying any attention. Now and then one of his agents would come and they would consult briefly in tones so low that the bystanders couldn't catch what was said.

'He's leaving everything to Jim,' I thought to myself, with a glow of pride. 'He's in so deep that he'll never get out unless Jim boosts him.' I felt a sort of pity for the quiet, pale man, with his sad dark eyes, for if Jim didn't succeed, I knew he was ruined. Jim would be, too, of course; but somehow that didn't seem so serious. He didn't care for money so much. There seemed little chance of failure. Merely to look at Jim was to gain confidence. The price of gold mounted steadily until it reached a hundred and forty-five. There were exclamations and excited talk in the office when this figure was announced.

'It's forty-five!' somebody called.

'Good,' said Jim. He reached for a pad on the table at his elbow and wrote a few words. He handed me the sheet. 'Take it in,' he said, 'and give it to Speyers.' I looked at the paper. It bore the following order: 'Put it to 150 at once. James Fisk, Jr.'

I hurried to the Gold Room. My pulses beat fast when I thought of what would follow the execution of Jim's order. I found the place in an uproar. I saw Speyers in the middle of a knot of struggling men down near the fountain in the middle of the pit. As I was not a member of the Board I couldn't go down myself, but I folded the paper, called a page boy, and told him to give it to Speyers. He wormed his way down to where Speyers stood and slipped the note into his hand. I watched him to make sure there was no mistake. As soon as he had read it Speyers began to hop around like a Shanghai rooster. His high, falsetto voice rose above the din. He took all the gold that was being offered by the men who surrounded him and at once began to bid for more – a hundred and forty-six, and hardly an offer. A silence fell upon the room. The medley of shouts and howls was stilled. Speyers's voice sounded loud and distinct in the hush:

'Forty-six for a million!' he shouted. There was no response.

'A quarter! a half! Forty-six and a half for a million!'

Somebody sold him two hundred thousand at a half and the pandemonium momentarily broke loose again, as others wildly offered to sell. But Speyers kept on bidding and the price crept up, fraction by fraction, until it touched a hundred and forty-eight.

I heard a man at my elbow tell another that some stock broker was going to shoot Speyers to put an end to his bidding because the quotations of stocks were crumbling. The rumor ran like wildfire through the packed room. Everybody began looking at his neighbor to see whether he carried a pistol. Speyers was no coward. As soon as the threat reached him, which seemed only a minute or two after I heard it, he came pushing his way up out of the well.

'Shoot me, will they?' he kept saying over and over. 'I'll give 'em a chance! I ain't afraid of 'em!' He pushed out of the Gold Room and into the Stock Exchange, followed by a curious gang. In the Exchange he rushed to the rostrum and turned his red, excited face to the crowd that thronged the floor. 'They tell me I'm going to be shot because I've been buying gold,' he screamed, and all the brokers stopped business to stare at him. 'All right! Here I am! Shoot away!' He was in dead earnest. Maybe he really expected to be shot; but he certainly did look funny waving his long arms like a distracted windmill. He was almost crazy with excitement; he was entirely so before the day was over. Drops of sweat stood on his face as he ran back to the Gold Room and rushed down into the pit. Gold was being bought at a hundred and fifty-two. As soon as he took this in, Speyers elbowed his way out of the Gold Room, much like a drowning man struggling to shore, and dashed over to Heath's office to report to Jim that he had put gold to a hundred and fifty.

'Vot shall I do now?' he demanded, wiping his face with his handkerchief. 'Do?' said Jim, 'Buy all the gold you can up to a hundred and sixty.' Speyers's eyes seemed to pop out of his head when he heard this. 'Do you mean a hundred and sixty?' he asked, not crediting his ears. 'Don't you mean a hundred and fifty?'

'No, I mean a hundred and sixty,' Jim replied coolly. 'Buy all you can at that price; but you won't get much. I've already given the same order to others and you'll probably be too late.'

The possibility of losing the center of the stage drove Speyers almost wholly distracted. He bounded out of the office and back to the Gold Room. I lingered behind, placing myself where Jim could see me, in case he should want me for anything. To all appearance he was entirely oblivious of the fact that he was driving Wall Street insane with uncertainty and fear and that failures were already being announced. These resulted from the inability of the shorts to put up the additional margins which the advancing price of gold demanded of them. They had to deposit currency, or certified checks, for the value of the gold they borrowed and every jump in the price meant more checks or currency. I noticed that brokers were now consulting with Gould in an endless stream. They were trying, as I found out later, to settle with him at some figure below the market. He was the chief lender of gold and he had given orders to his brokers to take the shorts into camp.

———♦———

If the shorts didn't have money to meet his terms, or if they were unwilling to meet them, they failed. The wide extent of the ruin of that day was shown by the Gold Bank records when it appeared that the statement of a single house would often report transactions with as many as thirty houses that had been forced to suspend before the day was over.

It seems absurd that the orders given by Jim and executed by that jumping-jack, Speyers, should have paralyzed business, as they did, from Boston to San Francisco. Wall Street's bedlam was only a sample. Thousands of men in every city were reading the astounding figures that came out on the ticker tape – figures that told them they were ruined. The fluctuations in the price of gold were so rapid that it was impossible to keep up with them. No speculator outside the Gold Room had a chance to protect himself. He gave his order to buy or sell, and after that he was in the hands of blind fortune.

Who could tell where these feverish pulsations in the price would lead? Fisk was declaring that gold would reach two hundred; maybe he was right. Perhaps the whisperings about a gigantic conspiracy among public officials, with President Grant at their head, to make fortunes by speculating in gold on the bull side, were true after all. Only the United States Treasury could smash the clique that was boosting gold, and the doors of the Treasury seemed to be fast locked. No wonder the men who had sold gold rushed to cover at the best prices they could get. And there sat Jay Gould in the midst of the stress, nodding and whispering and often shaking his head. And there, too, sat Jim, whacking the desk with his cane to call attention to the predictions he was making about the future course in the price of gold.

Gould didn't like the situation. He had heard that Seligman was selling gold and he knew that Seligman acted sometimes for Butterfield. 'He must know what he's doing,' he thought, and he sent a messenger to Butterfield to ask if anything had come from Washington. The man came back and reported that the General hadn't any news.

———♦———

There was excitement enough in the Gold Room before the excitable Speyers made his sortie into the Stock Exchange. When the price of gold reached a hundred and fifty, a panic seemed to sweep through men's minds. There was a general rush to buy. The heads of banks and of great commercial houses poured into Wall Street from every quarter. Telegrams clattered in from all over the country. The burden was: 'Buy! Buy! Buy!'

When Speyers got back to the Gold Room he plunged into a whirlpool of frantic excitement, where men were fighting with each other to save the remnants of their fortunes. Huge sums of gold were being bought and sold amid wild excitement by men distracted by the fear of ruin or crazed by the hope of enormous gains. Everybody seemed to be trying to buy gold.

'Sixty for any part of five million!' screeched Speyers, forcing his way down through the crowd toward the pit. In an instant the pandemonium was hushed. The babble of voices died away. Men looked at each other and turned pale. They knew that Speyers represented Jim. There was no response to his bid.

'A hundred and sixty-one for five millions, or any part of it!' screeched Speyers, flapping his long arms and glaring around with brown, protuberent, bloodshot eyes. The hands of the big clock on the wall were drawing together toward noon. Nobody offered gold at sixty-one.

'Sixty-two for five millions!' yelled Speyers, who had reached the rail around the fountain, among men who glared at him like wild beasts. Still there was no response. 'Sixty-two and a quarter – three-eighths, for five millions!' screeched Speyers again. This time there was an answer.

'Sold! One million at three-eighths.'

The announcement was like an electric shock. Men's hearts stood still while they tried to guess what was coming next. The bold seller was James Brown, a Scotch banker, not a speculator at all. He was acting as we learned afterward, for a coterie of merchants and bankers. Speyers at first could hardly believe that his offer had been taken. He stood with open mouth for an instant and then lowered his bid.

'A hundred and sixty-one for any part of five millions!'

'Sold, a million at a hundred and sixty-one!' said Brown in the same, strong confident voice. Speyers tried again – 'One hundred sixty for five millions, or any part!' he cried.

'One million at a hundred sixty! Sold!'

Speyers turned paler, if possible, than he had been before. A shout went up from the bears. It was dawning upon them that the bull clique was being attacked in earnest. The triumphant and terrifying rise in the price had been checked; the bids had fallen three points; could it be that the bulge had ended?

Instantly, a dozen men rushed violently upon Speyers offering him gold. They expected him to retreat, but to their horror he stood his ground. Jim had told him to buy all the gold he could get at a hundred and sixty and he carried out the order. In two minutes he must have bought nearly ten millions of gold. The offers ceased. Maybe there had been a mistake somewhere. Maybe a trap had been set for them. The sellers fell back with a sickening misgiving in their hearts. There was a stir in the fringes of the crowd. New men were forcing their way into the room, yelling offers of gold. In an instant the news ran from wall to wall: 'The Treasury's selling!'

The paroxysm which this intelligence caused seemed to drive out reason. Instantly, everybody was offering gold and nobody was buying – that is, nobody but Speyers. He went out of his head completely. He kept on bidding a hundred and sixty for gold, regardless of the offers. A few people sold to him as the price dropped, a point at a time, with no halt or recovery, through fifty to forty. In fifteen minutes it touched a hundred and thirty-three. The corner in gold was ended. The bubble had burst, leaving behind a litter of shattered fortunes and broken lives.

Of course, the thing had to collapse some time and it was lucky for us it lasted so long. If we could have had that entire day we'd have gathered in about all the cash there was in the city; but as it was, we didn't do so badly – at least, Gould didn't

———♦———

President Grant got back to the White House on Thursday night and he sent for Boutwell before he went to bed. They talked about the gold situation and what the treasury ought to do. They were agreed that the government should keep its hands off while the struggle was confined to Wall Street and to the bulls and bears; but that it should act if gold went much higher. When Jim began bidding up the price next morning – Black Friday – telegrams began to pour in from all over begging the President and the Secretary to order a sale of treasury gold to prevent a crash in the business of the country. The President wanted to sell five millions and Secretary Boutwell thought that would be enough. The President left it to him and he went back to the treasury and wired General Butterfield to announce the sale of four millions and the purchase of four millions of bonds. He didn't code the message and it went over both the Western Union and the Franklin wires. I've always thought that Brown and his crowd knew in some way that the message had been sent; maybe Butterfield gave them the news; he sold gold himself. Anyhow, Brown's first sale of gold was made ten minutes before the message reached the Sub-Treasury and he had sold seven millions down to a hundred and sixty before the news broke and the bottom literally fell out of the market for gold.

I ran to Heath's office as fast as my legs would carry me and burst into the back room. Jim and Gould knew that something had happened. 'The market's gone to hell!' I cried. 'Gold's going down a damn sight faster than it went up!'

'Well! Well! What's the matter with it?'

'Nothing, only Washington's sold four millions!'

'The hell you say!' Jim shouted, looking at Gould. 'I don't believe it. It's a damn lie!'

'It's the truth, straight from Butterfield.'

'What do you think, Gould?' Jim demanded. Gould looked at him seriously.

'I think it's true.' He replied, slipping down from his stool. 'I've been expecting it.'

'But Corbin said – '

'He didn't know.'

'Then he's a damned rascal!' Jim exploded, getting red in the face. 'Here I've been depending on his word. If he's been lyin' to me, I'll knock his head off!'

Gould stepped to his side and took him by the arm. 'Put on your coat,' he said. 'I don't think there's anything we can do here, under the circumstances. Let's go up to the office.'

'I'm going to find Corbin!' Jim shouted. 'I'll break every bone in his carcass for him. He's ruined me and he's ruined a thousand more with his damn lies!'

'I don't think it's quite so bad as that,' said Gould persuasively. 'Never mind about Corbin now. You can attend to him later. I don't like to hang around here any longer than I have to. Put on your coat!' There was a sound of angry voices in the outer office and Jim understood why Gould was impatient. He put on his coat.

'You're right,' he said, regaining his coolness. 'Rabbits, you linger around here for a while and let us know what happens.' Gould had opened the back door and in an instant it had closed upon them. They went in the nick of time. The other door opened and James, office manager for Heath and Company, put his head in. 'They're gone,' I told him.

He entered the room and behind him pressed a score of excited men, filling the room with themselves and their loud talk. The guards didn't try to stop them.

'Where's the scoundrel?' one demanded.

'Lynch him! String him up!' cried another.

'He's a thief!' shouted a third; and then all hands joined in, telling each other and all who cared to hear, what they wanted to do to Jim and why. Nobody said a word about Gould. The whole business was landed on Jim's shoulders.

When they found that Jim had gone, they poured again into Broad Street, yelling and shouting threats like wild Indians. I followed after them, nobody paying any attention to me. It was impossible to tell who had failed and who hadn't. The streets echoed with curses and threats against Jim. Everybody seemed to be blaming him for everything – not only for the sudden skyrocketing of the price of gold, but its still more sudden fall. There was confusion and madness everywhere. I was glad my friends had not attempted to brave it out. With the mob in such a temper, they could hardly have escaped.

♦

I made my way back to the Gold Room and there I found Speyers, looking like the last rose of summer, still bidding a hundred and sixty for five millions of gold. Nobody was paying any attention to him. Jim's last order to Speyers had been to buy all the gold he could get at a hundred and sixty and this was all the man remembered. I took him by the arms and shook him. 'Stop bidding!' I cried in his ear. 'Mr. Fisk wants to see you!' He turned his fishy gaze upon me, his mouth opened, and he collapsed at my feet. He was through for the day.

There were many others like him – driven almost if not quite insane by the terrible strain and by their losses. Some of them blew out their brains; I wonder that the list wasn't longer. I went round to Jim's house and entered by the back way.

'Do they miss us down there, Rabbits?' Jim asked, looking up from his desk with a rueful grin. I told him what the situation was and that everybody seemed to be crazy. 'I can't say I'm surprised,' Jim said. 'Between you and me, they're tin-horn sports. If they win, all right; but God save us when they lose! When a man goes into Wall Street, son, he's got to learn to do both and keep his face straight.'

'How did you come out?' I asked.

'The Lord and Jay Gould are the only ones that know,' he replied. 'Neither of them is sayin' a word for publication right now. All I can say is that I bought twenty or thirty million dollars worth of phantom gold and it melted away. I'm satisfied to leave it all to Gould. He's got a great head for figgers and he knows somethin' about the law, too – always an advantage in times like these.'

———♦———

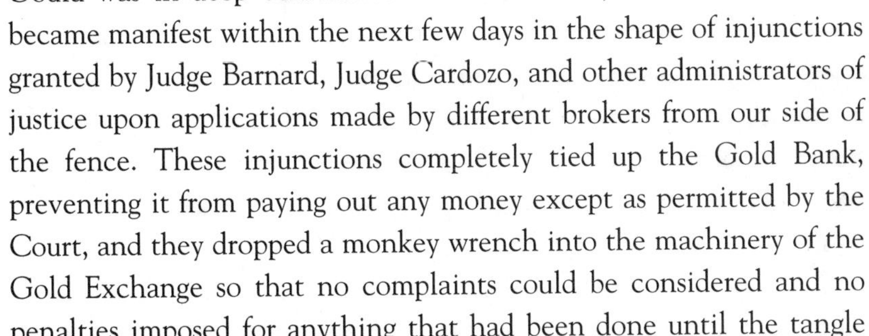

Gould was in deep conference with Shearman, the fruits of which became manifest within the next few days in the shape of injunctions granted by Judge Barnard, Judge Cardozo, and other administrators of justice upon applications made by different brokers from our side of the fence. These injunctions completely tied up the Gold Bank, preventing it from paying out any money except as permitted by the Court, and they dropped a monkey wrench into the machinery of the Gold Exchange so that no complaints could be considered and no penalties imposed for anything that had been done until the tangle had been straightened out. These legal measures gave time for private negotiations and understandings and the settlement of disputed claims out of court, so to speak.

There was a great howl when Jim produced Belden's letter which showed that his transactions had all been for Belden's account. Belden had failed and that left a good many people high and dry. They accused Jim of having repudiated his contracts. As Jim said, they were bad losers. They hated to be skinned at their own game and they never forgave Jim for having hung their hides on the fence, both bulls and bears alike.

Gould's resourceful tenacity saved every dollar that could be saved out of the wreck. After everything was over and done and the Garfield investigating committee of Congress submitted its report exonerating the President and his Cabinet from all blame, it turned out that he had clung to ten or twelve million dollars. He kept most of it; Jim, who had saved the day, got only a million or so out of it.

♦

Jim always insisted that President Grant had broken his promise not to sell any gold. He made no bones about charging complicity on the part of the President and prominent government officials in the operations of the clique. Toward the beginning of October, he sent for George Crouch, financial man of the *Herald*. He was then cooped up with Gould in the Grand Opera House where nobody could get to him without his consent whether to serve papers on him, beg for mercy, or shoot him. He gave George Crouch an interview which appeared in the *Herald* on October 8, two weeks after 'Black Friday.'

'You are aware, of course,' he said, 'that we have just passed through a great financial crisis. Everybody lays the blame on me. Now I've stood this just about long enough and I'm determined not to stand it any longer; so I'm just going to make a clean breast of it and expose the parties who got up the corner. I can make Rome howl at somebody else besides me – somebody you would never suspect of being connected with the affair.

'I do not deny that I was interested in the corner. Myself and my partner, Gould, were in the ring. Now, then, we are speculators. I had nothing to do with the concoction of the corner – it was all fixed before I was let into the secret. Now do you or does anyone else imagine that we should have risked millions, as we did, unless we had positive assurance that the government would not interfere with our operations?

'Of course we shouldn't. Well, then, I now tell you that we had something more than an assurance to that effect. Members of the President's family were in with us. The President himself was interested with us in the corner. That astonishes you, doesn't it?'

'Do you mean to say that President Grant was aware of the nature of your intended operations to bull gold?'

'Why, of course he was, and with him members of his family and parties holding high offices. And now I'll tell you how it originated and who started it. It was planned by Jay Gould and Abel R. Corbin, President Grant's brother-in-law. Why, damn it, old Corbin married into Grant's family for the purpose of working the thing in that direction. Corbin's next move was to secure his son-in-law's appointment to the sub-Treasury of New York, R. B. Catherwood, you know. Ultimately Corbin got Catherwood to withdraw in favor of General Butterfield on condition that Catherwood should have one-quarter of the profits. The first thing I did in the matter was to sound the President. I had several interviews with him on the subject and finally, with Corbin's influence, everything was arranged and we set to work.'

'What are you telling about it now for?'

'Because they went back on us and came near ruining us if we hadn't been smarter than chain lightning. We risked our millions on the assurance that the government wouldn't interfere. Grant got scared, however, when the crisis came, and gave Boutwell instructions to sell. And now I'll tell you what scared Grant. Kimber, a man who was in the pool with us, backed out at the last moment. He sold out and got short. Discovering that he had deceived us, Gould put up gold on him and broke him. Then Kimber leaked. Kimber's statement was telegraphed on to Grant and the result was Boutwell's order to sell. Now, up to the time when the government interfered with our operations I held in my hands the cards for fifteen millions, and should have made that if they had let us alone that day. But the crash came before I had made nine millions even.'

Jim testified later at great length before the Garfield Congressional investigating committee, but he didn't then charge the President with having gambled in gold. He did ask that Mrs. Grant and Mrs. Corbin be called as witnesses, but the committee didn't call them and in its report, while blaming Corbin and Butterfield, it denounced the effort that had been made to bring the President into the thing. My own opinion is that the President was ignorant of what was going on, but that Jim really thought he was in it.

♦

After the interview with George Crouch, Jim discussed it twice: once before the Garfield investigating committee's secret session in the basement of the Capitol, and once before a group of Washington newspaper correspondents. I got them together at the Willard so that they could ask Jim questions and give the people of the country whatever Jim would say about his appearance before the committee.

Before the correspondents Jim started with the initial words that passed between himself and the committee. 'In the first place,' he said, 'when I got downstairs, I called for the reading of their authority, my object being to see precisely what they were gunning for.

'Well, then General Garfield said, "Now you had better go ahead and state to the committee your version of the matter as you understand it, and when you are done, we will ask you what questions we please. What you will have to do is go into the history of the transaction." '

So Jim did. He outlined his connection with the Erie, mentioned Gould, explained in a few words the need of moving crops so that the road should get its legitimate business, and then told them about gold and how it entered into marketing our grain in Europe at a profit in the face of Mediterranean and Black Sea competition. All the time Jim was talking, Gould sat in the corner of the lounge and once in a while he put in a word to clinch a point, but mostly he listened as closely as any of the correspondents.

Then Jim told of the trip to Boston that the President, he, and Gould made on June 15, and how Gould and he tried to find out what President Grant's policy was going to be in the fall. The supper that Gould, Marston, and Jim gave Grant was their first real interview with him, and at that meeting it became evident that Grant then was on his march to specie payments and a lower price for gold. This struck Jim, Gould, and Marston like cold water.

'We went into an argument to convince him that something should be done to get off this crop at a high price – that it was his policy to sell gold at a high price for the foreign market. After we had been talking an hour and a half, he made one remark that I particularly remember: "It is well, gentlemen; the bubble might as well be pricked at one time as another," – as much as to say, "If we are to have a crash, it might as well be at one time as another." ' Jim stopped to laugh, and when he resumed his story, his smile was cunning.

'Our idea of crashes is to have it all milk and honey with us, and let the other fellow stand it. But – ' and he gave a comical sigh that the correspondents seemed to appreciate – 'Grant didn't seem to receive it quite that way.'

Then Jim talked of Gould's fear that Grant's policy would ruin them all, and showed how they got the notion that if matters were explained right to Grant, he might be induced to stop pursuing his theory. They tried to get together at Long Branch, but had no talk after all their effort. 'We wrote to Boutwell,' said Jim, 'that it seemed to be Grant's idea that he was traveling for pleasure. He didn't care to devote much time to business.'

Along in July, Grant was going by boat to Newport again. Gould wrote him a long letter, which Jim delivered to the President, and Jim went along on the boat and talked again with him. They arranged an appointment at Newport for the following Sunday. The first part of August, in the course of building the Paterson and Newark road, Jim and Gould got to know Catherwood, who married Corbin's daughter. Corbin, Gould knew before. Some time previously Catherwood had been mentioned as a possible assistant treasurer, but he probably was a little too near the family, and Gould and Corbin stopped backing him for the place and settled on Butterfield, who was appointed. Then Corbin got the notion that, through Butterfield, he could run the Treasury.

Of course, Butterfield felt under some obligation to Corbin, since he knew how he had come into the assistant treasurership. All of them decided that there was a lot of money to be made, especially by men who had their power of carrying. The whole country seemed to be set against gold going up. Gould talked a number of times with Corbin, Corbin with General Grant, and, once or twice, Gould with Grant. Corbin felt sure he could regulate the whole matter. 'That,' said Jim, 'was the beginning of this purchase of gold.'

At first Jim wasn't in it with the crowd. Gould and the others, financed mostly by Gould, bought about two million dollars' worth. Jim bought some at 137 on his own hook. Corbin told him that he, Corbin, had a million and a half of it and Mrs. Grant and General Porter half a million apiece. By the time gold got down to 131, about the fifteenth of September, Gould had what Jim called 'a pretty bag of it.'

'I said,' went on Jim, casting a smiling glance at Gould in his corner, 'Gould, if I had as much gold as you've got, and it stood me such a loss as I think it will stand you, I should think you'd invite all your able-bodied friends in to help bear the yoke.' The correspondents smiled, too. Gould, it seemed, was having a lot of talk with Corbin. But he didn't seem to want Jim in the deal with him and the others, Jim said.

Well, finally one day, Jim said to Gould, 'Have you got any understanding with Corbin, or have you carried out any of those theories with Grant that we talked about last July?' and Gould replied, 'Yes, there's no gold to come out of the government. We can put gold up to forty-five and I think we shall make money out of it, and we shall get our winter and fall transportation for our road. My idea is to go ahead.'

So Jim started to buy gold in earnest, but without any understanding about sharing Gould's loss or Gould his. With gold at 136¼, Jim bought what he felt he could carry. Gould had enough to sink a ship. With a letter from Gould, Jim went to Corbin and had a three-hour talk. Corbin told him things were going all right; that he had bought gold with Gould; that he had received and sent on to Washington a check for twenty-five thousand dollars; and that he was confident they were doing a great national good as well as helping the Erie's transportation; and that Corbin saw more money in the transaction than he had ever seen in his life.

This took them up to about September 21, the Monday or Tuesday before Black Friday. But, Jim said, he felt shaky about things. He kept needing to have his confidence renewed and Corbin renewed it.

Well, then Jim told of the trip William O. Chapin and I took to Washington, Pennsylvania, with Corbin's letter to General Grant, and how Grant took the letter out of the room with him – 'evidently as if to show it to Mrs. Grant or someone else,' Jim said – and how in about fifteen minutes Grant came back and said, 'All right,' and how we telegraphed, and the telegram read, 'Delivered. All right.'

On Thursday, Jim went round to see Corbin. Corbin said

everything was A-No. 1, that the letter had settled matters, and that the interests involved, national and otherwise, made everything safe.

That afternoon, with Gould and Jim buying through Belden's office, gold rose from 136 and five-eighths to 141. Part of the rise was due to the aftermath of a dinner the bears had given Boutwell. The evening papers carried statements that the government was interested and that there was a sharp, quick corner in gold, and that the government wouldn't sell. He went on to speak of the Belden letter, which played an important part in his own fortunes:

'Mr. Belden, who was then of the firm of William Belden, had seen so much gold bought for the last week that he made up his mind that we exactly knew our position or else we should not be caught in such a position as we were then. He said to me on the evening before Friday:

'Now, if you've got all this gold and you want any assistance, you'd better let me come in and help.'

'Said I, 'If you want to come in, we'll give you a hand in.'

'I haven't got time now,' he replied.

'I told him we would go to the back office at Heath's in the morning. 'I'll bring my broker in there,' I said, 'and you can give me a letter,' which he did. That letter was signed by William Belden and I understood that it gave me full, unlimited authority to make purchases and sales of gold during the day to any extent that I should deem advisable, and to report all such transactions as early as possible, with the understanding that the profits arising from the operations under such order' – Jim dropped into legal phraseology – 'were to belong entirely to Belden; and of course that he would bear the loss, if any should result, from the transactions for the day.

'On Friday morning Mr. Belden brought in one Speyers, introduced us, and said to me, 'Mr. Fisk, Mr. Speyers will execute any orders of mine that you give him.' And turning to Speyers, he said, 'When you've executed those orders you'll report to me.'

'Gold was then a hundred and forty-three and I said to Speyers that the sooner he was there, the quicker he'd get some of it, as it was then a little scarce.

'I told Speyers I didn't limit him. By the time he'd got out there, gold was sixty. He didn't see why, if gold would go up twenty or thirty in two or three minutes, it shouldn't go three hundred in half an hour, and so he commenced the assault on them at one hundred and sixty. Judging from what he told me, he got a pretty good lead on it at that.' This raised a laugh among Jim's hearers.

'That morning,' he went on, 'there had been an article in the *Times* in which the Administration was charged with being in league with us in putting up gold. Gould and I read it and we made up our minds that that article would be telegraphed to Grant and Boutwell. I looked right at it and it made me feel weak in the knees.

'We made up our minds that if it was laid on Boutwell's desk and on the table of the President, who had never speculated before this time, they'd be almighty weak. And, as I heard some ten or twenty minutes afterward, Mr. Boutwell went over to the Executive Mansion, and when he got back, there was a thunderclap struck us in the shape of a Sub-Treasury order to sell four millions of gold. I'd rather take forty millions of short gold than four millions of the real stuff!

'Speyers was meanwhile going it like sixty when the market caved right in. He – following what he thought was the right track, kept at one hundred and sixty.

'I saw him next without either coat or collar. He came right through the rooms saying "Mein Gott! Mein Gott! The whole thing's gone up! Mein Gott! I've got sixty millions at one hundred and sixty, and it is now one hundred and forty-one!"'

'We started uptown and the first thing I saw, on a bulletin board, was, "Queer pranks of the crazy brokers," and so on. We didn't know how it was; and of course, when we got uptown, we knew still less. We didn't know whether we were going to right or left. There never was any excitement like it!

'I'd got very bad by this time, and I said, "I'll step around and see this old villain Corbin, and see what he says about it."'

'I went into the house and the old man came down. I'll admit that I was pretty mad. When he got inside the door I said, "This is a pretty piece of business – you've set up to wipe us off the face of the earth!"'

'He said he'd only just heard of it! "I should think you might have heard it through the rumbling of the ground!" I said. "After giving you twenty-five thousand dollars more and after you had positively assured us that your message to the President, which our messenger took, had fixed the business – to serve us this way!" '

"Well!" says he, "my boy, how are you? How do you stand?"

"It looks as though we are ruined," I told him, "and we can't tell anything – whether we've got it, or somebody else has."

'I asked him if there was anything in the thing or whether the whole performance wasn't his own concoction. He stuck to his position, that he had done everything not to sell. After telling about seeing Mrs. Corbin several times, Jim went on: 'That is about the beginning and the end of the gold panic on the Black Friday of September twenty-fourth.

'The committee seemed very anxious to obtain from me whether any government official was connected with the affair. They repeatedly put this question to me: "Now, Mr. Fisk, will you state to the committee if any government officer was connected with you in the gold transactions in the City of New York?" "Now," said I "Mr. Chairman of the committee, I beg to tell you that I've told you under oath here exactly in what connection I consider the government officers of this country figured with me in that gold transaction."

'They were evidently trying to get out of me that no government officer was in it. Then they would make up their report that I said so. Every time they asked me the question, I said, "Gentlemen, I've stated to you the precise position in which General Grant stood which I derived from Mr. and Mrs. Corbin, and that is all the information you can get." I said to the committee that I had a great desire that they should examine Mrs. Grant and Mrs. Corbin – that I demanded it!'

4
Infatuation

The Commodore has Callers

The Commodore, with the aid and connivance of Drew and Eldridge, had got back out of the Erie the money he lost when he tried to buy a majority of the Erie stock in the open market and was tricked by Uncle Dan'l and Jim into swallowing a hundred thousand new shares fresh from the printing press. Jim thought it would be a good idea to sue him to get this money back so he began an action in December, 1868, after he and Gould had gained undisputed possession of the Erie.

David Dudley Field, his son, and Thomas G. Shearman conducted the legal proceedings. As a preliminary, Jim and Shearman called upon the Commodore and made a tender to him of the fifty thousand shares of stock that he had compelled the Erie to take off his hands. The suit which followed this formal tender called upon the Commodore to repay three million, five hundred thousand dollars that he had received in the settlement under the treaty, on the ground that it was illegal. Jim and Gould also filed suit against Work and Schell for the four hundred and twenty-nine thousand, two hundred and fifty dollars that had been paid to them under the treaty to recoup their alleged losses. While they were about it, they sued August Belmont for a million dollars which, they said, was the damage he'd done the Erie by suing its directors.

Finally, they brought a suit against Uncle Dan'l. They charged him with having bought Lake Erie boats from the railway company when he was a director years before and, after collecting from the company for services rendered to it by the boats, selling them back again to the company. They asked for the restitution of a million dollars for these characteristic transactions on the ground that they were fraudulent.

These proceedings all petered out as a result of a live-and-let-live understanding which was arrived at over legislation that both sides wanted. Jim and Gould wanted the Erie Classification Act to protect them against a possible loss of power in the board of directors. Vanderbilt wanted legal sanction for a stock dividend of eighty per cent on the New York Central and a bill that would permit him to consolidate the Central and the Hudson River Railroads. Each side withdrew opposition to what the other was after in Albany and each permitted the other to buy what it wanted from the legislature.

The origin of the classification idea I have already explained. Jim and Gould worked it for all it was worth. At the next election they put five dummy directors, salaried employees, into the board and created an executive committee of four members – Fisk, Gould, Lane, and Tweed which made meetings of the directors unnecessary. The executive committee was actually, of course, Jim and Gould. In its name, they ran the Erie.

Harlem Lane

I never knew a man who had greater confidence in himself than Jim had. He believed he could do whatever anybody else did, and he had a sneaking suspicion that he could do it a little better than the other fellow. That Jim succeeded in so many activities is proof of his ability and of the versatility of his active and tireless mind.

The completion of Central Park made trotting horses more popular than ever. No rich man was fully equipped unless he had a stable of fast trotters and knew how to drive them. Races upon which owners bet thousands of dollars were not uncommon. This was the kind of thing that Jim couldn't resist, especially as the Commodore was a conspicuous figure there. He and Josephine used to drive up there in his four-in-hand and then Jim would transfer to his trotting outfit while Josephine watched. Of course, Jim knew how to drive. He learned that when he was a boy, just as most of us did. But somehow he wasn't a success in Harlem Lane, I don't know why.

———♦———

It was well worth while to watch the crowds that gathered in Harlem Lane on fine afternoons. The road up there was filled with glistening horses and flashing coaches, buggies and all kinds of rigs, driven by their owners or by coachmen in livery. It was fun to watch the Commodore with his benevolent white hair, and his solid brother Jake, who didn't like him and didn't care who knew it. The financial sycophants used to get out of the Commodore's way and let him pass them, but Jake never did.

Robert Bonner, publisher of the *Ledger*, short, thick-set, with sandy hair and a cheerful countenance, owned the famous 'Auburn Horse' and the champion 'Dexter.' He and the Commodore were the leading amateurs of the road. William H. Vanderbilt, the Commodore's son and heir, and Frank Work, were rivals behind their trotters. 'Willie' was jealous to the tips of his flowing side whiskers of Work and there was a personal element in their trials of speed that gave them a special interest. Then there were Big Bill Tweed, not then known as a robber, George Baxter, three score and ten, like the Commodore, with the same patriarchal white hair and as rich as mud; John M. Tobin, a Wall Street rocket, thin, wiry, haggard; Frank Palmer, another patriarch, president of the Broadway Bank; Rufus Hatch, with a stylish team; Gould's partner Smith, tall, slim, sandy, and dozens of others. Even Gould had a fast pair of trotters but he didn't really care for trotting as sport; he went up to Harlem Lane because he thought it a good thing to be seen there.

In the horse world there was no coach that equalled Jim's. It was bright blue, with red running gear. That was a show! When the equipage went past with a load of pretty actresses, people stopped to stare. Jim was partial to this sort of turnout.

Edward S. Stokes

Jim first met Edward S. Stokes in the summer of 1869. Stokes was then twenty-eight years old, seven years younger than Jim. He was a handsome fellow, with black curly hair, black eyes, and a small black moustache. His manner was nervous and animated. He talked a blue streak. Wherever Ed Stokes was, in his opinion, was the middle of the stage. His thoughts ran mostly on racing and athletic sports. He was something of an athlete himself. He had a wide acquaintance among the horsemen and gamblers who made the Broadway saloons their hangout. Jim said he was a Philadelphian, and that he came of a good family.

Ed wasn't doing very well when he met Jim. Like many interesting and agreeable men, he could spend money faster than he could make it. He was always looking for a chance to get a fortune at one swoop, without working. Jim let him in on some Wall Street ventures in which he did well. It wasn't strange under the circumstances that he should tie up to Jim. He was around the Erie offices and the theatre at all hours of the day and night. If he wasn't in Jim's office, you'd be pretty sure to find him down in the bar-room on the ground floor of the Grand Opera House on the Twenty-fourth Street side. This branch of the establishment was intended especially for patrons of the theatre. Ed wasn't a drunkard but he liked a drink and he found in the bar-room the audience that he liked – men who could talk horse with him and that sort of thing.

I didn't take to him. With all his charm of manner, he didn't seem to me to be sincere. He treated me with indifferent condescension as though I were an outsider, when he took any notice of me at all. He was always careful about his dress. He carried this to the extent of dandyism, I thought; but Jim liked it. Jim liked clothes that attracted attention. It was a weakness of his. Ed was the only one of Jim's friends who always aroused my antagonism. His manner was so superior, so patronizingly rude, and his evident assumption of superiority to everybody else in everything, marked him as a spoiled child. He was selfish and vain and I noticed that if anybody happened to offend him, he would nurse a rancor that made him watch constantly for a chance to get even.

He had no conception of the value of money. He was even more of a prodigal than Jim and he spent every cent on himself, which Jim didn't. He was always borrowing from anybody who'd lend. His wasteful habits were known to his family, and his mother had reduced him to a small allowance after he had made a serious dent in her fortune, which wasn't large, after she became a widow.

There wasn't much love lost between Ed and his wife, although they had a pretty little daughter. They lived in the Worth House, at the corner of Fifth Avenue and Twenty-sixth. The story was that she fell in love with an employee of her father's and the old man wouldn't let them marry. He had some foolish idea that she could do better and he picked out young Stokes because of his society background, as the right match for her. I suspect that Ed married her more because he thought Southwick would make them a liberal allowance than because he cared much for her. He was so handsome that nine women out of ten, if they had been in her place, would have loved him; but she was in love already and that saved her. He became a man about town, as they were called – a well-dressed loafer – and she devoted herself to her little daughter.

♦

His mother, Mrs. Stokes, owned an oil refinery in Brooklyn. It hadn't been operated for some years and it was a good deal out of repair. She'd have been glad to sell it if anybody had made her a good offer for it, but nobody did. Ed told Jim about this refinery and Jim at once saw a chance to make money out of it.

'We'll form a company,' he said to his young friend. 'I'll be president and you can be treasurer. I'll furnish the capital to put the plant in working order and you get your mother to lease it to us. We'll pay her twelve thousand dollars a year. We'll bring in the crude oil over the Erie in tank cars at reasonable rates, refine it, and market the product.'

This was the plan that they carried out. The partners, with the advantage of low freight rates, and Jim's organizing skill, made money from the start. Ed began to give himself the important air of a successful business man of large affairs. He was insufferable! And he was so darn natty! His curls and moustache always shone with pomatum and he used to have his nails manicured every day.

Jim as an Impresario

After Jim got control of the Grand Opera House, he went into theatrical production with great enthusiasm. He had an idea that he could show the old heads how it ought to be done. It cost him a lot of money to convince himself that he didn't know everything about the drama. His theatrical plans were formed on a generous scale. While he was having the Grand Opera House done over with gilding and marble and frescoes, he bought the Boudoir Theatre on West Twenty-fourth Street and leased the Academy of Music at the corner of Irving Place and Fourteenth Street. The Academy was the largest theatre in the city.

He spent a lot of money fixing up the Boudoir Theatre and he made it so attractive that there was a great deal of talk about it. The bill at Pike's Opera House when Jim and Gould bought it with Erie money, was French comic opera. It wasn't a success and Jim took it off when he made extensive changes in the building. While this work was being done, he put Shakespeare's *Tempest* in rehearsal and produced it in the redecorated theatre with striking scenic effects. But it didn't pay. It had cost him thirty thousand dollars and he hated to take it off when he found that it was over the heads of his audiences, but he had to. He didn't have any better luck at the Academy of Music. There he produced the opera *Lurline,* with a competent company. When it didn't draw, he tried the experiment of having it sung in English one night and Italian the next, alternately. But he had to close the Academy doors after he'd lost twenty thousand dollars there.

The Boudoir Theatre was also costly to Jim. He put John Brougham, who had gained fame as actor and playwright, in charge there at first and called it Brougham's Theatre. After two months of bad business, he fired Brougham and changed the name of the place to the Fifth Avenue Theatre. Jim didn't get along with his managers. They were too temperamental for him and he for them. He couldn't work with Bergfeld or Tayleure any better than with Brougham, and his flare-up with Max Maretzek caused a sensation.

After trying English, French, German, and Italian companies in grand opera at the Academy of Music, he dropped that place of amusement by allowing his lease to lapse. He also abandoned the Fifth Avenue Theatre and leased it to another producer. He then concentrated on the Grand Opera House and had some success. He made money out of *The Twelve Temptations*, which he brought out in the winter of 1870. Jim varied its attraction by changing the ballet from blonde to brunette on alternate nights.

♦

It was Jim who made French opera bouffe popular in this country. He sent Maretzek to Europe with orders to get together a first-class company. Maretzek did a good job and brought back a company of capable actresses and 'leading ladies' enough to enable Jim to carry out an idea he had of giving the same part to three prima donnas in the same show – a different one in each act.

The trouble with Maretzek that made such a scandal was caused by the arrival of Christine Nilsson, who came here for a concert tour in 1870. Max had no contract with Jim, but he was rehearsing the opera-bouffe company. He was asked to conduct the first Nilsson concert. Jim heard of it and went up in the air. He looked upon the Nilsson company as a rival show, and he wrote a note to Max ordering him to keep away from it. He went to the concert to see whether his orders were being obeyed. There was Max conducting with all the assurance in the world. Jim foamed with rage, but he didn't do anything that night.

He gave instructions next day that he was to be notified as soon as Max showed up at the Grand Opera House for rehearsal. When he got word, he left his Erie desk and hurried down to the theatre, where he confronted Max among the actresses.

'What do you mean by conducting an opposition show when I tell you not to?' he demanded, with blood in his eye. 'You damn swindler! You thief! You liar! I'll show you who's running – '

Max interrupted at this stage by aiming a blow at Jim's nose. Jim ducked and they clinched. In a moment they went down amid the shrieks of the actresses and ballet girls. Stage hands pulled them apart. An inventory showed Max with a black eye and Jim with a rumpled shirt. That was the end of Max in Jim's productions. Jim was always in hot water in the show business. The theatre was no place for Jim. His talents didn't lie in that direction. But he hated to be beaten and, anyhow, he did give opera bouffe its start here.

♦

Josie's house was more Jim's home than his own lodging at No. 313 West Twenty-third Street, where he sometimes claimed a legal residence and where his negro valet, John Marshall, ruled, or Lucy's house in Boston, which was, after all, his real home. Jim took all his friends and associates to Josie's. Boss Tweed, Gould, Sweeney, Lane, and all of us who knew Jim well used to go to Josie's often. Jim and she gave a dinner there in the fall of 1868 to James McHenry, partner of Sir Morton Peto, the largest railway builder in the world. Boss Tweed and Fred Lane, two other Erie directors, were there. While Gould sometimes went to the house, he never went when he could avoid it. He didn't like Josie, and she knew it.

♦

There was a bowl of punch at Josie's on New Year's Day, 1870, and people were coming and going all day. Jim asked Stokes to drop in and he did. With much pride Jim introduced him to Josie but it appeared that he had already met her in Philadelphia, before Jim ever saw her. She was still Mrs. Lawlor then and Ed explained that was why, not having seen her, he hadn't identified her before.

A Hero to His Men

Jim was greatly admired by the employees of the Erie. But when there was a strike of brakemen and they made threats of violence, he sent Tommy Lynch up the line with a gang of New York toughs under orders to shoot down any man who offered resistance. This aroused great indignation among the strikers; but Jim himself followed Lynch, and the men he had ordered shot yelled and cheered him as soon as they saw who it was. This was a good example of his personal power over other men's minds.

In the public imagination it was always Jim who was running the Erie Railway. Gould occupied quite a secondary place. But in fact it was Gould who did the planning and Fisk who executed the plans.

Gould was content to let Jim have what glory there was, but he got and kept most of the profits. Jim made plenty of money too, but he didn't hang on to it. He counted on his ability to keep on making it.

♦

In the fall of 1870 Jim made a visit to the machine shops which the Erie maintained in Susquehanna, Pennsylvania. There were about six hundred mechanics there and quite a crowd of residents of the locality who had assembled to see the celebrated Prince of Erie. They watched him while he inspected the shop in his velvet coat and the velvet cap he wore while he was traveling. When he got through, they asked him for a speech and conducted him to a platform they had put up for the occasion. Jim climbed up there, took off his cap, and addressed the crowd.

'Fellow workmen and neighbors,' he began. 'I suppose you all read the newspapers. One day you may have inferred from what you read that this man Fisk was an angel from heaven; and on another day you may have read some other paper and thought that he was a devil from hell. Be that as it may, here I stand before you, plain Jim Fisk, either angel or devil, just as you choose to take me. Whatever I may be called, I'm a worker. I'm working and I have worked for the interests of the working men and of the public. I've worked for these interests untiringly and unceasingly. What was the Erie Railway six years ago and what is it now? You are the men who can best mark the vast improvement.

'Look at the improvements in your own workshops during that time and then judge of the time and money spent in carrying out the same kind of improvements along the whole line of the road. You mark the improvement of the road hour by hour, and you know how false are the impressions created by liars in white coats, whom God, for some inscrutable purpose, suffers to edit four-cent papers in New York!' There was great applause at this allusion to Horace Greeley, his famous white overcoat, and the *New York Tribune*, which had freely attacked the Fisk-Gould management of the Erie.

'You may not know, however,' Jim went on, 'that the author of these lies has eaten at the table of Cornelius Vanderbilt, and that these attacks are made in the interest of the New York Central and Pennsylvania Central Railroads. Were it not for the outrageous assaults of a portion of the press, backed by the influence and money of the competing lines who involved the road in an interminable series of lawsuits, we should have to-day a broad-gauge double track of steel rails from New York to Chicago, with the most comfortable cars and finest locomotives. The day is not far distant, however, when these will be accomplished facts! (Cheers.)

'I see before me men who, I will venture to say, are rising sixty years old, but who can't show as many gray hairs on their heads as can be found under the velvet cap that I wear. Sleepless nights and work that never ends are not your portion. Your homes may be humble, but your toil is over when you straddle the legs of your supper table. Don't think that all the work on this road is done at the vise and the lathe, for it ain't. The man who thinks that all Jim Fisk and Jay Gould have to do is to sit in a gilded office at one end of the road, and pass the time away by writing free passes and reading telegraph dispatches, has got a false impression.

'You enjoy your evenings in the presence of your families, while Jim Fisk and the heads of the road frequently spend the greater part of the night studying how to meet a debt of a hundred thousand dollars by noon the next day, when they don't know where to turn for twenty dollars; and all this, it may be, to feed you and your fellow workers. We have to study and work hard for your interests as well as our own, for our interests are combined! (Loud cheers.)

'I have been connected with the management of this road for some years, and this is the first time that I have enjoyed the privilege of meeting you. (Cheers.) You have my best wishes and shall have my best efforts for your welfare. If any of you ever come to New York, and I can assist you, I shall be most happy to see you. Good-bye!' (Loud cheers.).

Colonel of the Ninth

The title of colonel really belonged to Jim. The Ninth Regiment of the New York National Guard had come to a low ebb in 1870. It had only three hundred men and it was in debt besides. It occurred to somebody that Jim, with his love of gold lace and his bank account, would make a fine colonel. He was elected by the officers of the regiment on April 7, 1870, at a meeting presided over by General Varian, commanding the Third Brigade. Lieutenant-Colonel Braine, a veteran of the Civil War, who was devoted to the regiment and had been acting as its colonel, resigned to make way for a rich man who could get it out of its troubles.

Jim certainly enjoyed his military position and he made the most of it. In May, he invited the entire regiment to the Grand Opera House to see *The Twelve Temptations*. The guardsmen marched in, five hundred strong, with Jim dressed in a gorgeous uniform at their head, and with the band playing its loudest patriotic airs. The audience applauded; free champagne was poured at Jim's expense; it was a proud occasion.

Jim gave a prize of five hundred dollars to the company that should have most names on its roll on July first. On that date the strength of the regiment had risen to seven hundred men. They went into camp on August 20 for ten days at Long Branch. Out of compliment to his friend, Jim christened the camp 'Camp Gould.'

Another grand occasion came in February, 1871, when the regiment gave a ball at Jim's Academy of Music in Fourteenth Street. Society, with a capital 'S.' was conspicuous by its absence; but probably the hundreds who were there had a better time on that account.

———♦———

Jim took it into his head to show himself to his former acquaintances and associates in Boston as the commander of a military organization. He made up his mind to attend the celebration of Bunker Hill Day, Boston's chief celebration, on June 17, 1871, and he wrote to Mayor William Gaston a letter of introduction for a committee which he sent to Boston to confer with the local authorities there about the proposed trip of the Ninth. Jim asked that the 'hospitality of the city be extended to the Regiment.'

Jim's name was to Bostonians what a red rag is supposed to be to a bull. They hated, despised, and feared him all at the same time. His disregard of all that they held precious, his ignorance of the things that they regarded as necessary for all human beings of intelligence to know, and his genuine indifference toward them stuck in their crops.

Jim's innocent request that his regiment be received – and him with it – aroused derision all along the Back Bay and in the offices of the newspapers which depended on the Back Bay for their advertising and their patronage. The mayor didn't reply to the letter. He referred it to the Common Council, where it was made the subject of a debate filled with acrimony. The public attitude was reflected by the *Boston Advertiser*.

'The action of the Colonel of the Ninth New York Regiment,' it said, 'in asking for an official reception of this corps by the city of Boston, marks a new era in the history of effrontery. Such compliments are generally supposed to be tendered by the host rather than asked for by the guest!'

This treatment made Jim all the more determined to parade with his regiment in Boston on Bunker Hill Day. He therefore wrote to the governor asking permission to parade and the governor gave it as a matter of course. Thereupon Jim wrote to Mayor Gaston again telling him he was mistaken in supposing that he'd ask any favor of the City of Boston, that all he wanted was permission to parade, and he had it.

Jim asked the city to let him use the Common for a dress parade on Saturday and for a religious service on Sunday. The request was refused as though it had been an insult. Jim then wrote to the mayor of Charlestown asking if he could use Monument Square, in which Bunker Hill Monument stands, for his Sunday services. The aldermen of Charlestown refused this request on the ground that it would attract a crowd and create confusion, thereby causing the Sabbath to be broken. Very devout – Charlestown!

The regiment reached Boston on Saturday morning and was received with military honors by one of the Boston regiments. This rather relieved Jim's feelings, and he threw out his chest. The regiment took part in the celebration of the day and it was cheered all along the line of march. By this demonstration the great unwashed of Boston signified scorn for the Brahmins. In the evening, the band gave a concert on the Common, which attracted a crowd of thousands.

The next day it rained, so that Jim couldn't have worshipped out-of-doors anyway. He promptly hired the Boston Theatre and brought the regiment to it in omnibuses in the afternoon. He sat on the stage in full uniform with the chaplain. The theatre was packed with the Boston public. Jim was the best-advertised feature of Bunker Hill Day that year. The band played, the chaplain prayed and preached, and then Jim, in his glittering regalia, rose to speak. Great applause! He seized the opportunity to reply to the mayor and the common council which had been so merry at his expense, and through them to the blue-bloods of the Back Bay. He came back thick with honors.

♦

Jim's victory over the Boston Mutual Admiration Society was followed by a military experience from which he was lucky to escape with nothing worse than a sprained ankle and some wounds in his vanity – both painful, but not necessarily fatal. This occurred when the Orangemen attempted to parade on July 12, 1871, to celebrate their victory in the Battle of the Boyne. This parade was regarded by the Irish Catholics as a deadly insult; and it was, in fact, so intended. The Catholics promised to obliterate all Orangemen who should attempt to revive the shameful memory of what took place on the banks of the Boyne, and to demonstrate how much difference there was between the Irish river and the Hudson.

There were enough of them in the city to make good their threats. On Boyne Day of the preceding year the Orangemen had had a picnic in the woods up near Ninety-sixth Street, and they were attacked there by a gang of Irish Catholics who were working nearby. The picnickers were mostly women and children, who fled into Central Park and wherever they could find refuge, while the men made a stand. On this congenial occasion several were killed outright and many were wounded.

The affray caused a great outcry in the newspapers and pulpits. They demanded that the religious liberty guaranteed by the

Constitution should be upheld. When threats against the Orangemen were made in 1871, therefore, they aroused the strongest kind of protest from editors and clergymen. Mayor Hall and the superintendent of police attempted to avoid trouble by refusing to permit the parade. No doubt they were pusillanimously right; but Governor Hoffman took a different view. He didn't propose to allow New York to be dictated to by a mob. He came down from Albany and took personal charge of the turbulent situation. He ordered the militia, including Jim's regiment, to get ready, and soon after midnight, in a fever-heat of public expectation, he issued a statement from Police Headquarters in which he said:

'I hereby give notice that any and all bodies of men desiring to assemble and march in peaceable procession in this city to-day, the twelfth instant, will be permitted to do so. They will be protected to the fullest extent possible by the military and police authorities.'

♦

I was in Newport on July 12. I had gone there with some papers that Jim wanted Lucy to sign and I knew nothing about the street fighting until I saw the big scare stories in the papers next day when I got off the Fall River boat. These said that more than fifty people had been killed. I found out at the Opera House that Jim was in Long Branch and I went down there to find him. Sergeant Henry E. Page and Sergeant Sam Wyatt, of the Ninth, were in the list of dead, and Private Walter Pryor was among the mortally wounded.

Jim was in the Continental Hotel and Mrs. George Hooker, his half sister, was with him. He was propped up on pillows in a chair, with a bandaged foot and leg extended in another chair in front of him.

'I don't believe I was cut out for a military life,' he said gloomily, 'I ain't built for it, for one thing, because I can't run fast enough; and I haven't got the heart for it, for another. We ought to leave all our home fighting to the Irish. They'd rather fight than eat any time, and the more of each other they can kill off, the better they feel about it.

'There was a story going around that a big crowd of Orangemen was going to come across from New Jersey on the ferry and I told the governor about that. I advised him to order the boats to be stopped if they should try any such trick and he gave me authority to stop 'em. He said he expected he'd have enough to do to protect New Yorkers without trying to look after any Jersey orphans.

'I got down to the armory before eight o'clock next morning and I was there until I got word from the Opera House that a lot of men were coming over on the ferry. I went up to the Opera House, telegraphed to McIntosh and he stopped 'em.

'The orders were that the procession was to form at two o'clock behind two hundred and fifty police. A messenger came up from the Armory to the Opera House to tell me that my men were forming to get in line and I started down there on foot. The streets were jammed with people. I'd got almost to Twenty-fourth Street when they began to hoot and yell. I took to the middle of the street. I went on a ways further until I came in sight of the Sixth. The crowd was closing in behind as I went along, yelling like the devil. All of a sudden something whizzed past my head and I heard a shot. I got into the Sixth and kept on until I came to my own regiment.

'I sent a man to the Armory for my coat and sword and while I was waiting for the dry goods, I borrowed the Major's sword and took command. The parade started to move. Bricks and stones began to come our way and shots were fired. The orders were that the men were not to shoot unless they were shot at and that they were to pay no attention to stones and that sort of thing. If the crowd began shooting, they were to fire back without waiting for orders.

'Well, we stood everything until Pryor was hit in the knee by a bullet and Harry Page was shot down. I was standing close to him when he fell. We could hear volley firing up ahead and when Page and Pryor went down, my men opened up on the mob. We were marching a little ways behind the Sixth. The crowd on the east side of Eighth Avenue pushed in between and ran over us. I was standing there with Major Hitchcock's sword in my hand. Before I knew it, I was knocked down and trampled on and the regiment was scattered. A few of the men saw me and rallied around.

'When I tried to get up I found my foot was hurt so I could hardly stand on it. They carried me into a bakery, which was close by, on the west side of the avenue, and took me upstairs. They got the doctor for me, and he found that my ankle was out of joint. They took hold of it and yanked it back into place and then they went away to look after the wounded.

'I hobbled over to the window with Captain Spier. The avenue was full of Irish all swearing and fighting. Page's body lay where he had fallen and two of my men were standing guard over it. I saw the mob close in around them and one man lunging at them with a sword-cane. Then they caught sight of me. A big Irishman, with a hand on him like a ham, began to point up at the window. 'Here's that damn Colonel Fisk!' he yowled. 'Let's go up an' kill the bastard!' They made a push towards the door and I saw it was no place for me. I grabbed a heavy cane to help me along, somebody gave me an old coat, and I skinned out the back door.

'I guess I must have climbed over a dozen backyard fences before I got to the middle of the block. I thought it was safe there to come out into the street; I went through a house and looked back towards Eighth Avenue. The mob was still there, crazier than ever. What was worse, there was another mob coming down towards me from Ninth Avenue. I thought I was a goner.

'I made a quick survey of the landscape. I was in Twenty-seventh Street, halfway between the two avenues. On the other side of the street I saw a door that stood open and I managed to slip into it without being seen. There was a passage that led through to the back yard and I followed it. I stopped long enough to rub some dirt on my face as a disguise. The Ninth had killed a good many while it was defending itself and I knew they were after me to make an example. There was a high fence around the yard I was in, but I found a barrel to climb up on and I got over into the next yard. There were more fences and I don't know what else. At last I was so used up that I couldn't go any further and I made for an open door. Just as I was going to go in, somebody slammed it in my face. I looked around, saw a cellar window open, and crawled in there. The first thing I heard was 'Who the hell are you?' As soon as I could see, I made out a big, red-headed Irishman. He looked like Terence Burke who used to chase us when we were boys up in Bennington.

'Ain't your name Burke?' says I, just to break the ice. 'That's none o' your dom business' says he. 'The police are after me,' says I. That touched his heart. He gave me a drink and lent me an old pair of pants and an old hat and let me out into Twenty-ninth Street.

'The coast was clear. The mob had followed the parade into Twenty-third Street. I don't think they'd have known me any longer if they'd seen me; but anyhow I thought the best thing I could do would be to get a hack. There was one coming towards me and I hailed it. The man stopped. Just as I was getting in, I saw Gould inside. He didn't know me. His eyes got big like a scared cat's and he yelled to the driver to go ahead. "Hold on a minute!" says I. "Do you mean to say you don't know me, your own partner?" He looked sharp at me. "Is that you, Jim?" he says, sort of weak. I got in and he kept looking at me as though he didn't quite believe it was me after all. I'd had troubles enough. I couldn't go back to my regiment with the clothes I had on and I decided to come down here. I got a hack and that took me to the Pavonia Ferry, where I found one of our tugs. I went aboard of her and she took me to Sandy Hook. I came down here in the cars. I never took off those clothes till I got here.' Jim was pretty well scared that time. I think this experience sickened him of military doings. After it he was less active than he had been. His last appearance at the head of his regiment was on November 21, 1871.

♦

The results of the Black Friday disaster were felt for quite a while. After the crash speculation in gold didn't amount to much. The tangle was so involved that not all the lawyers in Wall Street could straighten things out. Jim and Gould simply put up the shutters and retired into the fastnesses of Castle Erie – the Grand Opera House. There they made settlements with their debtors and disputed the claims of their creditors.

Jim insisted that Speyers was acting for Belden and not for him and he refused to be responsible for the gold that Speyers had bought, especially for the purchases he had made at one hundred and sixty when gold was selling at one hundred and forty or less. All kinds of tricks were tried to serve legal papers on Jim in suits that were brought against him. Threats of personal violence were made against him by losers who'd been ruined. In view of this situation, Jim organized a patrol which ranged the sidewalks around the Grand Opera House and kept people moving.

Corbin disappeared. It was said that he had retired to Kentucky. After all had been said and done, I think that both Jim and Gould made money, Gould probably three or four millions and Jim perhaps a million, though I believe less than that. In spite of my efforts to keep the newspapers aware of Jim's good side, it got to be rather the fashion to speak of him either as a reprobate to be frowned upon by all good men, or as a mountebank. For this attitude, Jim himself was mostly to blame. He wasn't particular about the enemies he made.

When Chicago was swept by fire on October 8 and 9 of the next year, Jim took the lead in providing relief. He not only made generous cash donations but he had the officers and higher employees of the Erie Railroad and of the Narragansett Steamship Company raise money for the victims of the disaster. He had his six-in-hand hitched up and he drove it around the city collecting donations of food and clothing in the glittering drag, which was usually filled with his actresses. He put with others these supplies aboard an Erie train and rushed them to the sufferers in record time. But this activity didn't stop the jeering and jibing any more than his work in Boston for the wounded Union men at Antietam was remembered there when he wanted to parade on the Common with the Ninth Regiment.

♦

Another thing that hurt Jim's reputation was his intimacy with Boss Tweed and Tweed's Tammany accomplices. The Tammany Ring was beginning to go too far. The revolt of Sheriff Jimmy O'Brien in 1870 because Tweed wouldn't renominate him, and the attacks of the *New York Times*, were taking effect. Tweed was hand-in-glove with Jim, who had made him a director of the Erie, and they were tied up together in several business enterprises of a profitable sort.

Tweed had to pay for everything he got. They blackmailed him right and left. The 'Black Horse Cavalry' was organized in the legislature in Albany – a band of members who wouldn't vote for anything he wanted unless they were paid. Votes sold for from five thousand dollars each up to forty thousand. The Tweed charter cost him a million dollars in Albany. He got it all back, of course, out of the city treasury, and a great deal more. It was a good investment, but it drew attention.

It was hard to tell in those days who was honest and who wasn't. It looked sometimes as though nobody was above robbing the city if they got a chance. A list of eminent citizens, headed by Moses Taylor, sent a petition to the legislature in the spring of 1870 'to give to New York city a symmetrical and honest local government.' But it wasn't this guileless request, it was Tweed's million that got the charter through. He told Jim after the session that he'd had to give one man six hundred thousand dollars in cold cash for distribution before he could get the votes he needed. 'You ought to have sent down here for Gould,' Jim told him. 'He got our job done for us for a hundred thousand less than that.'

Jim had become a full-fledged Democrat. He attended the Tammany political meetings as well as the balls and social events of the Tammany leaders. He was a speaker at the Tammany ratification meeting on October 27, 1870, when Boss Tweed went to the Democratic rank and file for vindication. The reception that Jim got in Tammany Hall that night was like the reception he had in the Boston Theatre from the citizens there. Whatever he said or did, the common people never failed to cheer and admire him.

Light-O'-Love

Nobody could help liking Josie. She was always perfectly placid, for one thing. She made you feel that she was enjoying life, like a good-natured comfortable cat. Her face didn't show any sign of the experiences she had been through. She didn't talk about the past, as a rule. She seemed to have forgotten it. She hated disagreeable things. But one day, when I'd gone to her house to meet Jim, he was late and we sat talking while I waited for him. She told me something about herself.

This was in the Spring of 1870. What she told me about her engagement to James Carter and subsequent elopement, marriage and divorce from Frank Lawlor and her general feelings towards Jim made me feel uneasy on Jim's account, though I couldn't tell exactly why. I got the impression that Josie wasn't so bound up in him as she had been and I knew that it would almost kill him if she should quit.

♦

Jim had put Stokes on his feet. The arrangements under which the Brooklyn Oil Refining Company was operated made money and gave Ed a good income. He paid his mother twelve thousand dollars a year for the use of the property and the company allowed him twenty-seven thousand a year rent for it. The connection with the Erie was of great value to the company because the Erie gave rebates on the crude oil which it brought in and that enabled the company to undersell other refineries.

As I have said, Ed hadn't any idea of the value of money. He began to regard himself as a financial genius. He treated the refinery as though it belonged to him alone. He took advantage of his position as treasurer, to draw thirty-two thousand dollars out of it in the first four months. He wasted this money in various kinds of riotous living, but chiefly in betting on trotting races.

Jim remonstrated with him. He saw that Stokes hadn't any business head and by reorganizing the company, making it a corporation, he tried to fix things so that Ed couldn't steal any more money. Under the new plan Ed became secretary. But this didn't improve matters much. Ed managed to draw out thirty-seven thousand dollars more in the next six months. The fact that he needed the money was all the justification he thought necessary.

♦

While outwardly Stokes was as much Jim's friend as ever, I believe he was jealous of him and at heart his enemy almost from the beginning. Ed was stuck on himself. He couldn't bear to play second fiddle in anything. He believed he was better than any man he came in contact with and it secretly enraged him not to have everybody admit it. Jim had picked him up and put him on his feet, but it wasn't long before I ran across a story in the lobby of the Fifth Avenue Hotel that it was Stokes who was the benefactor and not Jim – that Stokes, having built up a prosperous business in refining oil in Brooklyn, had taken Jim in with him so that Jim might make some money through rebates at the expense of the Erie Railroad. I thought this reversal of the facts was a singular thing and I followed it up until I located Stokes himself as the author of it. I told Jim about it, but he only laughed.

When he didn't make headway in proving himself to be better than Jim was in business sense, Stokes turned his effort toward superiority in another direction, to a field where he was undoubtedly the better man. He began to pay court to Josie.

♦

Having got a home for herself, Josie began to consider how she could get Jim to endow it, so that she could feel herself safe for the future. Considering the large amounts of money that were passing through his hands, it seemed to her that a settlement wasn't an unreasonable hope. But Jim never had much of a surplus on hand. Besides, it was a pleasure to him to feel Josie's dependence on him from day to day. She understood how the land lay with him, but she resolved to try. She opened her campaign in the fall of 1869 and by January, 1870, it had reached a pitch of intensity where some decisive action was called for. She finally told Jim that unless he'd settle twenty-five thousand dollars on her, all was over between them. He put her off until, at the end of the month, she wrote to tell him that she would see him no more. She expected that this step would bring him to time, but it didn't.

Jim was in the habit of sending her notes from time to time, usually a hasty line with money that she wanted. She kept almost everything he wrote and eventually it was published. When he got her farewell letter, he wrote to her on February 1, a Sunday evening, as follows:

'My dear Josie – I received your letter. The tenor does not surprise me much. You alone sought the issue and the reward will belong to you. I cannot allow you to depart believing yourself what you write, and must say to you, which you know full well, that all the differences could have been settled by a kiss in the right spirit, and in after days I should feel very kindly towards you out of memory of the great love I have borne for you.

'A longer letter from me might be too much of an advertisement of my weakness, and the only great idea I would impress on your mind is how wrong you are when you say I have grown tired of you. Wrong! Wrong!'

Josie kept up the bluff for a week or two, but Jim held out and before long, she allowed him to persuade her to let bygones be bygones and begin afresh.

♦

Stokes first went to Josie's house with the infatuated Jim. Then he began to go there alone. He'd drop in to lunch or at odd times. Marietta Williams, Josie's cousin, was there too. She was a perfect foil for Josie – a pink and white blonde, with a turned-up nose, blue eyes, and vivacious manner. She had been married in Boston and she was discreet. I never knew where her husband went to, but he wasn't in sight anywhere.

There was a good deal of wax in the placid Josie's nature. Ed's conquest of her wasn't difficult. It could hardly be called a seduction. I think I know about when the event took place. It was along toward the middle of June, in 1870. Josie's warm skin took on a richer flush and her slatey, dark eyes began to have a dreamy look that I hadn't seen there before. Stokes at the same time became, if possible, more offensive. He stuck out his chest, fondled his little black moustache, dusted his patent leather shoes with his silk handkerchief, and laughed more loudly than usual. Of course, I didn't know anything positively and I didn't say anything to Jim. If a man is a fool to push in between husband and wife, he's a positive jackass to interfere between a man and his mistress.

♦

Jim didn't say a word to me, either, but he found something out before very long. He kept his troubles to himself. His love affair with Josie had been frowned upon by all his friends. Most of us had urged him to give her up. The thing had become known and the veiled allusions to it that the newspapers printed from time to time had made talk and brought a new special disrepute upon him that was different from the unflattering reputation he had already acquired by his financial doings. The fact that he had theatres had already aroused suspicions as to his morals. In those days all actresses were supposed by the godly to be prostitutes. So the general public easily believed the whispers about Jim's having a mistress and promptly gave him six.

When he found out about Stokes, Jim began writing letters to Josie. They explain just how matters stood between them. For instance, he had remonstrated with her and she had replied by reproaching him with making love to some of the actresses that he took out in his six-in-hand drag. She knew well enough that his idea in driving up Fifth Avenue with these women was to advertise his show but she had to have some answer and that's what it was. This was late in July, 1870. He wrote to her on August 10:

'My dear Josie,' he said, 'I cannot come to you to-night. I shall stay in town to-night, and probably to-morrow night, and after that I must go East. On my return I shall come to see you. Loving you, and *none but you*, I am, yours, ever, James.'

He drew a line under the words 'none but you' to assure her that her reproaches about the actresses had no foundation. He had told her that after two days he was going to Boston. But his jealousy prompted him to set a trap for her. Stokes was in Saratoga and had planned to go from there to Buffalo, following the races. Jim's next letter shows plainly enough what Josie did as soon as she thought his back was turned. It was written on August 14, four days after the other.

'Dear Josie,' he wrote, 'I found on my arrival at my office that the following dispatch had passed West last night: "E. S. Stokes, Buffalo and Saratoga Springs. Pay no attention to former dispatch. Come on first train. Rane." Of course *it means* nothing that *you are aware of*. But let me give you the author of it and my authority, and you will see how faithfully they have worked the case out after my departure last evening. Miss Peiris drove directly to Rane's office; from there to the corner of Twenty-second street and Broadway, where the above dispatch was sent, and from there to Rulley's. A third party was with them, but who left them there. Rane and Peiris – why should they need Stokes? What have I done that Nully Peiris should work against my peace of mind?

'P. S. Since writing the within, I understand a dispatch has reached New York, that he is on his way. James.'

Nully Peiris was among Josie's friends. She quickly came over to Jim's side of the fence knowing which side her bread was buttered on, and she told him things that made him ask Stokes to keep away from Josie's house. This appeal, which Jim made to Stokes as to a friend, not doubting that it would be heeded, filled Stokes with joy. He had won the victory he wanted. Jim admitted it by asking him to keep off.

'Ask me anything else, Jim,' he replied. 'Anything else in the world, I'll do; but I can't keep away from Josie. I love her – and she loves me!' Jim was struck all of a heap by this assurance. At first he didn't know what to say.

'I don't think it's fair, Ed, to take advantage of me like this,' he replied at last. 'You know I introduced you to Josie as my friend. Friends don't steal each other's sweethearts or wives – at least, they don't do it in Vermont, where I came from.'

'I knew her before you did, you know.'

'Maybe; but you didn't make love to her then.'

'I can't do it, Jim; you know what a woman she is. You ought not to ask me.'

'Very well,' said Jim shortly, and he turned his back. That was the end of their friendship.

Nobody who knew Jim would have expected matters to rest there, and they didn't. In a few days, Stokes got notice as secretary of the Brooklyn Oil Refining Company that the contracts between the company and the Erie Railroad, under which the company got its Pennsylvania crude oil cheap, had been abrogated. Then Jim sent him a proposal that he either sell out to the other stockholders his interest in the company, or buy them out. He made it plain that he didn't care for Ed as a business associate any longer.

Ed proposed to buy. He and Jim agreed on the purchase price, but the other stockholders didn't want Jim to get out and they refused to consent to the plan. Stokes asked Jim to meet him at Delmonico's to talk things over. This restaurant, which then was at Broadway and Chambers Street, was a favorite eating place of Ed's. Jim went there and of course their talk turned to Josie.

Stokes had a definite plan when he asked Jim to meet him. He wanted to get back the Erie contract. He thought Jim would make it a condition that he should let Josie alone in future, and that's just what Jim did do. Ed was ready. 'I'll tell you what we'll do,' he said. 'Let's leave it to Josie. If she says she'd rather have you, all right. I'll get out and stay out. But I don't see why this thing should interfere with business.'

'All right,' said Jim. 'I've got to attend a drill of the Ninth. I'll meet you at Josie's at half past ten.'

Jim hadn't seen Josie for several weeks. He had remonstrated with her because of what Nully Peiris had told him about Ed's visits, and she had countered with a renewal of her demand for a settlement. Jim had sense enough left to know that his hold over her, if he had any, was due to her need for somebody to support her rather than to affection and that if he made her independent of him, she would be saying good-bye. He reasoned that his only chance lay in getting Stokes to keep away. Then, he thought, Josie would come back and everything would be all right. He had really quit when Stokes proposed to leave it to Josie and he accepted with the idea of settling matters definitely, once for all.

Josie received him with friendly placidity, as though nothing had happened and invited him to have a glass of wine – his own – that she and Stokes were drinking. The thoughts that went through his head must have been unpleasant. 'Well, Josie,' he said when they were seated. 'I suppose Ed's told you what we're here for. Which of us is it to be?'

'You know I like you both,' Josie ventured.

Stokes leaned back in his chair and sipped his wine. He said nothing, but there was a faint smile on his lips as he watched the other two.

'I don't see why we can't all three be friends,' said Josie in her caressing voice, looking from Jim to Ed, and from Ed to Jim.

'No, Josie, it won't do,' Jim said positively. 'You can't run two engines on the same track in contrary directions at the same time!' But Josie refused to choose between them. In Josie's presence Jim's love for her returned. His eyes filled with tears when he begged her to come back to him and love him as she had at first, when they were both so happy. Ed's smile became more pronounced as he listened; but still he kept silence. Finding that he could get no decision from her, Jim rose to go.

'I'm through, Josie,' he said, 'I'll say good-night and good-bye at the same time. As for the Erie contract,' he added, turning to Stokes, 'I'll see that it's reinstated.'

He left Stokes in possession of the field. When he went to bed that night he flattered himself that he was done with nonsense and he was surprised to find that a weight was off his mind. He slept like a top.

It wasn't so very long before Josie wanted money. Stokes couldn't or wouldn't give it to her, so Josie's thoughts veered to Jim. She missed him and she turned on Nully Peiris for having told him about her. Nully wrote her a letter in which she explained what she thought of Josie. Josie pretended to believe that Nully had had the aid of Mlle. Montaland in composing this letter and she seized the opportunity to reopen negotiations with Jim by writing a complaint to him about it. As a matter of fact, Ed's interest in her wasn't quite so keen when she told him she had to have money as it was when Jim was paying the bills. He had even been borrowing from her.

Jim ought not to have answered Josie's letter. Any disinterested friend would have advised him not to if he had asked for advice, but he didn't. To tell the truth, he was still in love with her, and the bitterness of what he said in his reply betrayed him in every line. No 'Dear Josie,' simply 'Mrs. Mansfield.'

He began with some scornful remarks about her suggestion that Montaland had helped Nully to write the letter.

'But what think you of a woman who would veil my eye; first by a gentle kiss, and afterward, by deceit and fraud, lead me through the dark valley of trouble, while all this time I showed her nothing but kindness both in word and actions, laying at your feet a soul, a heart, a fortune and a reputation? But the mist has fallen, and you appear in your true light.'

Jim wasn't much on rhetoric, but he managed to get his meaning across. His letter shows how he loved her.

'I am aware that in your back parlor hangs the picture of the man who gave you the wall to hang it on, and rumor says you have another in your chamber. The picture upstairs send back to me. Take the other down, for he whom it represents has no respect for you.'

Then he invited her to continue the correspondence, infatuated as he was!

'If there are any unsettled business matters that it is proper for me to arrange,' he said, knowing that she must be hard up, 'send them to me and make the explanation as brief as possible.' He signed himself

'James Fisk, Jr.' without even a 'Yours truly.' Josie read his heart where he had exposed it so fully between the lines and she made haste to reply, as she knew he hoped she would, addressing him by the name he had signed, 'James Fisk, Jr.'

'I will send you the picture you speak of at once,' she wrote, 'the one in the parlor I will also dispose of. I know of nothing else here that you would wish. I am anxious to adjust our affairs so I write you this last letter.

'You have told me very often that you held some twenty or twenty-five thousand dollars of mine in your keeping. I do not know if it is so, but that I may be able to shape my affairs permanently for the future, that amount would place me in a position where I never would have to appeal to you for aught. I have never *had one dollar from anyone else*, and arriving here from the Branch, expecting my affairs with you to continue, I contracted bills that I would not otherwise have done. I do not ask for anything I have not been led to suppose was mine, and do not ask you to settle what is not entirely convenient for you. After a time, I shall sell my house, but for the present, think it best to remain in it. The money I speak of would place me where I should not need the assistance of anyone.'

A soft answer – no signature at all. She knew Jim. And no reference to Stokes except that he hadn't given her any money.

This correspondence began on October 1, 1870. Jim's reply was dated October 4. He didn't use any form of address at all.

'I wasted time enough to read over once more your letter and I determined to reply to it for the reason that, if it remained unanswered, you might possibly think I did not really mean what I said when I wrote, and suppose that I had somewhat repented of the course I had taken, or of the words I had penned. It is to remove any such impression that I again write to you, as I would have the language of my former letter and the sentiments therein expressed, stamped upon your heart as my deepest opinion of your character. No other construction must be put upon my words.'

Jim seems to have lost completely in those letters, and for the first time in his life that I know of, his semi-humorous way of treating even the most serious things.

'I turn over the first page of your letter,' he continued, 'I pass over the kind words you have written. Have I not furnished a satisfactory mansion for others' use? Have I not fulfilled every promise I have made? Is there not a stability about your finances to-day (if not disturbed by vultures) sufficient to afford you a comfortable income for the remainder of your natural life?

'You say you have never received a dollar from anyone but me, and you *will never* have another from me until want and misery bring you to my door, except, of course, in fulfilment of my sacred promise, and the settlement of your bills up to three weeks ago, at five minutes to eleven o'clock.

'You need have no fear as to my sensitiveness regarding your calling on anyone else for assistance. You may well imagine my surprise at your selection of the element you have chosen to fill my place (Stokes). I was shown to-day his diamonds, which had been sacrificed to our people at one-half their value, and undoubtedly, if this were not so, the money would have been turned over to you, that you might feel contented as to the permanency of your affairs. You will therefore excuse me if I decline your modest request for a still further disbursement of twenty-five thousand dollars. I very naturally feel that some part of this amount might be used to release from the pound the property of others in whose welfare the writer of this does not feel unbounded interest.

'You say that you hope that I will take the sense of your letter. There is but one sense to be taken out of it, and that is an "epitaph" to be cut on the stone at the head of the grave in which Miss Helen Josephine Mansfield has buried her pride. Instead of trying to answer this letter from your disorganized brain, or writing from the dictation of those around you to-day, simply take a piece of paper and write on it, the same as I do now, "Dust to dust, ashes to ashes Amen."'

This dramatic advice slid off the placid mind of Josie like water off a duck's back. He had offered to pay her bills up to the minute when he had abandoned the field to Stokes; and so she sent them to him. His valet, John Marshall, told him that she had instructed one man, Bassford, to change the dates of purchases so as to make him pay for things she'd really bought after their separation. He accused her of this when he sent her the money to pay for what he regarded as his fair share of the bill, and in his exasperation he added – 'I had supposed you "honest" but I find that a trace of that virtue does not even cling to you!'

It was there that he put his foot in it. Josie came back with indignant denials. He felt that he might have wronged her by his suspicions, and like all generous men, he exaggerated his possible offense out of all proportion. He made haste to apologize in a letter that he sent on October 20, addressing her as 'Madam.'

'You know I would not wrong you,' he wrote, 'and I would take back all my acts when there could be a shadow of doubt that you were right and I was wrong.

'I sent John to Bassford's and they told him that the dates of the bills should not be changed. But what does it matter whether it is so or not? I cannot *feel* you would do it, and something says to me: "This was one of the things she was not like." So I pass it by, and if the letters of last night or to-day are not like me, you can wash the bad act out from your memory and leave but the one idea – that I want to do my duty and fulfill every unsettled relic.

'We have *parted forever*. Now let us make the memory of the past as bright and beautiful as we can; for on my side there is so little to cherish that I cling to it with great tenacity and hope from time to time to wear it off. You know full well how I have suffered. Once you knew me better than anyone on earth. To-day you know me less. It is the proper light for you to stand in. It is all you desire on your side. It is all you deserve on mine.'

Before he signed this letter with his initials he said 'I am yours ever, etc., etc.' and he added to it the following postscript:

'I would have liked to have answered your letter in full, but, as you say, I have not a well-balanced brain and I know I could not do justice to a letter of that kind, so refrain and content myself to let the sentiments of it "know and fret me."'

———♦———

On the strength of this display of relenting, Josie got Jim to come to see her. She told him she was sorry for all the pain he had suffered; she didn't see why they couldn't keep on being friends. I think she was truthful in this – she actually didn't see why they couldn't. She appreciated all he had done for her, she told him. She hoped he wouldn't think so harshly of her. She was ready to give him all he had ever had from her again. The result of his call was another love letter, written October 25, without any 'Madam,' or 'Dear Josie.'

'Why should I write to you again?' Jim began. 'There comes another and another chapter until I get weary with the entire affair. I would forget it, and no doubt you would the same. Who supposed for an instant that you would ever cross my path again in a spirit of submission and with a contrite spirit! You have done what you should be sorry for, and I the same for permitting it.'

Jim talked from his heart with Josie, but he wrote to her from his brain. He knew what he ought to do, but try as hard as he might, he couldn't get resolution enough up to do it.

'You acted so differently from your nature that I forgive you,' Jim continued, 'and you even went so far as to bring my mind to bear on how I could take you back again. First the devil stood behind, and my better reason gave way for the moment, and I came away, telling you I would see you no more. When your better character comes in contact with mine, we are so much alike that much of what is said, like last night, had better have been unsaid.

'All now looks bright and beautiful, and my better nature trembles at ideas that were expressed last night. But that I should have left on your mind an idea that you could control me, is erroneous. You have gone out from one element and have taken another (Stokes) and for you to turn back, either when you are situated that way, or when even you could say that element had gone, should make no difference to me. It was you that took the step and you should and shall suffer the consequences.

'You might suppose you could love two, and perhaps more, elements and make them hover near you. Certainly you did last night and – for shame! – I was one of them! But it will *never* occur again! For once, let us be honest. You went that road because it looked smooth and pleasant, and mine looked ragged and worn. Now, a mistake cannot be found out too soon. I can see you now as you were last night, when you talked of this man, and do not deceive yourself –

you love him! Cling to him. Be careful what you do, for he will be watchful. How well he knows *you cheated me!*

'And now, as I know precisely how you stand from your own lips, I will treat him differently. Although you would not protect him, I will. While he is there, and until his memory is buried forever, never approach me, for I shall send you away unseen. Ever be careful that you do not have the feeling that you can come back to me, for there is a wide gulf between you and me. I would not hold a false hope out to you. I shall not trouble you more in this letter. You have the only idea I can express to you. You know when you can see me again, if ever.

'The risk for you is too great. Loving, and suited as you are, cling to him for the present, and when your nature grows tired of that, throw him off. Don't begin plotting to-morrow. Take tomorrow for thought, and be governed by this letter, for the writer has much of your destiny in his hands.'

———♦———

This was the longest of all his letters. It shows that he understood perfectly what Josie's character was – a light-o'-love, who never could be satisfied with one man, or even one man at a time. It's easy enough to understand Josie but it isn't so easy to understand why Jim didn't treat her for what he knew her to be. Everybody knows that attachments like his are not uncommon. Jim was no fool and no weakling. He knew he ought not to love Josie but he couldn't help loving her. That he tried to break away from her – that he used all his willpower to escape, and couldn't, is equally plain. The only explanation that can be given is that it was his fate that his love for her was stronger than he was; and of course, that explains nothing; it's merely a statement that it was so.

But Josie understood quite well how the land lay. Stokes had no money. She saw that he didn't love her; that he was capable of loving only himself. I think that they agreed together that Josie should go back to Jim.

She told him that Stokes had left forever, that she was through with him for good and all – and Jim took her back.

5
Disaster

Stokes Collects Money

When the year 1871 began, Jim was almost thirty-seven years old. Josephine acknowledged twenty-three and was really thirty-one. Stokes was nearly thirty. His wife and daughter had been sent to Europe by her father to avoid his neglect and escape his insults.

Stokes moved to the Hoffman House in July and proceeded to enjoy himself as a grass widower. He didn't have to make much of any change in his routine. He was always wanting money and always trying to win it by gambling, when he had anything to bet with. Finding himself, as usual, short of cash around New Year's Day he went to the Devoe Manufacturing Company on January 7 and collected twenty-seven thousand, five hundred dollars, which he appropriated. It was Brooklyn Oil Refinery money. He boasted of this theft among his friends, from whom he did not attempt to hide his venomous jealousy of his benefactor.

As soon as the other stockholders in the oil company found out what he had done, they got out a warrant for him, accusing him of embezzlement, and he was arrested in the Hoffman House on that same day, which was a Saturday. He was kept in jail over Sunday and bailed out on Monday. He spent his time spreading a story that he had been arrested, not for theft, but because Jim was jealous of Josie's love for him. The case was heard by Judge Dowling, who dismissed the complaint against Stokes on the ground that, while the Brooklyn Oil Refining Company was a corporation in form, it was in reality a partnership and, under the law, the appropriation of company money by a partner didn't constitute embezzlement. A good many people, not knowing very much about it, believed that he was a victim of Jim's supposed malice.

♦

Fortified by this interpretation of the law, Ed next seized the refinery, put eighteen men on guard there, and had a secret pipeline laid to draw off the oil from a tank that held fifty thousand dollars' worth of it. He planned to convey this oil to the tanks of another refinery. Jim got wind of this clever piece of knavery and he sent a hundred men across the East River in the quiet hours of Sunday morning. They attacked the refinery, battered their way in, threw out the Stokes defenders, and took possession. Stokes felt foolish. He tried three times on Sunday to regain his foothold, and each time he was repulsed. Jim held the fort.

♦

Both sides knew that the business couldn't very well be carried on under such conditions. Jim and Byers, treasurer of the company, reopened negotiations to buy Stokes out and get rid of him. He needed money, as usual, and he finally agreed to get out if they would let him keep the twenty-seven thousand five hundred dollars that he had collected from the Devoe company and pay him fifteen thousand dollars more, with an additional six thousand dollars for his mother. He got the money and gave up his stock in the company. With this payment he had taken a hundred and thirty thousand dollars out of the concern in two years, which wasn't so bad considering that his mother supplied the plant and Jim furnished all the capital, besides running the business.

Boss Tweed's Downfall

Boss Tweed and his Tammany Ring were having everything their own way when the year 1871 dawned upon a changing world. It didn't look as though anybody could shake him. We didn't understand so clearly then that the newspapers – the reasonably honest ones – are the real rulers in this country. Most of them were with the Boss. The Republican *Tribune* admired him and the *Sun* even proposed, perhaps ironically, that a subscription be started to build him forthwith a memorial as a public benefactor. Tweed had sense enough left to squelch this project. But the *Times* had convinced itself that he was a thief; all that it needed to convince others was some proof. The Boss and the rest of them felt secure, but they worked hard to make themselves more so.

♦

Jimmy O'Brien, a sandy-haired, loose-lipped professional public servant, had been sheriff of the County of New York. In those days, this was the richest office in the city. But Jimmy couldn't keep money. At the end of his term he didn't have a dollar left, but he had something else and that was a claim against the city for three hundred and fifty thousand dollars. Boss Tweed said 'no' and Jimmy turned against him. That was in 1870. He was energetic, and he had a good many friends in politics and they set on foot a new Democratic organization that they called the Young Democracy. It started with a rush. Its leaders were Tammany men and they had votes enough in the Tammany general committee to force Tweed to call a meeting, as he was bound to do when a certain number of members signed the request. If this meeting had been held, it would have put Tweed out as boss. He had his friend, Police Commissioner Henry Smith, forbid the meeting on the ground that it might cause another riot, and with this breathing space, he went to Albany and bought the votes to put through the Tweed charter, which made him supreme and saved him for the time being. It cost him a million dollars cash. But he had to buy off Jimmy O'Brien after all.

The sheriff had a man named Copeland put into a job in Comptroller Connolly's office for the purpose of getting proofs of thievery that he could use to blackmail the Ring. Copeland did copy some suspicious figures, but he was fired before he got all that Jimmy wanted.

Samuel J. Tilden, who was showing hostility to the Ring, took it into his head that he wanted to go to the state assembly from Jimmy's district and Jimmy consented. O'Brien then sent word to Tweed that he could control Tilden and he promised to divert him if Tweed would buy his claim against the city. He said he'd pay the money back as soon as the city paid him. At first the Boss wouldn't listen; but he changed his mind and finally bought half the claim for cash. He had to borrow the money. Connolly bought the other half. Jimmy never called off Tilden; he couldn't. However, everything continued to look rosy. It was 'business as usual.'

The Ring was making ready to provide itself with a valuable set of respectable accomplices by paying the Viaduct Railroad the five million dollars that the legislature had authorized it to convey to that corporation out of the city treasury, when Watson, one of the leading padded-bill go-betweens, went out sleigh-riding in December, 1870. He was smashed up; in a week he was dead, and his death sealed the fate of the Tweed regime.

Watson had risen to be one of the chief workers in Comptroller Connolly's office. His job when he died was given to Stephen C. Lyons, Jr., who was already on Connolly's payroll, and the vacancy caused by the promotion of Lyons was filled by the appointment of Matthew J. O'Rourke as county bookkeeper. O'Rourke was of a literary turn and he'd been writing stuff for one of the newspapers. He had noticed that the city was paying enormous rents for National Guard quarters. When he got into the finance department of the city, he found out that these payments were really money that was being stolen and he copied the records which showed it. He tried to sell this information here and there, but the newspapers turned up their noses at it until he got around to the suspicious *Times*. George Jones, who owned that paper, saw in it the proof that he had long wanted to get hold of, and he bought it. On top of this the *Times* purchased the evidence extracted by Jimmy O'Brien's man Copeland from Connolly's books. It hired O'Rourke to write up the Ring, and O'Rourke cut loose early in July, 1871.

He showed that in three years, the Ring had paid a million a year to a paper called the *Transcript*, owned by Tweed, and to the New York Printing Company, which Tweed had formed. He charged that three and a half millions had been spent for repairs to the Tweed courthouse – enough to put up and furnish five such buildings – and that the firm of Ingersoll and Company in two years had actually received five million, six hundred thousand dollars for furniture and carpets for the same courthouse. The other newspapers promptly rushed to the defense of the Boss and the Ring; but O'Rourke's figures carried more weight than all the sarcastic comments of rivals. He had the goods.

The Boss didn't rise to the occasion. When a reporter asked him what about the court house, he replied by putting his famous question: 'Well, what are you going to do about it?' That reply set all the journalistic tin pans and cowbells going harder than ever.

♦

The city got pretty well stirred up. Tilden and other Democrats who had sense enough to get in out of the wet, called a mass meeting on September 4. William F. Havemeyer presided and there were no less than two hundred and twenty-seven vice-presidents and fifteen secretaries under the umbrella with him. Among them were a number of the Viaduct Railroad crowd. Joseph H. Choate, a Republican, offered a resolution which created the famous Committee of Seventy.

Filled with zeal for reform, the committee proposed to descend upon Connolly's office and seize the vouchers which would reveal rascality. But when they went to get the vouchers, they couldn't find them. The incriminating documents had vanished overnight. 'Burglary!' yelled the Ring, but it came out that they had been burned in the attic of the City Hall, where the comptroller's office was in those days.

When the ashes were discovered, Mayor Hall loudly demanded the resignation of Comptroller Connolly. Connolly said the way to get him out was by impeachment and conviction. He refused to vacate without those formalities. But his worst fears regarding the intention of his friends to make a scapegoat of him were soon confirmed and on the advice of Havemeyer he appointed Andrew H. Green deputy comptroller and gave him the run of his office. By doing this, he turned the tables. Mayor Hall tried to make out that he had resigned, but that didn't work.

The mayor then tried another tack. He announced that 'the gross attacks of a partisan journal upon the credit of the City should be answered by a full report from a Committee of Citizens.' He expected the same kind of report that the Stewart committee had made and he was surprised and pained when the committee, on October 27, made a report in which it found that the city debt was being doubled every two years; that three million, two hundred thousand dollars had been paid for armory and drill room repairs costing a quarter of a million; that eleven million dollars had been paid for work on the courthouse that was worth less than three millions; that similar discrepancies appeared in the payments made for lumber and printing; that the payrolls were stuffed with loafers 'whose services were neither rendered nor required' and finally, that warrants and vouchers had been altered and payments made on forged endorsements. The lid was off!

♦

Jim had been opposed to the appointment of the Mayor's committee. 'You've got too many enemies against you,' he told the Boss. 'There are some very smart gentlemen among them. The best thing you can do is to pack up and get out.'

'We've got the courts,' Tweed said; 'we've got the city, we've got the Governor, and we can have the Legislature when we want to buy it. I don't see a damn thing to get scared over!' But Jim was right. There were some long heads in the opposition. Tilden saw that the Tweed domination of the Democratic party in the state was certain to be overthrown and that the party would be wiped out unless it got in first and cleaned house. He also saw that the man who led in the housecleaning would inherit the leadership. He made up his mind to be that man.

Connolly was persuaded that Tweed, Hall, and Sweeney were going to unload on him and that he ought to save himself. He wasn't a smart man and he agreed to do what Tilden advised.

Mayor Hall's demand for Connolly's resignation marked the first crack in the Ring. Connolly knew then he'd been thrown overboard and sought refuge with the enemy. Sweeney took account of stock and came to the conclusion that Tweed was doomed. But he had a cunning brain and his way to safety was devious.

John Foley, a citizen, started a suit on September 7, 1871, against the city to prevent the audit or payment of any more claims. He named Mayor Hall, Comptroller Connolly, Tweed, and Sweeney specifically among the defendants. He filed his complaint before our friend Justice Barnard. That worthy jurist issued an injunction which brought the Ring to its knees because it cut off the supply of funds. Tweed had made his property over to his family and when Barnard slammed the doors of the city treasury, he didn't know where to turn. He was indignant about Barnard.

'The damn fool thinks he can get out with a whole skin!' he fumed to Jim. 'He's got an idea, even, that he's going to be governor before he gets through! He knows damn well that Foley can't sue without the consent of the attorney general. He's making his own law as he goes along. But he might as well be right. We're broke and if we had to depend on borrowing a nickel, we'd starve to death! Pete's as much cut up over it as I am.'

Pete was Peter Sweeney. Nobody ever found out exactly, but there are reasons for believing that it was Sweeney who inspired the Foley suit and who got Barnard to issue the injunction by dangling the governorship in front of his nose. It looked as though the proceeding would send Connolly to jail, and maybe the mayor and Tweed besides. With attention thus diverted, 'the Squire' – Sweeney – might find a loophole for escape.

There was a great outcry against the injunction. The pay of an army of city employees, the cohorts of the Ring, was stopped. Incited by the Tammany leaders, feeling ran high against reform. Women and children, who were innocent, were being made to suffer. It became necessary to modify the order so that salaries and wages might be paid and money borrowed by the city for this purpose, and Justice Ingraham did it.

Tweed determined to seek vindication at the polls for himself and his associates. There was to be an election on November 7 to choose a new legislature, state officers, judges, and aldermen. He felt sure of victory. His supporters rallied around him.

———♦———

The Committee of Seventy had Mayor Hall indicted in October. It also indicted Tweed and had Charles O'Conor made a deputy attorney general to prosecute him. O'Conor was assisted by William M. Evarts and Wheeler H. Peckham. His bail was fixed at one million dollars. Then came the election. The Boss used all his resources, but the battle went against him, even with the Republican aid that was freely given. It was a body blow; but he himself was re-elected to the senate by nine thousand majority. The enthusiastic declaration of his followers in the Fourth District had meant something.

Sweeney resigned his office of president of the Park Board on November 1. His brother Jim had been indicted and had fled to Paris. The 'Squire' was also indicted and he skipped to Canada, whence he proceeded to Paris to join his brother, who later died there.

'Slippery Dick' Connolly was heartbroken when he was indicted. He had resigned his office on November 20, so that Andrew H. Green might be appointed in his place. He understood that immunity had been promised him by Tilden and he continued to visit his office. He was arrested there by Sheriff Brennan – who was no friend of his – on November 25. Tilden said he was 'surprised' although, like Tweed's, the arrest was made on the strength of an affidavit he himself had signed. Bail was a million dollars. Connolly offered to settle for that sum and the offer was refused. O'Conor wanted half a million more. Mrs Connolly, when she heard that, remarked 'Richard, go to jail!' and he went. He got out on the last day of the year, under bail for a million, and went to Europe. He had about six million dollars. He never came back, and a later decision of the Court of Appeals that his arrest had been illegal made his bail worthless. 'Slippery Dick' was lucky.

My friend Mayor Hall was another lucky one. He was put on trial. A juror died and he was tried again. This time the jury disagreed and they let him go free. He lived to a ripe old age, always charming, enjoying life, and practicing his profession as a lawyer in the city.

After his brother's death, 'Squire' Sweeney came back and settled with the state for four hundred thousand dollars out of his brother Jim's estate. That fixed him up all right.

But Boss Tweed was punished. His downfall was fast. He was indicted for felony on December 16 and released on five thousand dollars bail by Justice Barnard. He resigned the office of Commissioner of Public Works. Everybody was against him. He was tried. The jury didn't agree and he ran away to California. He was fool enough to come back to stand trial again, and this time he was convicted. Justice Noah Davis sent him up for twelve years. The Court of Appeals let him out after he had served one year.

As soon as he got out, he was arrested in a civil suit and held in three thousand dollars bail. The warden let him go to his home in Fifth Avenue for dinner and he fled to New Jersey, where he hid in a farm house behind the Palisades. Then he moved to a fisherman's hut near the Narrows, called himself 'John Secor,' and visited Brooklyn. In a schooner he fled to Florida and got to Cuba in a fishing smack. There he was recognized, but he got on board the *Carmen*, a Spanish barque, which took him to Vigo, Spain. In Vigo he was arrested on an identification made possible through a cartoon of Thomas Nast's and delivered to the American man-of-war *Franklin*, which landed him here on November 23, 1876. They put him into Ludlow Street jail, and there he died of diabetes on April 12, 1878. He lies buried in Greenwood Cemetery.

Ceda Talks to Jim

Not long after Jim had been persuaded to take Josie back, Ceda came down for her winter visit. She was very much upset when I told her what I knew about what was going on. I didn't know the whole truth because Jim's letters to Josie hadn't yet been published.

'That Mrs. Mansfield will get Jim into some serious trouble yet,' she told me. 'She's treacherous; do you suppose it would do any good for me to speak to Jim?'

'I don't think it would,' I said. 'We all have, but it hasn't changed him any. He knows he's a fool about Josie; but then, you might try; it can't do any harm.'

'I guess I will,' said she. 'I shouldn't feel satisfied, somehow if I didn't.' The next day she carried out her intention and Jim, I think, appreciated her anxiety for him and her motive in trying to reason with him; but it had no result.

Ceda was overcome by his weakness. I think almost all women, and a great many men, can't get over the feeling that people can do what is good for them if they only want to. 'But I should think he'd *see* what she is!' Ceda remonstrated when I had laboriously tried to explain all this to her. Jim understood it. He knew what was the matter – and he couldn't save himself.

Jim's Triumph at Bennington

Some matter of business took Jim to Albany early in August and he got it into his head to attend the Ninety-fourth Anniversary celebration of the Battle of Bennington, which was fought on August 13, 1777. He hadn't been back there since he used to drive his famous four-in-hand peddler's wagon through the town.

This trip was Jim's only return to Vermont during his lifetime. He had left the state a young man, poor, vigorous, ambitious, to seek his fortune, and he had found it. The Benningtonians showed more real interest in Jim than they showed in the politicians who were there and the guests who had been invited to orate to them. Jim did plenty of handshaking at the tavern.

A stand had been put up on the hill where the battle was fought, and copiously draped with flags. Somebody got Jim a seat on the platform. He was the center of observation of the townsmen and farmers, who looked at him and wished they had his money. The committee and the more refined persons who sat with Jim on the platform, didn't seem to notice that he was there.

The orator of the day was J. K. Herbert, who did the subject spread-eagle justice in a manner that aroused his hearers to loud enthusiasm. Music by the band followed, but the populace didn't disperse. Instead they raised a cry for Jim, who, after some hesitation – not much – rose and stepped forward. It was noted that, as he advanced, Governor Seth B. Hunt, Governor Stewart, and other gentlemen present, moved to the rear of the platform, got into carriages, and were driven away. This may have been a coincidence. At any rate, it didn't trouble Jim any. The audience had remained.

'Fellow-citizens of Bennington!' he began, and there were cheers. 'Fellow-citizens of Vermont! Fellow-citizens of New York – of everywhere and all creation! (Cheers.) I thank you for this compliment, which I shall always esteem as one of the proudest relics of my life! (Cheers.) It is some years since I have visited this place and I come back to it with pleasure, for it was here that I made my first trade – of a jack-knife! (Applause.)

'I started out in life here; and if I have succeeded in any degree, it is because I have shown something of the spirit of the men who fought at Bennington. 'Up, boys, and at 'em!' is a good motto for everybody! (Loud cheers).

'My career has perhaps been a varied one; but I have always tried to do right. Whenever I have failed in that direction, it was because of circumstances which no man could control. But, as I have said, I am glad to be here and to celebrate with you the day that is so memorable in the history of old Vermont!' (Loud and prolonged cheers.)

That was a day of triumph for Jim in spite of the loftiness of the 'better element.' The same thing had happened in Boston when he went there on Bunker Hill Day. It always happened when the rank and file were able to show their admiration.

♦

A great many thousand shares of Erie stock had been sold in England to buyers who expected it to pay dividends. When they didn't get any, they grew restless and finally combined with outsiders in this country to form an Erie Stockholders' Protective Association. The exposure of the Tweed Ring's stealings from the city was made much of by our enemies in Erie to bring discredit and distrust upon us. Boss Tweed and Squire Sweeney were dropped from the board of directors. They themselves saw the necessity for it. Perhaps this wouldn't have done any harm if the Erie hadn't had to borrow money by selling its bonds; but it had to get money to pay for the permanent improvements and extensions that were being made.

At this stage of events, Gould began to talk things over with William Butler Duncan, a broker who was interested in straightening out the twisted affairs of the Atlantic and Great Western Railroad, which was owned in England. Duncan knew what the feeling was there against the Erie management.

'You can't sell any Erie bonds over there until you've cleaned house,' he told Gould. 'You might as well make up your mind to that. You've got to get rid of Jim Fisk, first of all, and then elect a new board of directors that will show there's been a complete new deal. Put in the right men, and you won't have any trouble selling your bonds.'

Gould turned this proposal over in his mind and he consulted with Levi P. Morton, banker and afterward governor. The final result was that, on December 11, 1871, he wrote a letter to Morton and Duncan in which he proposed to reorganize the Erie board of directors by procuring the resignation of the board then in office and substituting a new board which he named. This new board was headed by himself and it included August Belmont, John Jacob Astor, and representatives of all the trunk line railroads. Gould suggested that 'the permanent organisation of the company be selected by Messrs. William Butler Duncan, Levi P. Morton, and myself.'

♦

Jim's name wasn't mentioned anywhere in this letter. Gould proposed to leave him out in the cold. He knew what Jim had done and was doing to build up the Erie. He knew that Jim had ventured every dollar he had in the world in the perilous operations that ended in Black Friday, and that he owed his own escape from ruin to Jim's boldness and skill in forcing up the price of gold and keeping it there until he could get out of the trap he had got himself into. But Gould didn't say a word to Jim about his negotiations with Duncan and Morton until everything had been agreed to and Duncan was on his way to England to get the English crowd to accept the plan.

Coming as it did on top of his troubles with Josie and Stokes, the knowledge that his reign as Prince of Erie was ended and that he was about to be ousted from the offices that he had fitted up and decorated, seemed, all things considered, like a blow below the belt. Gould explained that they had reached the end of their rope and that something radical had to be done. He tried to show Jim that the change in Erie didn't mean the end of their partnership, and that he'd make more money outside than in. Jim listened to him; but he knew well enough that Gould had decided to drop him in order to save himself.

'All right,' he said at last. 'If you've got the heart to ask me to get out, I'm through.' His voice sounded heavy and discouraged and tired. Gould looked at him with his inscrutable black eyes as Jim put on his hat and went out; but he said nothing more. Jim had trusted him completely; if he hadn't – but the events of the next few weeks make speculation foolish. They changed everything.

Stokes Wants More

Stokes soon lost or spent the money he had received for his share in the Brooklyn Oil Refining Company. He had to have more. The easiest way to get it that he knew of was to get it out of Jim's pockets, using Josie as an accomplice. He had no serious difficulty in getting Josie back. She simply couldn't resist him. Her promises to Jim went overboard with scarcely a qualm. An affidavit was made in October by Richard E. King, who had succeeded John Marshall as handy man in Josie's establishment when Jim made Marshall his valet. One of his duties was to wait on the table.

'When I went to live at the house of Mrs. Mansfield,' he swore, 'I was told to keep away from John Marshall and all Mr. Fisk's party, and Mr. Fisk, and have nothing whatsoever to do with them, and that that was a condition of my keeping my place. When I went there to live, I found that Mr. Stokes and Mrs. Mansfield were living there together as man and wife. They occupied the same room when they retired at night, and in all respects conducted themselves toward one another as is customary for married people to do.

'The principal subject of conversation between Mrs. Mansfield, Mr. Stokes, and Mrs. Williams, who I believe is a cousin of Mrs. Mansfield, was the manner in which they proposed to make money out of Mr. Fisk by means of letters from him to said Mansfield, which she said she had, and statements by said Mansfield of conversations between Mr. Fisk and herself, by selling the same to newspapers, or compelling him to pay them money to prevent the same from being made public, and they said they could get a large amount of money out of Mr. Fisk in that way.' These were the letters that Jim wrote to Josie. I have given some of them already to show how overmastering his love for her was. King went on to explain in his affidavit that he had heard Josie promise Stokes to give him the letters and let him make all he could out of them if he would stick to her and take care of her for the rest of her life.

When she gave him the letters, King swore, she urged him again to make all he could out of them and to take care of her. Stokes promised. He was enthusiastic about the letters. He thought there was big money in them.

This affidavit gives a glimpse of what was going on behind Jim's back in Josie's house after Stokes took Josie away from him again. From King's outline, it's easy enough to fill in the details. I think Jim felt Josie's second desertion even more deeply than he had felt the first. It showed him how completely in Stokes's power she was and how little room there was to hope that he could ever win her back. He looked ten years older.

'Well, Rabbits,' he said, 'thank God this business is over and done with at last. Josie can't keep away from Stokes. She's as bad about him as I've been about her; but I guess it's time now to wind things up.' I shook his hand and congratulated him, though I had my private misgivings about there being any real ending.

It wasn't long before Stokes showed his hand. He hired a lawyer, Ira Shafer, who served on Jim a claim for two hundred thousand dollars, which he said was due Stokes as his rightful share of Brooklyn Oil Refinery profits. Jim retained William H. Morgan to defend him, and it then appeared that Stokes proposed to use all the letters that Jim had ever written to Josie as evidence in support of his claim. There wasn't a word in them about the Brooklyn Oil Refining Company and nothing whatever to support Stokes's claim, which hadn't a leg to stand on, anyway. But the use of them as evidence would make them public, and Stokes expected Jim to settle his claim rather than permit that.

He was right. Jim didn't want the letters published. Morgan proposed referring the claim to arbitration, binding Jim to pay whatever award should be made. Stokes agreed and asked for Squire Peter B. Sweeney as arbitrator. Jim objected to Sweeney, and Stokes then wanted Clarence Seward. Jim took Seward. A condition of the arbitration was that Jim's letters should be given up and Stokes on April 12, sent them to Squire Sweeney with a brief note. Sweeney was to be the custodian of them.

After hearing Stokes in support of his claim and listening to Jim in opposition, and reading the arguments made by the lawyers, for and against, Seward found that there was no basis for any claim growing out of the oil business. But he said that Jim ought to pay Stokes something for having had him arrested in the embezzlement charge. He thought ten thousand dollars would be about right to square this. Jim made no objection, but Stokes wanted more. He asked for five thousand dollars for Shafer, and Jim said all right and paid it.

The net result of all this legal work was that Jim gave Stokes fifteen thousand dollars to get his letters back. Stokes accepted Seward's award and signed it on June 30, 1871, together with a release of Jim from any further liability in connection with the oil refinery. 'Finis!' said Jim, when Morgan gave him this release. 'Now let the dead past bury its dead!'

♦

The award that Seward had given Stokes didn't last him and Josie long. At the end of two months, they found themselves once more in need of funds. They turned to Jim. He was their unfailing source of supply.

In one of the letters that Josie wrote to Jim, she spoke of an impression that he 'held some twenty or twenty-five thousand dollars' of hers in his keeping, and asked him for it. He refused to give her the money on the ground that she would use it to redeem Stokes's diamonds, which had been put up by Stokes for a loan. She now doubled the amount, no doubt at Stokes's instance, and sued Jim for fifty thousand dollars.

In September Stokes also hired Marsh and Wallace to bring suit before Justice Ingraham to have the Seward award set aside and his claim for two hundred thousand dollars reopened. Stokes went around town bragging that Judge Ingraham was a friend of his and that he'd have Jim's letters, which his lawyers had got from Squire Sweeney in order to show them to Justice Ingraham, published in the *Tribune*.

Justice Ingraham wasn't so much of a friend. He refused to set aside the Seward award and reopen the oil refinery claim. He read Jim's letters, and when he rendered his decision on the application that Marsh and Wallace had made, he handed them back to the lawyers.

Blackmail

It was evident enough that we hadn't heard the last of Jim's letters. Stokes was determined to get Jim to buy him off again and that was the aim of his attempt to have the Seward award set aside. I knew Morgan, Jim's lawyer in the reference of Stokes's claim, had a copy of them and, with Jim's consent, I got it from him.

I was astonished when I read the letters to find nothing in them that was in the least damaging to Jim. His opposition to their publication was being attributed to something incriminating to him in the management of the Brooklyn Oil Refining Company. Stokes had made people believe that if what was in the letters should become known, Jim would go to jail and that that was the reason why he'd been willing to pay fifteen thousand dollars to have them kept secret.

'There isn't a thing in any of these letters that's even discreditable to you,' I told him, 'except that you were too generous to Josie.'

'I know it,' he said.

'Then why don't you give them yourself to the newspapers and let them be published? That would stop Stokes and at the same time show everybody what a liar he is.'

'I can't do it, Rabbits; I can't paste up on the wall some of the purest thoughts that ever stirred me for the world to laugh at! This is my *heart* that you want me to make a show of! I won't do it!'

He was obstinate for a long while, but I kept at him and got Belden and Ceda to advise him to give out the letters and put an end to the talk about them. He confessed everything to Lucy and that mild soul forgave him with tears. But it wasn't until he found out that Stokes had actually given the letters to a Brooklyn newspaper man, James Pooton, to be sold to the press that he gave way. He sent Shearman, who lived in Brooklyn, to get Justice Pratt there to enjoin Stokes and Josie and Pooton from making the letters public; and he told me to go ahead and have copies made of them for publication. He proposed to give them out with a statement over his own signature in which he said:

'This will amuse a great many heartless people, but I am satisfied to let them laugh. For much that I have done, I have been justly blamed, and I have been ridiculed for much more. In this correspondence, which was an insult to one of the purest women that ever lived, I have been more guilty than in anything else. I have sought and obtained the forgiveness of my wife. Now let the world laugh!'

But in the eleventh hour, he changed his mind again and told me not to give the letters out. Destiny played with him just as a cat plays with a mouse; and finally pushed him along to meet the fate that awaited him. If he had checkmated Stokes by publishing the letters, he would have escaped; but he tried other means.

Jim talked with King and got from him the statement of what had been going on in Josie's house before Stokes attempted to use the letters. The cold-blooded conspiracy that the boy described stirred Jim's fighting spirit. 'Rabbits,' he said, 'I'll be damned if I'm going to give 'em the satisfaction of having those letters published! I'll die in the last ditch with my boots on before I do it! I want you to go to Albany and get Frank Lawlor to tell you what really happened out there in California when Josie says he eloped with her.'

'I'll go if you want me to,' I said, 'but do you really think it's worth while? Wouldn't it be better to take away the only weapon they've got against you by giving out the letters?'

'I'm going to show 'em that Jim Fisk isn't a laughing stock! So help me God, I'll put 'em behind the bars! You go ahead.' So I went, and I found Lawlor not reluctant to talk. He didn't like the way Josie had always put him in the wrong.

'I never eloped with her at all,' he said. 'There isn't any truth in that story. I met her first in 1863, when she was a pretty and attractive girl. She was all right then, but I didn't have any idea of marrying her.

'I was playing an engagement in Virginia City, in Nevada, when Warren, Josie's stepfather, and her mother, tried to blackmail D. W. Perley. He was a rich man and he must have been sixty years old or more from what Josie's told me. He was in their house and in the parlor alone with Josie when Warren came in with a revolver in his hand and threatened him. The story was that Perley jumped out of the window with almost no clothes on and that Warren had surprised him at a critical moment. It made a great scandal out there.

'Josie told me all about it when I got back to San Francisco. She said she was afraid her mother and stepfather would try to use her to get money out of Perley and that she relied on me for protection. I said I didn't know how I could protect her unless I married her and that I couldn't do that; but she begged me and finally I married her to save her from her own parents.'

'Didn't you live with them after you were married?'

'No; I never spoke to Warren from that day to this, and I wouldn't let Josie speak to him. She never saw her mother out there again, either, but once, and that was just before we left California for New York. I was fond of her, but I never cared for her so much that I couldn't give her up easily when I found she was going astray.'

'When was that?'

'It was when we were living in New York after we came East from California. I had some reason to suspect her and I told her one day that if she went wrong, I wouldn't have anything more to do with her. But I couldn't stop her, and I saw that I couldn't stay with her any longer without becoming a laughing stock for everybody that knew us; so I left. That was sometime in 1868.

'Have you seen her since the divorce?'

'I have not. I made the mistake of my life when I married her; but anybody might have done the same thing under the same circumstances. I have no ill feelings towards her. I believe she was innocent in the Perley blackmailing affair in San Francisco; if I hadn't believed it, I never would have married her.'

I reported to Jim what Lawlor had said and he had me tell William A. Beach, whom he had retained as his lawyer in Josie's suit for fifty thousand dollars, about it. In his answer to Josie's claim, he submitted the affidavit that King had sworn to.

The publication of King's statement enraged Stokes to such a degree that he swore out a warrant for Jim's arrest for libel. Jim appeared before Judge Bixby in the Yorkville Court and gave bail on November 18, 1871.

Josie didn't want to take the witness stand against Jim. Either she had still some fondness for him, with the veering inclination that is common among women of her amorous nature, or she shrank from the questions she knew Jim's lawyers could ask. Maybe both reasons had weight with her. Anyhow, she wasn't there when the case was called and Jim, who had come to court in naval uniform, had to come again. But she was on hand when the matter came up on November 25. The questioning wasn't finished that day and Judge Bixby adjourned the hearing and there was truce over New Year until January 6, 1872. Stokes had got John McKeon to help John R. Fellows, assistant district attorney, present the case against Jim, and he was a fighter. With him on one side and Beach on the other, quick action couldn't be expected.

♦

Josie's complaint, which was sworn out in the Yorkville Police Court before Justice B. H. Bixby, denied the conversations that King swore he had overheard about how to get money out of Jim for his letters. There was some sparring between the lawyers about the letters that were causing all the trouble. Stokes had given them to Squire Sweeney, who held them until Justice Pratt, when he granted the injunction against their publication by Stokes and Pooton, ordered him to hand them over to John D. Tuthill, of 213 West Twenty-first Street, whom he made custodian of them. Judge Bixby signed an order directing Tuthill to produce them; but the custodian couldn't be found. So the letters seemed safe for the time being, at any rate. Jim's former bosom friend and the woman who was mistress of them both, by turns, realized that they were gone and that probably the chance of getting them back was slender, at best.

♦

There was much interest in the questioning of Stokes and Josie which everybody knew would take place when the hearing on their libel charge against Jim was resumed. Jim couldn't stay to see Josie exhibited for what she really was and finally driven to tears before a room which was jammed by a curious crowd. So he left and went back to the Grand Opera House. It was Saturday afternoon and he had to approve payrolls and clean up his desk, and he was planning to go down to the Grand Central Hotel to see Mrs Morse, widow of that friend of his who killed himself by breaking his neck when he was bathing in Lake Pontchartrain.

Another thing he had to look out for was a loan of a quarter of a million dollars that he had promised to make to the police department so that the men could get their pay. The zeal of the reformers who were driving Tweed and his crowd out of the city trough because they had been too greedy, tied up the city funds so that salaries couldn't be paid. Jim knew what it was not to have a cent, with the month's bills coming in, and he offered to advance the money so that the salaries could be paid on Monday.

Toward four o'clock in the afternoon he had cleaned up all his work. He put on his coat and was going out when a clerk came in with some salary checks to be signed.

'More checks?' Jim asked, halting and looking back.

'Only a few,' said the clerk, 'They could wait.'

'No, I'll sign 'em,' Jim said. 'The men have earned the money and they ought to have it.' He went back to his magnificent desk and signed the checks without taking off his coat or hat. A boy brought word that his clarence was waiting.

'All right, sonny; tell John to hold his hosses – I'll be there in a jiffy.'

He stopped for a moment in the glittering bar-room at the foot of the stairs. 'Mix me up a lemonade, Dave,' he said to the barkeeper. 'A man needs a little refreshment after a hard day's work!' Dave grinned and watched with admiration while Jim drank. So did four or five other men, customers, who were standing at the other end of the bar. Then Jim walked out across the tesselated marble floor, got into his clarence, and drove away along Twenty-third street into eternity.

Murder

Stokes left the Yorkville courtroom in company with John McKeon, his lawyer, and Assistant District Attorney Fellows in the carriage that Jim had given Josie. She and Etta drove home in Colonel Fellows's clarence. Stokes's face was white and his eyes burned with rage. Not only had he been shown by the lawyer's questions to be something strongly resembling the 'fancy man' of a prostitute but Josie, after maintaining her composure until almost the very end, had broken down at last in a flood of angry tears.

This was all the result he had got from the libel complaint he had had Josie make against Jim. Justice Brady had made permanent the injunction against the publication of Jim's letters to Josie that Justice Pratt had granted temporarily, and they were beyond his reach. The appeal to the law that he had thought so clever, had yielded only shame and bitter humiliation. Anger glowed in his brain like a hot coal.

The three men drove to Delmonico's and went in there to luncheon. They finished and Stokes got up to go. As he did so Justice Barnard came in and told Colonel Fellows that the Grand Jury had just indicted Stokes and Josie for attempted blackmail of Jim, and that warrants were out for their arrest. Stokes heard, but the others said afterward that they couldn't tell whether he had or not.

He went out alone into Broadway and got a public coupe. 'Take me to the Hoffman House,' he said, and before he realized that they had started, they were there. He noticed by the clock that stood on a post in front of the Fifth Avenue Hotel that it was about half-past three. He left the coupe, went to his room, and got a revolver. It had chambers for four cartridges. It was loaded. He put it into the pocket of his cream colored Alexis overcoat and went back to the waiting coupe. 'Where to?' asked the driver, Lawrence Corr.

'To 359 West Twenty-third Street.' He thought he might see Josie once more before he did it. The coupe turned west into Twenty-third Street. They were passing the Grand Opera House. He leaned forward and looked up at the front of the building which he had so often entered as the bosom friend of the man who was now his relentless enemy. He saw Jim's carriage waiting.

Where could he be going in his carriage? They had reached Josie's in the middle of the block. He was going down to see Mrs Morse, of course! He had overheard him tell Spencer in court that morning that he was going there. What a fool he was to forget it! The Grand

Central Hotel just the place! He rapped on the glass and Corr pulled up his horses. 'Drive me down to Broadway and Fourth Street,' he said; and the coupe swung around. Fisk always went in by the Ladies' Entrance; he'd come up the stairs –

The coupe stopped. They must have driven fast. No – it was almost four o'clock. He paid and walked down Broadway. He went into the hotel by the Ladies' Entrance. Some loungers sitting in the window glanced at his cream colored overcoat and at the little cane he carried. 'He's a dresser,' said one to another, nodding at him as he walked up the broad staircase leading to the second floor where the ladies' parlor was.

Nobody on the second floor! What luck! Any minute now he'll be here. Maybe he's there now. Let's see –

♦

John Redmond, a young Irishman, was cleaning the glass in the Ladies' Entrance door at ten minutes after four o'clock. A carriage stopped at the curb and a man wearing a large cloak lined with red got out. It was Colonel Fisk. He knew him well. He stopped wiping the glass and opened the door for him.

'Hello, John; is Mrs. Morse in?' Colonel Fisk asked.

'No, sorr, she's gone out an' the oldest girl's gone with her; but the other wan is in her grandmother's room, sorr.'

'Tell her I'm here and ask whether she can see me.'

'I will, sorr.'

Jim didn't wait but went on upstairs ahead of the boy. There were two left turns in the stairs and two landings. Jim had almost reached the top when he heard a low voice, vibrating with hatred, exclaim –

'Now I've got you!'

He looked up and saw the cream-colored overcoat. It was Stokes! He was standing at the top of the stairs, almost within arm's reach. He had one arm stretched out. Good God! There was a pistol in his hand! No chance to escape in that narrow space! No chance to reach him!

Crack! Crack! Two pistol shots. Jim felt the first bullet strike him in the body and his legs gave way under him. 'Oh!' he cried. 'Don't!'

He got to his feet. The second shot hit him and went through his left arm. He fell again and slipped down to the second landing, five or six steps. Again he got up and this time he walked to the bottom of the stairs. He saw people beginning to collect there, at the sound of the shots, and he decided to go back up. John helped him to the top and into a room there.

Thomas Hart, bell boy, was on his way up to the fourth floor to answer a call. He saw a figure in a light-colored overcoat creep stealthily along the wall, stop at the head of the stairs, and look cautiously down, and with his left arm resting on the banister, fire two shots from a pistol. Then the man turned and walked quickly toward the main stairway, throwing the pistol into one of the ladies' parlors as he passed.

Hart followed. The man noticed him. 'There's a man shot. You'd better go and see!' he said. 'Yes,' said Hart, 'and you're the one that shot him!' He kept on following.

In the confusion, in spite of the boy's presence of mind in keeping after him, Stokes might have got away. He went down the big staircase into the lobby of the hotel and turned towards the barber shop, which had a door opening at the back into Mercer Street. Before he could go out he was seized.

'That's the man that shot me,' said Jim, when Stokes was led upstairs to the sofa on which he lay. 'That's Stokes; he wanted my life!' It was the end. They took Stokes away and locked him up. He drew a long breath. A weight was off his mind. At last he had proved his superiority over that rascal! He looked down at his lavender colored trousers and his patent leather shoes. He had shown that common clown what it meant to get in the way of a gentleman! He felt himself a martyr.

♦

'Jim Fisk's been shot!' The news ran through the city like an electric shock. From city to city – and from every city, in widening circles, through towns and villages to remote hamlets and solitary hillside farms – the news spread. 'Jim Fisk's been shot!'

Everybody knew Jubilee Jim, no matter whether they had ever seen him or not. They knew him just the same, and they liked him. They liked the way he had refused to bow to the intellectuals of Boston; they approved when he drove the Credit Mobilier crowd out into the open; they were delighted when he declined to kowtow to the majestic Commodore. He did exactly what they'd have liked to do themselves if they'd been able. They were proud of his Yankee smartness. At bottom, their amused admiration for him was founded on the conviction that he had a good heart – that he'd give the shirt off his back to relieve distress, and that he wouldn't squeeze nor rob a poor man.

If Stokes, pluming himself in his cell, could have felt the heat of indignation that his sneaking act of cowardice aroused against him all through the country, and even in England, where Jim's peculiar qualities were less well thought of, he would have been scorched to a cinder.

The fatal news reached Lucy at No. 74 Chester Square, in Boston, in the form of a telegram from Colonel Hooker, Jim's brother-in-law, who had been Belden's partner up to the crash of Black Friday. Poor statuesque Lucy melted into helpless tears and was hurried to the train by the efficient Fanny Harrod. Jim wasn't dead yet but Lucy knew in her heart that he was going to die and every faculty was absorbed in the hope of reaching him before he went.

———♦———

Meanwhile a posse of doctors were busy around Jim, who was conscious and not in much pain. Mrs. Morse and her daughters and his half-sister, Minna Hooker, came to see him, and so did Gould and Tweed and others. Tweed had been released from jail the day before, Friday, by Justice Cardozo under a million dollars bail.

'Hadn't you better send for Comer to take charge of any private papers you may have in your pockets?' the wary Tweed suggested. He meant John H. Comer, Jim's secretary.

'No; I haven't got any private papers with me,' Jim said. 'They're all public papers. I don't care who sees them.' He was referring to fifteen one hundred dollar bills that he had in his pocket when he was shot.

♦

There was intense excitement in and around the Grand Central Hotel that Saturday night. Broadway was packed with people waiting anxiously for news and held back by the police from forcing their way in to exhibit their sympathy at Jim's bedside. The wound in his left arm didn't amount to much, but the bullet that had entered his abdomen had four times perforated the intestines. They probed for it several times, but couldn't find it. Finally Jim insisted that they should let him alone until they could get hold of Dr. Lewis A. Sayre. He was a noted surgeon. Jim always wanted the best he could get when he bought professional service. That was the reason he got David Dudley Field to look out for his legal affairs.

Field had been sent for and he reached the hotel soon after Tweed got there. Jim asked him to draw up his will and this was soon done. It was brief. It left everything to Lucy, who was directed to pay three thousand dollars a year for the support of Jim's father and stepmother, and annuities of two thousand a year each to the two Morse girls, Minnie and Rosie, until they married. The only other bequest was a hundred thousand dollars in stock of the Narragansett Steamship Company to Minna. Lucy and Eben D. Jordan were made executors of the will, which was witnessed by Shearman, Gould, and Dr. F. Willis Fisher, the house physician of the hotel. When this had been attended to, Coroner Young came in with a jury of six men, who took Jim's ante-mortem statement. Jim told how he had come to the hotel that afternoon and how Stokes had lain in wait for him and shot him.

Around eleven o'clock, when the crowd thinned out, the doctors held a consultation and decided they couldn't do anything more then. Jim seemed to be fairly comfortable. His fever came toward morning. Lucy got to the hotel at a quarter past seven o'clock Sunday morning, with Comer and the competent Fanny Harrod. Lucy couldn't restrain her grief when Mrs. Morse met her at the head of the stairs. But Jim didn't hear her cries and laments. He was unconscious and breathing hard. 'Can nothing be done to save him?' wailed Lucy, with her arms around his neck. 'O God! If you must take him, take his soul!'

When Jim's breathing stopped, the troubled look left his face, which assumed a grave and peaceful expression. The undertaker, assisted by John Marshall, with tears running down his black cheeks, put the body in a coffin and the people in the hotel were allowed to take a last look. The clerks and messengers sobbed; everybody was in tears.

The coffin lid had been screwed down when Gould and Shearman came in. They asked to have it lifted again and that was done. Both of them cried like women. The crowds in the streets, which had gone home during the night, came back again in full force at daybreak. They stood dumbly staring at the hotel, snatching at scraps of news, until word came at eleven o'clock that Jim was dead.

Tweed had stayed up with the watchers until one o'clock. He came in again as the body was being removed and he followed the coffin, hat in hand, all alone, while it was taken down to the Mercer Street entrance and put in the hearse that carried it to Jim's modest home in West Twenty-third Street.

There, after the autopsy, a committee of the Ninth Regiment took charge of it. The crowds that had watched the Grand Central Hotel now choked Eighth Avenue and Twenty-third Street. They gazed at the Grand Opera House, and at Jim's house, where his body lay, and they marched staring past Josie's house, further along toward Ninth Avenue, in the hope of catching a glimpse of her. They hated her unanimously.

♦

It was made known finally that Jim would lie in state in the Grand Opera House next morning before he was taken to Brattleboro to be buried there, and then a good many people went home. But again the streets were packed when Jim was carried for the last time into the Opera House Monday morning and placed on a catafalque in the foyer of the theatre. An unbroken line of people filed in from Twenty-third

Street, past the coffin buried in flowers, with its military guard of honor, looked bareheaded at Jim lying quietly there in his colonel's uniform, and filed out through the Eighth Avenue entrance. There was much weeping, especially among humble people whom Jim had helped.

Then the entrances were closed and the Episcopal funeral service was read by Chaplain Pratt, of the Ninth, amid the sobbing of Lucy, Minna, and other women. This ceremony was finished at two o'clock, and the coffin, draped in an American flag, was escorted into the street by six commanders of Third Brigade regiments. The Ninth was drawn up, facing the Opera House, and the famous band, in which Jim had taken so much pride, played a wailing dirge when his coffin was brought out and placed in the waiting hearse.

The music changed to a dead march and a platoon of a hundred policemen started east through Twenty-third Street. Every inch of space on the sidewalks and in doorways was filled with a grieving crowd, which stood in complete silence, hats off, while the procession passed. Flags draped with black crepe were displayed from roofs and windows. Behind the police marched the band and then scores of Erie employees, with crepe tied around their left arms. Then came the Veteran Corps of the Ninth Regiment, Lieutenant-Colonel Braine and his staff, and the regiment itself, marching in a triple line. Behind this was the slowly moving hearse, drawn by four black horses, heavily caparisoned, like the hearse, in black, and followed by Jim's spirited black horse, led by a tall negro and carrying an empty saddle, with Jim's spurred military boots, toes turned backward, in the stirrups. The officers of the Third Brigade and officials of the Erie followed the charger, and then a line of carriages a quarter of a mile long, with Gould in the first one.

Deliberately and solemnly through the silent throng of watchers, the procession moved in the wintry air to Madison Avenue where it turned up to Twenty-seventh Street and then east again to the New Haven Railroad depot at Fourth Avenue. It was an impressive sight – just the kind of thing that Jim would have enjoyed taking part in if he could have been on the back of his horse instead of where he was.

When the Ninth Regiment reached Madison Avenue and Twenty-sixth Street, it broke ranks and stood at attention in two long lines, between which the hearse passed. The coffin was placed in a car that had been heavily draped with black. Lucy, Minna, members of committees, and others got into other cars, also draped, the horses were hitched on, and the cars were drawn up to Forty-second street, where they were coupled together into a funeral train.

At every station along the line to New Haven and up the beautiful, snow-covered valley of the Connecticut River to Brattleboro, crowds were waiting to watch in silence with bared heads while the train went by. They all knew Jim or felt that they did. Above Hartford there were many who had known him in fact in the days when he drove his wonderful peddler's wagon down from Vermont through the hills. They were all sorry that he was dead.

♦

The train got into Brattleboro about midnight. Almost the entire population was waiting to meet it. Jim was carried to the Revere House, where once he had been a waiter boy, and his coffin, laden with flowers, was deposited for the rest of the night. The officers of the Ninth as a guard of honor took turns watching in two-hour shifts. Brattleboro people pressed their noses against the windows of the hotel in the hope of seeing Jim, but it wasn't until daylight came that they were allowed to enter. As had happened in New York, most of those who passed the coffin left it with wet eyes, and many of them with sobs.

The coffin was carried to the Baptist Church at eleven o'clock and Jim lay there in state until the second funeral at one. The building was packed to the doors with the townspeople and with the delegations that came from New York and from Boston. The Boston special train arrived just before the service, with Eben Jordan and other friends from that city on board. Jordan was much affected. I never saw men cry at any other funeral as they did at Jim's. Chaplain Pratt, although he had been sick, came to Brattleboro so that he might speak at the final funeral service.

'I have known him only a short time,' he said, 'but in that short time I found him to be my friend, and I have been led hither because I found in him that which attracts us to a man, as goodness and truth always attract us.

'He who lies before you was no common man. As to his faults, I will not speak of them. A censorious world will do them ample justice. He had denunciations enough from those who never looked into his merits. It is but natural that a man of his strong characteristics should have had strong faults as well as strong virtues. When his good qualities are balanced against his bad, I venture to say that we will at least have an equipoise; we will find them at least up to the average.

'I will speak of those virtues which were most manifest in him. He was magnanimous by nature, and he never consulted his means when he wished to do a good deed. Colonel Fisk was generous to a fault. He once remarked to me, "I care little for money for its own sake. I want it in order to be enabled to do good to others." He gave his money to the poor – to such as truly needed it. When he was lying a corpse in the Grand Central Hotel, a lady holding a child by the hand attempted to force her way into the room. "For six months," said she, "he has kept me and my child from starvation, and I have never seen his face. I want to look upon my noble benefactor."

'Another peculiarity was his independence and manliness of character. Colonel Fisk knew how to say "I will" and "I will not." He always expressed the sentiment of his soul in spite of all opposition. This is a virtue which cannot be too highly commended. There was nothing of the hypocrite about Colonel Fisk. Whatever he did was open and above board. Those doings which shock public sentiment are not to be commended, but conscientiousness is.

'No matter what the maledictions of the press may have been, and no matter what those persons whom he has beaten at their own game may have said against him, they have all had the manliness to come forth in the last few days and acknowledge his virtues. The crowded hotel, the immense and respectable assembly in the streets, their sad faces as we passed in procession show that where true virtue exists, the world is ever ready to acknowledge it.

'We have every reason to believe that he gave testimony to his faith in Jesus. We may hope that, although not professing that name during life, his prayer has been heard and accepted at the throne of the Almighty.'

♦

For the last time, the coffin was carried to the hearse and the funeral proceeded up the icy hill, through the frosty air, to the cemetery. Jim had bought a plot on the southern edge of the cemetery, on the brow of a steep decline where trees were growing. He didn't think he would be the first to lie in it. When we were gathered around it, the coffin was lowered with the usual words of committal from the minister, and then we left the gravediggers to finish their work. More than once, as he walked through the snow to the cemetery gate, Pop Fisk turned and looked back at the grave shaking his head as though he couldn't understand. It didn't seem possible to him that Jim could die. But Love, his wife, small and wrinkled, in her heavy crepe veil, took him by the arm and led him on.

Almost everybody who had come up in the funeral trains from Boston and New York went back in them after the burial. I had intended to go, too, but Ceda kept me. She had been much overcome by the ceremonies and her eyes were red. She lived in a neat white house, with leafless lilac bushes at the door and a southern window full of geraniums and other plants.

At supper we talked about Jim. Ceda wanted to know everything I could tell her about what brought on the murder. She had feared a catastrophe, but not that! After we left the table, we sat before an open fire in the pleasant south room and I went on with my story while I smoked a cigar. I told her in detail of Jim's life in New York. Ceda listened attentively. Of course she knew about all these things, but it seemed to interest her to hear me tell of them from first-hand knowledge. At last, 'He loved life,' said she.

She asked me about Josie and Lucy. 'You know, Rabbits, I was always interested in both of them,' she said. So I went into Jim's relations with them, too. It was hard to tell her about Stokes, but I did it. Finally it came time to go. 'Shall I see you before you start back to New York?' she asked. I told her that I shouldn't leave Bennington till the day after the next, and I promised before that to see her and bid her good-bye.

♦

The next afternoon was gray and overcast. It was my last chance to go out to the cemetery and see that things had been left as they should be. From the livery stable down town I hired a cutter and a quiet mare that Ceda and I had driven before, and set out. Snow began to fall as I drove along. Soon I had left the town behind, and in perhaps twenty minutes I reached the cemetery gate. There I drew to one side of the road, tied the horse to a hitching post, blanketed her, and started to walk up the snow-covered path to the plot where Jim lay. The snow, a little damp, caked under my feet and made walking difficult. Once or twice I thought I saw footprints here and there, as if someone had come before me, but I gave little heed to them.

At last I started down the narrow, scarcely discernible footpath that led to Jim's plot. Everything was white and gray and black in the failing light; there were no other colors. Then as I came in sight of what I knew must be the newly mounded grave, already covered with the snowfall, I saw a figure beside it. At first I thought it was a child. Then, as I drew nearer, I could just barely see that it was Ceda, on her knees beside the grave.

I stopped in my tracks. I couldn't go on – not just then. Many things came back to me. I thought of her as a girl in pigtails and straight gingham dress watching us boys play Indians with Jim as chief. I thought of her during the war, of the Ceda who had done so much for those wounded soldiers, Yankees and Rebs alike, of the Ceda I had loved so long. If anyone in this world knew her, I did.

As I stood looking at her, the snow began to fall faster and the night grew deeper. Ceda rose to her feet, turned toward the path, and seemed to catch sight of me. I thought she started back a little, but, if she did, she recovered herself as I spoke her name and advanced toward me, slipping a little on the uncertain ground. We drew nearer one to the other, and when we met she extended her left hand. The other was in her muff. 'Rab!' she said. She groped for my arm. I could not see her face, but I knew it was wet with tears.

We turned into the main path that led to the gate. When we had walked part of the distance, Ceda stopped and looked back toward the grave. We could no longer see it, hidden in the dark and the snow.

'He's gone,' she said.

Postscript

The fortune of almost a million dollars that Jim left for Lucy was all gone when she died in South Boston in February, 1912, at the age of seventy-six. She'd been living there for years in a little frame house with her sister, on fifty dollars a month from a block of houses in Main Street in Brattleboro that Jim gave her long before he died. She made this property over to Colonel Hooker to look after for her. He lived in Brattleboro. Her capital oozed away in driblets. A big slice of it went in the 'restitution' that Gould made to the Erie when he lost control to the Britishers a few weeks after Jim was murdered; and another slice went when Lucy loaned a quarter of a million to a hotel man, who failed. She and her sister looked after each other, doing their own washing, cooking, and mending. Lucy had two 'strokes' before she died. She never complained; but Fanny Harrod, who married, was indignant at the way everybody conspired to rob her, and especially at the failure of Gould, with all his millions, to make any provision for her.

◆

Pop Fisk died in 1883 in Brattleboro, when he was seventy-one years old. He and Love, his second wife, lie beside Jim in the Brattleboro cemetery.

◆

Commodore Vanderbilt left a fortune of more than a hundred millions when, in 1877, he made way for his son Willie at the age of eighty. He remained triumphant, dominating, and unshaken until he breathed his last breath.

♦

Uncle Dan'l Drew went to his reward one night, in 1879, at the home of his son in Forty-second Street, just east of Fifth Avenue, at eighty-two years of age. He had been a bankrupt for several years, but he was still hoping to get back into Wall Street and to make a fortune there.

♦

Gould was a nervous wreck when he died in 1892 in his Fifth Avenue house. He was fifty-six years old and he left behind him a fortune of more than seventy millions.

♦

Josie was hooted out of Boston when she went there after selling what she had in New York after Jim was dead. Then she went abroad and picked up a living at her trade in Paris and at various European watering places. In 1891 she astonished the world by marrying a rich American, brother of the Vicountess Falkland, Robert Livingston Reade. He left her after a year or two with an allowance and she came back to Boston, where she had a stroke in 1899. Then she went to Philadelphia for a while; and she was last recorded out in South Dakota, where she was asking to be admitted in 1901, to a Catholic Home. By that time nobody seemed to care what became of her.

Stokes was tried for Jim's murder and the jury disagreed. He had the best lawyers. It took all his father was worth to pay for the first trial. He was tried again and sentenced to be hanged; but his conviction was set aside by the Court of Appeals. This time the expense was borne by an uncle, who was persuaded to it by W. E. D. Stokes, his son, and Ed's cousin. Ed repaid him by quarreling bitterly with him.

On his third trial he was finally convicted of manslaughter. For this, he was sentenced to six years and served four, getting out of Sing Sing in 1876. The man who stood by him and paid for the third defense was Cassius M. Reed, proprietor of the Hoffman House, who had taken a fancy to the young Adonis, which wasn't shared by his wife, a wholesome young Irish woman. It cost Reed sixty thousand dollars before Ed got out of prison, and Reed was the only person at the gate to greet him. He brought him home and kept him at the Hoffman House until people began to shake hands with him once more, although Delmonico never would have him in his restaurants after the murder. Reed financed a paving company for him, and, when it failed, sent him to California. There he drove a fast trotter named 'Eva.' John W. Mackay wanted her and offered twenty thousand dollars for her. Ed wouldn't sell, but in a day or two, he presented her to Mackay.

Then Mackay began to cherish him; let him buy the Victorine silver mine, which he and Reed sold in Europe at a big profit. Ed and Mackay went in with Reed managing the Hoffman House. Ed started branch restaurants down town to get even with Delmonico for being so particular about not having murderers in his place. Mackay employed him to buy up stock in the Bankers' and Merchants' Telegraph Company. Ed cheated him and Mackay sued him and got out of the Hoffman House connection. Reed found that he had been helping himself to the hotel money. He tried to stop these larcenies, just as Jim had, by changing the partnership into a corporation in which he held two-thirds of the stock and Ed one third. Reed put two hundred thousand dollars into it; but Ed froze him out somehow and Reed found himself in a boarding house hall bedroom, suing for some of the money out of which he had been bamboozled by his attractive young friend.

Stokes, all alone, couldn't seem to make things go. He sold out to a syndicate, and moved into a house at No. 209 West Seventy-ninth Street. He was sixty-one years old when his sister took him away to her home in St. Nicholas Avenue in the last stages of Bright's disease. This was in 1901, while Josie was seeking shelter in South Dakota. Ed died and it was then found that he had been living in Seventy-ninth Street with a woman who said they'd been married in Canada, secretly, the year before. Stokes didn't change much as long as he lived.

It was said of him that after he murdered Jim, he never would lie down to sleep unless there was a light burning near his bed and a servant within call. He was afraid of Jim's ghost.

♦

The citizens of Brattleboro paid Larkin Mead twenty-five thousand dollars for an impressive monument of Italian marble which they erected over Jim's grave. On one side of the shaft is cut a portrait medallion of Jim as he looked when he was alive. At the four corners of the massive base sit four marble young women. One has a locomotive carved on a chaplet which encircles her brow. She represents railroading. The second represents commerce by water. The third figure typifies the stage. The fourth stands for trade in the broadest sense. Thousands of visitors have looked upon this memorial of one of the most noted of Vermont's sons, and a good many of them have carried home chips of Italian marble which they managed to break off and steal as souvenirs. They have made the monument more fitted to commemorate Jim's career – striking from many aspects, picturesque, but blemished.

Index

About TEXERE

TEXERE seeks to become the most progressive and authoritative voice in business publishing by cultivating and enhancing ideas that will illuminate the global business landscape. Our name defines the spirit of our vision: TEXERE is the ancient Latin verb 'to weave.' In an increasingly global business community, we seek to create an intersection where authors and readers can share the best thinking and the latest ideas. We want to leverage the expertise and insights of leading thinkers by weaving them with TEXERE's capability to deliver them to the marketplace.

To learn more and become a part of our community visit us at:

www.etexere.com

and

www.etexere.co.uk

About the Typeface

This book was set in 11/15 Goudy.